ISLAM

HIJACKED

BY

MARWAN HACHEM

Printed in the United States of America

First Printing 2022

ISBN: 978-1-0881-1708-8

بِسْمِ اللَّهِ الرَّحْمَنِ الرَّحِيمِ

In the Name of Allah—the Most Compassionate, Most Merciful.

INTRODUCTION

In a world that slipped back to darkness, it's time to stop and go back to the roots and original bases; Islam is a religion that thrive on science, love, and passion for humanity. The Holy Quran is the base of Islam, my book is an invitation to every Muslim, every man of clothes, every person who loves knowledge to take a minute and rethink where we are now and how we got here and what we can do to correct this path. No disrespect meant to anyone or any religion because I believe in all of them; my problem is with the people who appointed themselves as Gods. The message is pure intention based on love and knowledge, and if anyone has an issue with it, they must search and prove and correct the mistakes in this book, after all, I am not perfect.

"When something goes wrong, those who has the ability to take actions, has the responsibility to take actions."

Acknowledgments

First, thankful to God for giving me more than I deserve, always. God always does good to humans, but only a few of us take the time to realize the blessing they are living in.

Thank you to my friends, Zaher Said, Ammar Aljenini, and my brother, Mostapha, who supported me and discussed these matters for years together and reviewed the very first draft of this book.

Thank you to Claire Foster and Dr. Chahrour, who inspire me to speak even if everyone is against what you think.

This book has been under discussion for many years and studying the facts and arguments, till finally we sharpened our point of view and supported it with evidence.

Thanks to everyone who read this book, whether they like it or not but reading it with an open mind.

Finally, thank you for your time and effort to read and, take the points I have mentioned and build on them or make corrections. And with all my heart, ask God for guidance for me and all humanity.

TABLE OF CONTENTS

بِسْمِ آللَّهِ آلرَّحْمَـٰنِ آلرَّحِيمِ

In the Name of Allah—the Most Compassionate, Most Merciful.

QURAN AND ISLAM

وَقَالَ آلرَّسُولُ يَـٰرَبِّ إِنَّ قَوْمِى آتَّخَذُواْ هَـٰذَا آلْقُرْءَانَ مَهْجُورًا ٣٠

The Messenger has cried, O my Lord! My people have indeed received this Quran with neglect.

Al-Furqan30

9

QURAN:

It's a lively miracle that has been around for 1500 years, and it will be for many years till the judgment day, and in every era, we find more about this miracle. God sent many prophets and messengers, some we all know and some we might never know. The message is constant: to preserve humanity and surrender for all Mighty. Imagine this scenario that God created Adam, and he didn't send prophets or messengers how the humans would have evolved? Cannibalism is normal, killing is normal, and stealing is normal; who will know what is right or wrong? Before Prophet Muhamad PBUH came with the message, they used to bury the girls!!

God sent many prophets with virtue to teach people about right and wrong. And all the messages that God sent via the Holy books match despite the followers of each book hating and fighting the followers of the other book. Only if they take time to read the books, they will find that it's one message came to Abraham, Moses, John Jesus, and Mohamad PBUT.

If Quran came with Adam, it would have been lost a long time ago, so in order for the Quran to come, there is a preparation needed to be made to get the humans ready through many prophets and messages so the final book will include everything.

What makes Quran the miraculous??

There are many things that make the Quran Miraculous; some we know, and some are yet to be found because there is no limit to God's wisdom.

Human Creation

ثُمَّ خَلَقْنَا ٱلنُّطْفَةَ عَلَقَةً فَخَلَقْنَا ٱلْعَلَقَةَ مُضْغَةً فَخَلَقْنَا ٱلْمُضْغَةَ عِظَٰمًا فَكَسَوْنَا ٱلْعِظَٰمَ لَحْمًا ثُمَّ أَنشَأْنَٰهُ خَلْقًا ءَاخَرَ ۚ فَتَبَارَكَ ٱللَّهُ أَحْسَنُ ٱلْخَٰلِقِينَ ١٤

"Then We developed the drop into a clinging clot ˻of blood,˼ then developed the clot into a lump ˻of flesh,˼ then developed the lump into bones, then clothed the bones with flesh, then We brought it into being as a new creation.' So Blessed is Allah, the Best of Creators."

Almumenon 14

How a man from the desert knew this 1500 years ago without doing any research or surgical procedures and testing for different times of development of a baby in the woman's womb??

Yes, you can say it's a coincidence, but how many coincidences do you need before you realize he couldn't possibly come up with what is written?

DEEP OCEAN

أَوْ كَظُلُمَـٰتٍ فِى بَحْرٍ لُّجِّىٍّ يَغْشَىٰهُ مَوْجٌ مِّن فَوْقِهِۦ مَوْجٌ مِّن فَوْقِهِۦ سَحَابٌ ۚ ظُلُمَـٰتٌ بَعْضُهَا فَوْقَ بَعْضٍ إِذَآ أَخْرَجَ يَدَهُۥ لَمْ يَكَدْ يَرَىٰهَا ۗ وَمَن لَّمْ يَجْعَلِ ٱللَّهُ لَهُۥ نُورًا فَمَا لَهُۥ مِن نُّورٍ ٤٠

"Or ˹their deeds are˺ like the darkness in a deep sea, covered by waves upon waves,¹ topped by ˹dark˺ clouds. Darkness upon darkness! If one stretches out their hand, they can hardly see it. And whoever Allah does not bless with light will have no light!"

An-Noor 40

This just discovered recently about waves at the bottom of the ocean, although he didn't go to the ocean!

THE BEE

وَأَوْحَىٰ رَبُّكَ إِلَى ٱلنَّحْلِ أَنِ ٱتَّخِذِى مِنَ ٱلْجِبَالِ بُيُوتًا وَمِنَ ٱلشَّجَرِ وَمِمَّا يَعْرِشُونَ ٦٨

"And your Lord inspired the bees: "Make ˹your˺ homes in the mountains, the trees, and in what people construct."

An-Nahl68

ثُمَّ كُلِى مِن كُلِّ ٱلثَّمَرَٰتِ فَٱسْلُكِى سُبُلَ رَبِّكِ ذُلُلًا ۚ يَخْرُجُ مِنۢ بُطُونِهَا شَرَابٌ مُّخْتَلِفٌ أَلْوَٰنُهُ فِيهِ شِفَآءٌ لِّلنَّاسِ ۗ إِنَّ فِى ذَٰلِكَ لَءَايَةً لِّقَوْمٍ يَتَفَكَّرُونَ ٦٩

"And feed from ˹the flower of˺ any fruit ˹you please˺ and follow the ways your Lord has made easy for you. From their bellies comes forth liquid of varying colors, in which there is healing for people. Surely in this is a sign for those who reflect."

An-Nahl69

From their bellies, not one but more than one! How??

The **crop or honey stomach** is a special expandable structure located between the esophagus and the true digestive tract of the worker bee.

The crop stores collected nectar until the worker is ready to return to the hive. No true digestion happens in the crop. <u>**Honey is not bee vomit**</u> , as you may read elsewhere.

This ability to carry raw nectar in the crop back to the hive is important. Without the special part of a worker bee, they would not be able to produce honey.

Did Mohamad PBUH dissect the BEE??

THE MOSQUITO

إِنَّ ٱللَّهَ لَا يَسْتَحْىِۦٓ أَن يَضْرِبَ مَثَلًا مَّا بَعُوضَةً فَمَا فَوْقَهَا ۚ فَأَمَّا ٱلَّذِينَ ءَامَنُوا۟ ۞
فَيَعْلَمُونَ أَنَّهُ ٱلْحَقُّ مِن رَّبِّهِمْ ۖ وَأَمَّا ٱلَّذِينَ كَفَرُوا۟ فَيَقُولُونَ مَاذَآ أَرَادَ ٱللَّهُ بِهَٰذَا
مَثَلًا ۘ يُضِلُّ بِهِۦ كَثِيرًا وَيَهْدِى بِهِۦ كَثِيرًا ۚ وَمَا يُضِلُّ بِهِۦٓ إِلَّا ٱلْفَٰسِقِينَ ٢٦

"Surely Allah does not shy away from using the parable of a
mosquito or what is even smaller. As for the believers, they know
that it is the truth from their Lord. And as for the disbelievers,
they argue, 'What does Allah mean by such a parable?' Through
this ˹test, ˺ He leaves many to stray and guides many. And He
leaves none to stray except the rebellious.

Al-Baqara26

Mosquitoes are relatively small insects, measuring an average of
just more than 6mm long and weighing about 2.5 milligrams.
They're divided into three basic parts: the head, thorax, and
abdomen.

Head: The **head** is crammed with sensory equipment that helps
the mosquitoes find and feed on people and animals.

Compound eyes They have two large **compound eyes** covered
with tiny lenses called ommatidia that can detect even slight
movement. On the top of their heads, they also have **ocelli**,
simple photosensitive eyes that detect variations in light.

Antennae: Their **antennae**, long feathery organs, jut forward from their heads and contain sensory receptors that detect carbon dioxide in human breath from the distance of more than 100 feet. The maxillary palp between the antennae picks up the odor of octanol and other chemicals released in human sweat.

Proboscis: Right in the middle, also between the antennae, is the **proboscis**, a long-serrated mouthpart used to pierce the skin and suck out blood. The proboscis holds two tubes, one that injects saliva containing an anticoagulant and mild painkiller and a second that actually draws the blood.

Did He also dissect the mosquito??

The Universe

لَا ٱلشَّمْسُ يَنۢبَغِى لَهَآ أَن تُدْرِكَ ٱلْقَمَرَ وَلَا ٱلَّيْلُ سَابِقُ ٱلنَّهَارِ ۚ وَكُلٌّ فِى فَلَكٍ يَسْبَحُونَ ٤٠

"It is not for the sun to catch up with the moon,[1] nor does the night outrun the day. Each is travelling in an orbit of their own."

Yaseen40

For so many years and till 1979, the whole world thought that the sun stay still and doesn't move, while 1500 hundred years ago, the Quran specified that everything in the universe is swimming, not just moving but swimming!!

A: If you imagine looking down on the Milky Way, the sun is located nearly 27,000 light-years from the center, about halfway between the center and the edge of our disk-shaped galaxy. Looking from the side, the disk is relatively flat, and the sun is currently located about 55 light-years above the plane of the galaxy's disk. Over time, the sun orbits the center of the galaxy, sketching out a roughly circular path (again, looking down from above) that takes about 230 million years to complete at a speed of about 137 miles (220 kilometers) per second.

With respect to its axis of rotation, the sun is moving through the galaxy tipped at an angle of about 60° from the galactic plane. This also applies to the planets orbiting the sun, just like the disk of our galaxy, if you look at our solar system from the side, the planets orbit the sun in a relatively flat plane. Essentially, the sun and the plane in which the bodies of the solar system orbit around are both tilted forward by 60° as they move through the galaxy.

It's perhaps also worth noting that the sun doesn't appear to trace a flat circle — in one plane only — as it moves around the galaxy. The sun actually appears to bob up and down through the disk (we are up right now, above the plane of the disk) as it moves, with a period of about 60 million years.

Please watch:
https://www.youtube.com/watch?v=KUdIQ7kvD7w

HOLY QURAN: MANY MIRACLES

Language miracles (set the rules for the Arabic languages, it's impossible for one man to put rules for a whole language).

Historic miracles (explains some of the historical events, also, it's impossible for a man in the desert to know about).

Numeric miracles (mathematical miracles taught us the math. the positions of words in the Quran based on numerical values. It's miraculous to be put that way even if you used computers for that).

Universe miracles, health miracles, knowledge miracles, and so on. Since it's the book of God, why not read it over and over many times till it sinks.

EASY AND SIMPLE

Do you know that God has mentioned in the Quran four times that the Almighty made the Quran easy for understanding, is there anyone reading it?

وَلَقَدْ يَسَّرْنَا ٱلْقُرْءَانَ لِلذِّكْرِ فَهَلْ مِن مُّدَّكِرٍ

"And We have certainly made the Quran easy to remember. So, is there anyone who will be mindful?"

17 22 32 40 Al-Qamar

This Ayah has been mentioned four times in the Quran, OMG!!! How many times do you want God to tell you more before you start reading the Quran?

There is Ayat in Quran if you read it, you will not understand it but believe me nobody else will, no man of cloth will, too. The miracle of the Quran is for every era, so 1500 years ago, they didn't know what Equinox is or the baby in the woman's womb as the Quran specified it.

There is some Ayat in Quran; even if you read it will not make sense to you. You will not understand it! but let me assure you, nobody will.

I stated earlier, every era has their discoveries about Quran. What we know now was never known or understood 1000 years ago, but people believed in the Quran and kept reading it.

Now we are more knowledgeable, and we have the technology under our fingertips to help us. Why not explore the greatness of this book??

Some Ayat in Quran you will not, or the men in cloth will be able to explain because this explanation belongs to God alone and these Ayat just to give us an idea, not to take it; and explain it in any graphic way or different meaning.

هُوَ ٱلَّذِى أَنزَلَ عَلَيْكَ ٱلْكِتَـٰبَ مِنْهُ ءَايَـٰتٌ مُّحْكَمَـٰتٌ هُنَّ أُمُّ ٱلْكِتَـٰبِ وَأُخَرُ مُتَشَـٰبِهَـٰتٌ فَأَمَّا ٱلَّذِينَ فِى قُلُوبِهِمْ زَيْغٌ فَيَتَّبِعُونَ مَا تَشَـٰبَهَ مِنْهُ ٱبْتِغَآءَ ٱلْفِتْنَةِ وَٱبْتِغَآءَ تَأْوِيلِهِ ۗ وَمَا يَعْلَمُ تَأْوِيلَهُ إِلَّا ٱللَّهُ ۗ وَٱلرَّٰسِخُونَ فِى ٱلْعِلْمِ يَقُولُونَ ءَامَنَّا بِهِ كُلٌّ مِّنْ عِندِ رَبِّنَا ۗ وَمَا يَذَّكَّرُ إِلَّآ أُوْلُوا ٱلْأَلْبَـٰبِ ٧

"He is the One Who has revealed to you ˹O Prophet˺ the Book, of which some verses are precise—they are the foundation of the book while others are elusive.¹ Those with deviant hearts follow the elusive verses seeking ˹to spread˺ doubt through their ˹false˺ interpretations—but none grasps their ˹full˺ meaning except Allah. As for those well-grounded in knowledge, they say, 'We believe in this ˹Quran˺—it is all from our Lord.' But none will be mindful ˹of this˺ except people of reason."

Al-Imran7

The Quran translation is wide and unlimited because some of the facts are known, and some yet still to come. The miracles are limitless in the Quran, and we can go on and on about it, can't fit it in one book, or some of it not revealed to us yet; just highlighting two very important ayahs.

THE CHALLENGE

First is the miracle that God challenges all the creatures to come with one surah like Quran,

أَمْ يَقُولُونَ ٱفْتَرَىٰهُ ۖ قُلْ فَأْتُواْ بِسُورَةٍ مِّثْلِهِ وَٱدْعُواْ مَنِ ٱسْتَطَعْتُم مِّن دُونِ ٱللَّهِ إِن كُنتُمْ صَـٰدِقِينَ ٣٨

"Or do they claim, "He[1] made it up!"? Tell them ˹O Prophet˺, "Produce one surah like it then, and seek help from whoever you can—other than Allah—if what you say is true!"

Yunis 38

وَإِن كُنتُمْ فِى رَيْبٍ مِّمَّا نَزَّلْنَا عَلَىٰ عَبْدِنَا فَأْتُواْ بِسُورَةٍ مِّن مِّثْلِهِ وَٱدْعُواْ شُهَدَآءَكُم مِّن دُونِ ٱللَّهِ إِن كُنتُمْ صَـٰدِقِينَ ٢٣

"And if you are in doubt about what We have revealed to Our servant,[1] then produce a surah like it and call your helpers other than Allah, if what you say is true."

Al-Baqara 23

فَإِن لَّمْ تَفْعَلُواْ وَلَن تَفْعَلُواْ فَٱتَّقُواْ ٱلنَّارَ ٱلَّتِى وَقُودُهَا ٱلنَّاسُ وَٱلْحِجَارَةُ ۖ أُعِدَّتْ لِلْكَٰفِرِينَ ٢٤

"But if you are unable to do so and you will never be able to do so then fear the Fire fueled with people and stones, which is prepared for the disbelievers."

Al-Baqara24

I hope when you read this, you realize the challenge; that nobody could or can do that ever!! Will that imply for Hadith??

THE LAST PROPHET

The second challenge: the Holy Quran said Muhammad PBUH is the last Prophet!

1500 years Later still no prophet?

مَّا كَانَ مُحَمَّدٌ أَبَآ أَحَدٍ مِّن رِّجَالِكُمْ وَلَٰكِن رَّسُولَ ٱللَّهِ وَخَاتَمَ ٱلنَّبِيِّنَ ۗ وَكَانَ ٱللَّهُ بِكُلِّ شَىْءٍ عَلِيمًا ٤٠

"Muhammad is not the father of any of your men,¹ but is the Messenger of Allah and the seal of the prophets. And Allah has ˹perfect˺ knowledge of all things."

Al-Ahzab40

One of the best stories I have ever heard, and I will like to share it with you, there lived an old man with his grandson, the grandson asked him, why you keep reading the Quran and you never memorize it? The Oldman asked the grandson to go and fill an old dirty basket he used to carry coal, with water from the beach, so the grandson attempted to do that, and every time he did that, by the time he got to his grandfather, the basket get empty as it leaked through. After 10 attempts, the grandson gave up and said, I can't do it, what a waste of time! Then the grandfather asked him to look at the basket and said; it became very clean, you don't have to memorize the Quran, but very surely, it will cleanse your soul and make you strong against ignorance and temptation and help you heal physically and mentally.

وَنُنَزِّلُ مِنَ ٱلْقُرْءَانِ مَا هُوَ شِفَآءٌ وَرَحْمَةٌ لِّلْمُؤْمِنِينَ ۚ وَلَا يَزِيدُ ٱلظَّٰلِمِينَ إِلَّا خَسَارًا ٨٢

"We send down the Quran as a healing and mercy for the believers, but it only increases the wrongdoers in loss."

Al-Isra82

Islam is a religion of peace, and it surrendering yourself to GOD in every matter, and to God only. It's easy and simple, just believe in God as the supreme power, the creator, and He has no partners, and you are guaranteed heaven. To be Muslim, all you have to do is surrender to God.

THE FORGIVENESS

إِنَّ ٱللَّهَ لَا يَغْفِرُ أَن يُشْرَكَ بِهِ وَيَغْفِرُ مَا دُونَ ذَٰلِكَ لِمَن يَشَآءُ ۚ وَمَن يُشْرِكْ بِٱللَّهِ فَقَدِ ٱفْتَرَىٰ إِثْمًا عَظِيمًا ٤٨

"Indeed, Allah does not forgive associating others with Him ˹in worship˺,[1] but forgives anything else of whoever He wills. And whoever associates others with Allah has indeed committed a grave sin."

An-Nisa48

إِنَّ ٱللَّهَ لَا يَغْفِرُ أَن يُشْرَكَ بِهِ وَيَغْفِرُ مَا دُونَ ذَٰلِكَ لِمَن يَشَآءُ ۚ وَمَن يُشْرِكْ بِٱللَّهِ فَقَدْ ضَلَّ ضَلَٰلًا بَعِيدًا ١١٦

"Surely Allah does not forgive associating ˹others˺ with Him ˹in worship˺,[1] but forgives anything else of whoever He wills. Indeed, whoever associates ˹others˺ with Allah has clearly gone far astray."

An-Nisa116

It's mentioned twice in the same surah An-Nisa, wow! How great is God to forgive us for all the sins, except we make partners to God. Isn't God the most merciful? His mercy is beyond our imagination. On another thought, if God is that merciful, why we can't be; if we believe in God? Why it's always like my way or the death? How come the men of clothes can't get together and study and discuss and correct each other and accept the facts only?

GOD

Nobody can grasp the concept of worshiping God, the creator. Let me explain; if I asked the whole world, can you draw the God? What do you think the best outcome would be? Maybe a giant man or cloud or even shapes have nothing to do with the concept of supreme power or the creator. We are not at the level to discuss that. Even no matter what we think God is look like, God doesn't look like it. There is nothing like GOD. Everything we know or we draw, it's a manipulation for God creature - the fly, the ant, the bee, the animals, the earth, the sky, the plant, the planets, everything our mind copying and trying to manipulate so literally. We can't draw something we never witnessed, but we believe in God as the supreme power of the creator. And this is the task the God wants us to do; just believe and have faith.

فَاطِرُ ٱلسَّمَـٰوَٰتِ وَٱلْأَرْضِ ۚ جَعَلَ لَكُم مِّنْ أَنفُسِكُمْ أَزْوَٰجًا وَمِنَ ٱلْأَنْعَـٰمِ أَزْوَٰجًا يَذْرَؤُكُمْ فِيهِ ۚ لَيْسَ كَمِثْلِهِۦ شَىْءٌ ۖ وَهُوَ ٱلسَّمِيعُ ٱلْبَصِيرُ ١١

"ˈHe isˈ the Originator of the heavens and the earth. He has made for you spouses from among yourselves, and ˈmadeˈ mates for cattle ˈas wellˈ—multiplying you ˈbothˈ. There is nothing like Him, for He ˈaloneˈ is the All-Hearing, All-Seeing."

Ash-Shuraa11

Let us just have faith in the creator who loves us and spread this love with all mankind instead of waging wars against each other's over what??

As Humans, for years, search for God, and; although God sent prophets, few believe them; because, as humans, we need to worship something or someone we can see, we believe in material things. Some worshipped the sun or the stones or the rain. They create Gods for everything they can imagine; although the prophets came told them that there is one God almighty and if there is many Gods, they will fight between each other.

GOD PARTNERS

مَا اتَّخَذَ اللَّهُ مِن وَلَدٍ وَمَا كَانَ مَعَهُ مِنْ إِلَٰهٍ ۚ إِذًا لَّذَهَبَ كُلُّ إِلَٰهٍ بِمَا خَلَقَ وَلَعَلَا بَعْضُهُمْ عَلَىٰ بَعْضٍ ۚ سُبْحَٰنَ اللَّهِ عَمَّا يَصِفُونَ ٩١

"Allah has never had ˹any˺ offspring, nor is there any god besides Him. Otherwise, each God would have taken away what he created, and they would have tried to dominate one another. Glorified is Allah above what they claim!"

Al-Mu'minun91

We always, as humans, like personification. We like statues and anything we can tend to, whether it's grave or picture or place, or even a human. All humans are equal in Islam; no one is better than other, only Infront of God, whether a believer or disbeliever.

I would like to share a story; I met an engineer who was working for Chrysler company, and he retired. So over dinner, we were talking about now he is retired and how he will spend his time. The answer was, I follow the Buddha religion, and I am very interested in religions, but while I was reading about the religion Judaism, Christianity, and Islam. It's interesting that I realized that the three religions are the same way; they hate each other's, and what is the difference between them?? He spoke?

My answer was that it's basically easy and simple! Let's say you are in love with a girl; you are very far, and you send her a letter, but she doesn't know how to read. The mailman read the letter to her, but she fell in love with the mailman. God sent many Prophets to humanity and messengers with one message on different stages, different eras, Jewish fell in love with Moses PBUH and David PBUH, and Christian fell in love with Jesus PBUH and Muslims fell in love with Muhamad PBUH. It's God who we should fall in love with. All the messengers and prophets are Messengers (Mailmen), they lived and died but God is not. God is Almighty the creator; doesn't live or die, God is the life, the first, the Last, the supreme power. The gentleman then asked how about Muslims, there is Sunna and Shiite? I answered it's simply the same concept, but some people fell in love with the messenger, and others fell in love with his cousin.

The point behind the story is God, who we worship and believe in. We believed in all messengers and books and angels and judgment day where we will be asked.

ءَامَنَ ٱلرَّسُولُ بِمَآ أُنزِلَ إِلَيْهِ مِن رَّبِّهِ وَٱلْمُؤْمِنُونَ ۚ كُلٌّ ءَامَنَ بِٱللَّهِ وَمَلَـٰٓئِكَتِهِ وَكُتُبِهِ وَرُسُلِهِ لَا نُفَرِّقُ بَيْنَ أَحَدٍ مِّن رُّسُلِهِ ۚ وَقَالُوا۟ سَمِعْنَا وَأَطَعْنَا ۖ غُفْرَانَكَ رَبَّنَا وَإِلَيْكَ ٱلْمَصِيرُ ٢٨٥

"The Messenger ˹firmly˺ believes in what has been revealed to him from his Lord, and so do the believers. They ˹all˺ believe in Allah, His angels, His Books, and His messengers. ˹They proclaim, ˺ "We make no distinction between any of His messengers." And they say, "We hear and obey. ˹We seek˺ Your forgiveness, our Lord! And to You ˹alone˺ is the final return."

Al-Baqarah285

MEANING

So go back to Islam to understand the meaning of it, you can translate it as surrender to God, and both Christianity and Judaism believe the same thing; surrendering to God. Islam started the day Adam PBUH was created, till now, all the prophets surrender to God.

إِنِّى وَجَّهْتُ وَجْهِىَ لِلَّذِى فَطَرَ ٱلسَّمَـٰوَٰتِ وَٱلْأَرْضَ حَنِيفًا ۖ وَمَآ أَنَا۠ مِنَ ٱلْمُشْرِكِينَ ٧٩

"I have turned my face towards the One Who has originated the heavens and the earth—being upright—and I am not one of the polytheists."

Al-An'am79

DARWINISM

One of the theories we keep hearing about is the evolution theory of Darwinism. Darwinism subsequently referred to the specific concepts of natural selection, the Weismann barrier, or the central dogma of molecular biology.[2] Though the term usually refers strictly to biological evolution, creationists have appropriated it to refer to the origin of life or to cosmic evolution, which are distinct to biological evolution.[3] It is therefore considered the belief and acceptance of Darwin's and his predecessor's work in place of other concepts, including divine design and extraterrestrial origins.[4][5]

Islam agrees with this evolution theory,

وَإِذْ قَالَ رَبُّكَ لِلْمَلَٰئِكَةِ إِنِّى جَاعِلٌ فِى ٱلْأَرْضِ خَلِيفَةً ۖ قَالُوٓا۟ أَتَجْعَلُ فِيهَا مَن يُفْسِدُ فِيهَا وَيَسْفِكُ ٱلدِّمَآءَ وَنَحْنُ نُسَبِّحُ بِحَمْدِكَ وَنُقَدِّسُ لَكَ ۖ قَالَ إِنِّىٓ أَعْلَمُ مَا لَا تَعْلَمُونَ ٣٠

"'Remember' when your Lord said to the angels, "I am going to place a successive 'human' authority on earth." They asked 'Allah', "Will You place in it someone who will spread corruption there and shed blood while we glorify Your praises and proclaim Your holiness?" Allah responded, "I know what you do not know."[1]

Al-Baqarah 30

So, there were Humans on earth before Adam PBUH and, in similarity, looked like Adam PBUH, and the human used to act in an animalistic way and had no speech ability whatsoever. The angels know that because they can see that, but a little less, they know about Adam PBUH.

EVIDENCE

وَٱلتِّينِ وَٱلزَّيْتُونِ ١

By the fig and the olive ˺AT-Tin1

وَطُورِ سِينِينَ ٢

and Mount Senyin, AT-Tin2

وَهَٰذَا ٱلْبَلَدِ ٱلْأَمِينِ ٣

and this secure city ˹of Mecca˺!˼ AT-Tin3

لَقَدْ خَلَقْنَا ٱلْإِنسَٰنَ فِى أَحْسَنِ تَقْوِيمٍ ٤

Indeed, we created humans in the best form. AT-Tin4

ثُمَّ رَدَدْنَٰهُ أَسْفَلَ سَٰفِلِينَ ٥

But We will reduce them to the lowest of the low AT-Tin5

Charles Darwin is best known for his theory of evolution through natural selection. Darwin's work was first made public in 1859, it shocked the British religious establishment, and while today it is accepted by virtually all scientists, evolutionary theory is still rejected by many Americans often because it conflicts with their religious beliefs about Divine creation, but then we may tend to think of Darwin's theory of evolution is anti-religious you may be surprised to learn that Darwin theory and the holy Quran share some commonalities. Let's start by taking a closer look at the theory; the theory has two main points - first, all life on Earth is connected and related to each other's trace back their separate lines of descent of all organisms that ever lived. They will converge to a single point of origin the beginning of Life. Charles Darwin was reluctant to publish his views on the origins of Life. His only speculations on the subject and known from a private letter to his friend and colleague Joseph Hooker in which he speaks of a Little warm pond in which the first molecules of Life could have formed. The holy Quran written over 1400 years ago tells us that all life on Earth is connected and related to each other when it says And we God made from water all living things second this diversity of life is a product of modifications of populations by natural selection where some traits were favored in an environment over others and the holy Quran tells us that the history of creation is a history of both creation and selection when it says your lord creates whatever he wills and selects, the holy Quran also tells us that the prophet Adam PBUH was brought to prophecy by selection when it says indeed Allah God selected Adam and Noah and the family of Abraham and the family of Imran above all up people at the heart of Darwin's theory of evolution is the notion of copying and the variations it creates meaning that it is copying results in several evolutionary successive stages similarly the holy Quran tells us that God created us in successive stages when it says what is the matter with you that you do not hope for Honor from Allah when he created you in successive stages. Charles Darwin believed that humans evolved in Africa and that the root of the human tree was very deeply ingrained there and in 1962 our Roots were shown to be definitively in Africa geneticists are able to identify certain genetic sequences or markers in each of us and cross reference it with a number of ever growing international databases where there's a match there's likely a common ancestor and genetically speaking all markers points to Africa with the mapping of the human genome in 2003 combined with thousands of people around the world submitting their DNA for testing there's now mounting physical proof that we all started in Africa before migrating around the world furthermore advanced DNA testing combined with recently unearthed discoveries a bolstering the belief that if you look back far enough all living human beings are the descendants of a small innovative and ambitious set of people on the African continent and the holy Quran confirms this when it says in a very short chapter of only eight verses, by the fig and the olive by the mountains of Sinyin and by the secure City of Mecca we have indeed created the human in the best directed shape then we returned to the lowest of the low except those who believed and did righteous deeds for them there is a reward unending so what's it causes you to deny the recompense the day of Resurrection, is not Allah the most just of Judges. let's take a look at exactly how this short chapter about figs, olives, and the mountain of Sinyin explains the origins of humankind so let's talk about figs; you know that sweet mushy fruits that come from an inwardly blossoming flower in an article for BBC earth published on the 17th of January 2017 Mike Shanahan writes that fig trees have not only witnessed history but have shaped it wild figs trees first grew in Africa around 80 million years ago humans have been eating figs throughout history figs not only nourished animals but the year-round presence of ripe figs would have helped sustain our early human ancestors. High-energy figs may have helped our ancestors to develop bigger brains; there's also a theory that suggests our hands evolved as tools processing which figs are soft and therefore sweet and rich in energy while the first humans benefited from fig biology their descendants mastered it and where exactly does the world fig tree called Ficus vastea, grow? In or near the Horn of Africa, and it's primarily endemic to

Ethiopia's. and now for olives, whose tree has been called the tree of Life. In an article on the Australian broadcasting corporations website, on the 7th of February 2013 Dr. Besnard of the French national center for scientific research explains it his researchers concluded that three main branches of wild olives split from a common ancestral tree at least 1.5 million years ago now on to mountains in the New York times by Carl Zimmer or May 30th 2013 Zimmer states that in the hearts of evolutionary biologists, mountains occupy a special place it's not just their physical Majesty mountains also have an unmatched power to drive human evolution our ancestors moved to high altitudes and their experience natural selection that has reworked their biology like the adjustment of hemoglobin levels, for example, this is the most extreme example in humans that you can find said Rasmus Nielsen an evolutionary biologist at the University of California at Berkeley humans have adapted to mountainous environments just as Charles Darwin predicted. An BBC News article in March 2015 revealed that it was search team led by professor Brian Vilmore from the University of Nevada in Las Vegas have discovered what they called the most important transition in human evolution this this is the transition from tree dweller to upright walker, this transition happened and was discovered in Ethiopia human evolution also known as harmonization is the evolutionary process that led to the emergence of anatomically modern humans beginning with the evolutionary history of primates which appeared at least 18 million years ago and leading to the emergence of homo erectus or upright man which was the first creature to stand fully upright, so what do all these findings in all these articles have to do with that short chapter of the Quran we mentioned simply put, the holy Quran points to Africa and tells us that the history of the upright man's evolution started with the evolution of primates at least 80 million years ago and led to an upright man at least one and a half million years ago how exactly does the holy Quran do this by swearing by the fig which first grew in Africa around 80 million years and by the olive which lived from its common ancestral tree about 1.5 million years ago and by the mountain of Sinyin which is found in Ethiopia and now called Choke mountain and finally by swearing to Mecca the land of Islam that God created the human in the best directed shape the word Taqwim being used in the original Arabic of the verse means erected, which means to raise and set in an upright or vertical position and God says after that we then return the human back to the lowest of the low and now scientists are searching for our ancestors in the afar desert of Ethiopia which coincidentally happens to be the lowest point in Ethiopia the lowest in Africa and the lowest point on the planet, this is how a brief chapter of eight versus summarizes millions of years of human evolution in a book revealed 1400 years ago by God, for how could the prophet Muhammad PBUH have known about the link between the creation of humans in an erected shape and the millions of years of evolution that took place between the appearance of the fig and the Olive and how could he have known about the link between the creation of humans in an erected and an African Amharic mountain in Ethiopia? or even about the location of the mountain of Senyin that has for years been wrongly translated as the mountain of Sinai in Egypt, and that we just recently discovered thanks to satellite mapping? In short, he could not have known. So, where is this mysterious mountain that turns out to be of great significance? The mountain of Senyin is in an Amharic town that is not even known by most Ethiopians, it's now called choke mountain and can be found in the Ethiopian Highlands located in the Amhara national, regional State, East Gojjam zone northwest of the town of Debre Markos. Administratively the area belongs to two Veridas districts Sinan and Machakal where Senyin is. It's about 330 km north of the national capital Addis Ababa by road. This highland lies at a latitude of 2,386 m above sea level. Many of the rivers of the upper Nile originate from this mountain range; the total of 59 rivers and many springs are identified in the upper catchments of choke mountain the climate of the choke mountain region between February and May are known to be warm. During this period, the average temperature could reach up to 17.80 Celsius, whereas during the coldest months between June and August, the average monthly temperature reaches 15.60 Celsius. In chapter 2, verse 38 of the holy Quran, God tells us that there is an order for all of mankind to descend when he States we God said, Descend from it all of you and when guidance comes to you from me GOD whoever follows my guidance there will be no fear concerning them nor will they grieve the word it here refers to the paradise where Adam and Eve descend form it that may mean that the paradise where Adam and Eve lived before they sinned was on Earth and located at a height above sea level. This nicely fits the characteristics of the mountainous of Senyin, now called choke mountain in Ethiopia, Africa, and also happens to be the place where humans first evolved. In short, the holy Quran simply confirms the African roots of the human family tree. So long before Darwin even used evolution as a mechanism to explain diversity and the development of species, the holy Quran itself addressed the emergence diversification, and origins of life on Earth.

This article is well explained by Claire Foster

Claire Foster speak about Islam
https://www.youtube.com/watch?v=82a0tj_rOmU

This video shed light on this matter in more detail.

Once you Build an open Base for the people, to blindly believe in what humans say, and disregard what God said, then it is easy to Hijack any religion. Hadith is considered what Human said against Quran what God said. Some will argue that the Prophet didn't come with this stuff from his own mind, but God taught him, and that is completely true about the message of the Quran, not about a guy after 200 years telling lies and rumors about the Prophet; that goes against Quran. I am not Saying all the Hadith is wrong, and since the Hadith is the gate for Evil to add lies and rumors, it's better to close that door and go back to our indestructible castle, the Holly Quran.

KNOWLEDGE

Islam is the religion of knowledge; when Europe was sinking into the dark ages, the Islamic world was living golden ages, where all the inventions and science took place.

Muḥammad ibn Mūsā al-Khwārizmī[note 1] (Persian: محمد بن موسى خوارزمی, romanized: *Moḥammad ben Musā Khwārazmī*; c. 780 – c. 850), or **al-Khwarizmi** was a Persian polymath from Khwarazm,[6][7][8][9][10][11] who produced vastly influential works in mathematics, astronomy, and geography. Around 820 CE, he was appointed as the astronomer and head of the library of the House of Wisdom in Baghdad.[12]:14

Ibn Sina (Persian: ابن سينا; 980 – June 1037 CE), commonly known in the West as **Avicenna** (/ˌævɪˈsɛnə, ˌɑːvɪ-/), was a Persian[4] polymath who is regarded as one of the most significant physicians, astronomers, philosophers, and writers of the Islamic Golden Age,[5] and the father of early modern medicine.[6][7][8] Sajjad H. Rizvi has called Avicenna "arguably the most influential philosopher of the pre-modern era."[9] He was a Muslim Peripatetic philosopher influenced by Greek Aristotelian philosophy. Of the 450 works he is believed to have written, around 240 have survived, including 150 on philosophy and 40 on medicine.[10]

Ḥasan Ibn al Haytham, Latinized as **Alhazen**[10] (/ælˈhæzən/;[11] full name *Abū ʿAlī al-Ḥasan ibn al-Ḥasan ibn al-Haytham* أبو

علي، الحسن بن الحسن بن الهيثم; c. 965 – c. 1040), was
an Arab mathematician, astronomer, and physicist of the Islamic
Golden Age.[12][13][14][15][16] Referred to as "the father of modern
optics,"[17][18] he made significant contributions to the principles
of optics and visual perception in particular. His most influential
work is titled *Kitāb al-Manāzir* (Arabic: كتاب المناظر, "Book of
Optics"), written during 1011–1021, which survived in a Latin
edition.[19] A polymath, he also wrote on philosophy, theology,
and medicine.[20]

Abu Abdullah Muhammad ibn Battutah (Arabic: أَبُو عَبْدُ اللهِ مُحَمَّدُ
بْنُ عَبْدِ اللهِ اللَّوَاتِي ٱلطَّنْجِي بْنُ بَطُّوطَةُ, romanized: *Abū ʿAbd Allāh
Muḥammad ibn ʿAbd Allāh al-Lawātī al-Ṭanjī ibn
Baṭṭūṭah,* /ˌɪbənbætˈtuːtɑː/; 24 February 1304 –
1368/1369),[a] commonly known as **Ibn Battuta**, was
a Berber Maghrebi[1][2][3] scholar and explorer who traveled
extensively in the lands of Afro-Eurasia, largely in the Muslim
world, traveling more than any other explorer in pre-modern
history, totaling around 117,000 km (73,000 mi),
surpassing Zheng He with about 50,000 km (31,000 mi)
and Marco Polo with 24,000 km (15,000 mi).[4][5][6] Over a period
of thirty years, Ibn Battuta visited most of southern Eurasia,
including Central Asia, Southeast Asia, South Asia, China, and
the Iberian Peninsula. Near the end of his life, he dictated an
account of his journeys, titled *A Gift to Those Who
Contemplate the Wonders of Cities and the Marvels of
Travelling,* commonly known as *The Rihla.*

Many more Muslim scholars on all subjects, till the men of
the clothes, entered the Hadith into the likelihood of Islam and
accused this scientist of infidelity; and spread the ignorance in the
Muslim communities; just, to gain ruling here or there and they
became worse than the devil himself. The men of clothes start

providing these rules with different approval and writing different Hadith to please their rulers. They divided the Islam empire into pieces and ruined what the pioneer Muslims achieved, and all what has left for us is the ignorance and reminiscing on the past. All of that happened just because we, as **Claire Foster** said, left the book on the shelf collecting dust and we followed the devils in clothes.

ISLAMIC GOLDEN AGE

The **Islamic Golden Age** was a period of cultural, economic, and scientific flourishing in the history of Islam, traditionally dated from the 8th century to the 14th century.[1][2][3] This period is traditionally understood to have begun during the reign of the Abbasid caliph Harun al-Rashid (786 to 809) with the inauguration of the House of Wisdom in Baghdad, the world's largest city by then, where Muslim scholars and polymaths from various parts of the world with different cultural backgrounds were mandated to gather and translate all of the known world's classical knowledge into Aramaic and Arabic.[4]

The period is traditionally said to have ended with the collapse of the Abbasid caliphate due to Mongol invasions and the Siege of Baghdad in 1258.[5] A few scholars date the end of the golden age around 1350, linking with the Timurid Renaissance,[6][7] while several modern historians and scholars place the end of the Islamic Golden Age as late as the end of the 15th to 16th centuries meeting with the Islamic gunpowder empires.[1][2][3] (The medieval period of Islam is very similar, if not the same, with one source defining it as 900–1300 CE.)[8]

Is it a coincidence that during that Golden Era, then Bukhari decided to collect Hadith, from God knows whom, 194 years after the prophet died?? Why? All these years, the Muslims were living in prosperity, and they were advanced in science and life, and suddenly Hadith happened. Does he even speak the language? And how come most of the Hadith speak of about one person heard from another and so on that I heard the prophet saying!! Because of this info, the prophet whispers to one guy only! Wow!

No Offense

With all respect to Muslims who care honest about carrying the message, all we are saying; is that for the years after the prophet, many things happened. The Islamic state was divided into multi states, and every ruler of each state started making their own rules to fit their needs. Even the states started fighting each other's like how it used to be before Islam! The greed and the power-hungry persons killed Muslims more than others (even the grandson of the prophet got killed over power, and no Muslim questioned that?) Once the Islamic states divided, they became weak; then the Tatar and Moguls invaded, then the crusade war, and so on, many lies could be fabricated in the name of Prophet. The only thing that can't be fabricated is the Holy Quran. In all fairness, we need to validate the Hadith with Quran; if it matches, it's fine, but if it totally changes the meaning and comes up with nonsense, we should know it's fabricated Hadith.

Some will debate why you wait for the western civilization to discover something and then claim that discovery to the Quran, it's easy and simple, we were going to discover it a long time if it wasn't for the alteration in the path of Islam, which redirected all the effort from science into fiction through Hadith. We killed science by ignorance, and we waited till the western civilization took where we reached at and built on it! The problem is not in the West, it's in ourselves, and that will not change the fact the Quran is a knowledge book, not a fictional story.

أَمْ تَحْسَبُ أَنَّ أَكْثَرَهُمْ يَسْمَعُونَ أَوْ يَعْقِلُونَ ۚ إِنْ هُمْ إِلَّا كَالْأَنْعَٰمِ ۖ بَلْ هُمْ أَضَلُّ سَبِيلًا ٤٤

"Or do you think that most of them listen or understand?[1] They are only like cattle—no, more than that, they are astray from the ʿRightʾ Way!"

44 Al-Furqan

Recently I watched short interview for a man of clothes who claim that if you follow Quran, you are disbeliever because you have to follow the sunnah of Prophet! And he says God said to follow the GOD and The Prophet. It's the ignorance itself in man, who came first in the order the GOD or the prophet? So, you follow what GOD said to the fullest then follow the prophet and anything that said about prophet goes against what GOD said its fabrication.

NOAH PBUH

One of the stories that the Quran sheds the light on, too, is NOAH PBUH, where everyone thinks that the whole universe got covered with water and NOAH PBUH ship carried from every animal's pair. It's not true. The flood happened in a certain region, and it could be somewhere on Turkish border with Iraq, just in that region, not the whole world. And the ARK that NOAH PBUH built was just wooden boards connected to each other's, and the type of animals he carried with him were domestic animals; that he needed to survive this period and reproduce in that region. So basically, his family and few of people with him and few animals he need to survive after that. God stated 8 pairs of sheep, goats, camels, oxen. Noah has been sent to his own people only not to the whole world, and he took the animals at that town. Not the whole world animals.

وَحَمَلْنَـٰهُ عَلَىٰ ذَاتِ أَلْوَٰحٍ وَدُسُرٍ ١٣

"We carried him on that ˹Ark made˺ of planks and nails,"

Al-Qamar 13

حَتَّىٰ إِذَا جَاءَ أَمْرُنَا وَفَارَ ٱلتَّنُّورُ قُلْنَا ٱحْمِلْ فِيهَا مِن كُلٍّ زَوْجَيْنِ ٱثْنَيْنِ وَأَهْلَكَ إِلَّا مَن سَبَقَ عَلَيْهِ ٱلْقَوْلُ وَمَنْ ءَامَنَ ۚ وَمَآ ءَامَنَ مَعَهُۥ إِلَّا قَلِيلٌ ٤٠

"And when Our command came and the oven burst ˹with water˺,¹ We said ˹to Noah˺, "Take into the Ark a pair from every species along with your family—except those against whom the decree ˹to drown˺ has already been passed—and those who believe." But none believed with him except for a few."

Hud40

قِيلَ يَـٰنُوحُ ٱهْبِطْ بِسَلَـٰمٍ مِّنَّا وَبَرَكَـٰتٍ عَلَيْكَ وَعَلَىٰ أُمَمٍ مِّمَّن مَّعَكَ ۚ وَأُمَمٌ سَنُمَتِّعُهُمْ ثُمَّ يَمَسُّهُم مِّنَّا عَذَابٌ أَلِيمٌ ٤٨

It was said, "O Noah! Disembark with Our peace and blessings on you and some of the descendants of those with you. As for the others, we will allow them ˹a brief˺ enjoyment, then they will be touched with a painful punishment from Us."

Hud48

God clearly stated other people weren't on the Ark!!!

Because Noah PBUH got send to his own people not to the whole world!

Finally, the most important message is Islam is not a religion of violence as they like to show, and some will bring versus from Quran about fighting; so, let us examine this. Muhammad PBUH stood his ground to defend his beliefs and his message, and he is not the first one to throw a punch; but he was in a defender position at all times, and the verses of Quran encouraged him to fight for his right and defend himself but not to kill and force people to become Muslim or believers but once they are they have every right to defend themselves same with any other religion as long as you don't be unfair and unjust and wage war for a barbaric reason. Although history deleted this truth about Islam and pictured Islam as that barbaric religion that encourage killing and war, it's not true. And that is a challenge for every man in the world to prove the opposite.

وَقَٰتِلُوا۟ فِى سَبِيلِ ٱللَّهِ ٱلَّذِينَ يُقَٰتِلُونَكُمْ وَلَا تَعْتَدُوٓا۟ ۚ إِنَّ ٱللَّهَ لَا يُحِبُّ ٱلْمُعْتَدِينَ ١٩٠

"Fight in the cause of Allah ˹only˺ against those who wage war against you, but do not exceed the limits.¹ <u>Allah does not like transgressors.</u>"

Al-Baqarah190

ٱلشَّهْرُ ٱلْحَرَامُ بِٱلشَّهْرِ ٱلْحَرَامِ وَٱلْحُرُمَٰتُ قِصَاصٌ ۚ فَمَنِ ٱعْتَدَىٰ عَلَيْكُمْ فَٱعْتَدُوا۟ عَلَيْهِ بِمِثْلِ مَا ٱعْتَدَىٰ عَلَيْكُمْ ۚ وَٱتَّقُوا۟ ٱللَّهَ وَٱعْلَمُوٓا۟ أَنَّ ٱللَّهَ مَعَ ٱلْمُتَّقِينَ ١٩٤

"˹There will be retaliation in˺ a sacred month for ˹an offence in˺ a sacred month, and all violations will bring about retaliation. So, if anyone attacks you, retaliate in the same manner. ˹But˺ be mindful of Allah, and know that Allah is with those mindful ˹of Him. ˺"

Al-Baqarah 194

Is Muslims timing for fasting right??
Why Quran specified Ramadan for fasting??

The **Hijri year** (Arabic: سَنة هِجْريّة) or **era** (التقويم الهجري *at-taqwīm al-hijrī*) is the era used in the Islamic lunar calendar. It begins its count from the Islamic New Year in which Muhammad and his followers migrated from Mecca to Yathrib (now Medina). This event, known as the Hijrah, is commemorated in Islam for its role in the founding of the first Muslim community (*ummah*).

In the West, this era is most commonly denoted as **AH** (Latin: *Anno Hegirae* /ˈænoʊ ˈhɛdʒɪriː/, 'in the year of the Hijra') in parallel with the Christian (AD), Common (CE) and Jewish eras (AM) and can similarly be placed before or after the date. In predominantly Muslim countries, it is also commonly abbreviated **H** ("Hijra") from its Arabic abbreviation *hā'* (هـ). Years prior to AH 1 are reckoned in English as **BH** ("Before the Hijrah"), which should follow the date.[1]

A year in the Islamic lunar calendar consists of twelve lunar months and has only 354 or 355 days in its year. Consequently, New Year's Day occurs ten days earlier each year relative to the Gregorian calendar. The year 2022 CE corresponds to the Islamic years AH 1443 – 1444; AH 1443 corresponds to 2021 – 2022 in the Common Era.[a]

Definition[edit]

See also: Lunar calendar and Solar calendar

The Hijri era is calculated according to the Islamic lunar calendar, whose epoch (first year) is the year of Muhammad's Hijrah, and begins on the first day of the month of Muharram (equivalent to the Julian calendar date of April 19, 622 CE).[2]

The date of the Hijrah itself did not form the Islamic New Year. Instead, the system continues the earlier ordering of the months, with the Hijrah occurring around the 8th day of Rabi al-Awwal, 66 days into the first year.

Predecessors[edit]

By the age of Muhammad, there was already an Arabian lunar calendar with named months. Likewise, the years of its calendar used conventional names rather than numbers:[3] for example, the year of the birth of Muhammad and of Ammar ibn Yasir (570 CE) was known as the "Year of the Elephant".[4] The first year of the Hijra (622-23 CE) was named the "Permission to Travel" in this calendar.[3]

Establishment[edit]

17 years after the Hijra,[3][5] a complaint from Abu Musa Ashaari prompted the caliph Umar to abolish the practice of named years and to establish a new calendar era. Umar chose as the epoch for the new Muslim calendar the hijrah, the emigration of Muhammad and 70 Muslims from Mecca to Medina.[6] Tradition credits Othman with the successful proposal, simply continuing the order of the months that had already been established, beginning with Muharram.[citation needed] Adoption of this calendar was then enforced by Umar.[7]

The prophet fasted Ramadan the same month every year for many years till he died, and according to the Arabic months!

Why they changed Ramadan dates after the prophet died??

Questions to be asked? How has that ruined Ramadan?

- Who changed the Arabic years to Hijri years????
  (Arabic years like Hijri years depend on the moon, but
  Arab used to correct the year every 2 years and 8
  months by adding a month, so everything goes back to

normal similar to leap year where Feb comes at 29 days)
- The Arab used to add a month every two years and 8 months; to straighten the year back to normal.
- Why spring first and spring second come in winter? It defeats the purpose of the name.

EQUINOX

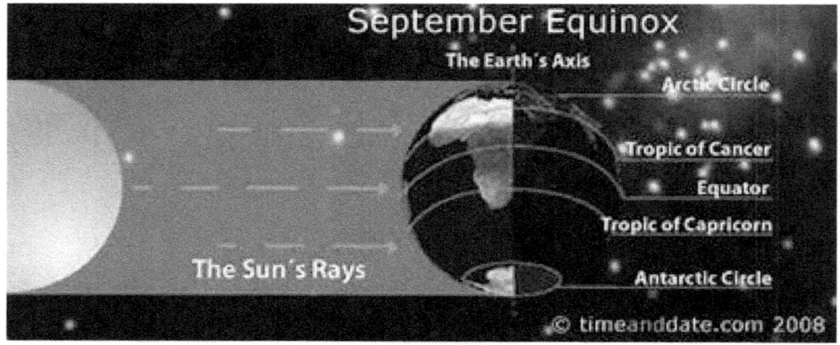

Equinox phenomena happens on Sep 23rd:

An equinox is an event in which a planet's subsolar point passes through its Equator. The equinoxes are the only time when both the Northern and Southern Hemispheres experience roughly equal amounts of daytime and nighttime. On Earth, there are two equinoxes every year: one around March 21 and another around September 22. Sometimes, the equinoxes are nicknamed the "vernal equinox" (spring equinox) and the "autumnal equinox" (fall equinox), although these have different dates in the Northern and Southern Hemispheres. The March equinox is the vernal equinox in the Northern Hemisphere, and the autumnal equinox in the Southern. The September equinox is the autumnal equinox in the Northern Hemisphere and the vernal in the Southern. **The Science of the Equinoxes** During the equinoxes, solar declination is 0°. Solar declination describes the latitude of the Earth where the sun is directly overhead at noon. (The Equator, of course, is 0° latitude.) So, equinoxes are the only times of the year when the subsolar point is directly on the Equator. The subsolar point is an area where the sun's rays shine perpendicular to the Earth's surface—a right angle. Only during an equinox is the Earth's 23.5° axis *not* tilting toward or away from the sun: the perceived center of the Sun's disk is in the same plane as the Equator. Before and after the equinox, the subsolar point migrates north or south. After the March equinox, the subsolar point migrates north as the Northern Hemisphere tilts toward the sun. Around June 21, the subsolar point hits the Tropic of Cancer, (23.5°N). This is the June solstice, after which the subsolar point begins to migrate south. After the September equinox, the subsolar point continues to move south as the Southern Hemisphere tilts toward the sun. Around December 21, the subsolar point hits the Tropic of Capricorn (23.5°S). This is the December solstice. As its name suggests, an equinox indicates equally illuminated hemispheres, with the solar terminator equally dividing the Earth from north to south. (The solar terminator is the shadowed line indicating daylight and sunlight on a globe.) A true equinox would indicate 12 hours of both day and night. Although the equinoxes are as close to this phenomenon as happens on Earth, even during the equinoxes day and night aren't exactly equal. This is largely due to atmospheric refraction. Atmospheric refraction describes the way light seems to bend or deviate from a straight line as it passes through Earth's atmosphere. Atmospheric refraction is a result of increasing air density, which decreases the velocity of light through the air. Due to atmospheric refraction, we are able to see the sun minutes before it actually rises and sets. *Equatorial Regions.* The Equator, at 0° latitude, receives a maximum intensity of the sun's rays all year. As a result, areas near Earth's Equator experience relatively constant sunlight and little equinoctial variation. Equinoxes and celestial seasons generally have less impact than climate-driven patterns such as precipitation (rainy seasons and dry seasons). *Mid-latitudes* Seasonal variation increases with latitude. Atmospheric refraction also increases the disparity in the "equinox" length of day and night. At about 30 latitudes, day is about eight minutes longer than night. *Polar Regions* Atmospheric refraction is most dramatic in the Arctic and Antarctic, with daylight extending about 12 hours and 16 minutes. In this way, the equinoxes in polar regions signal the slow change from "midnight sun" to "polar night." "Midnight sun" describes the phenomenon in which the sun never dips below the horizon, keeping the region bathed in sunlight 24 hours a day. "Polar night" describes the opposite phenomenon, a time in which the sun never rises, keeping the region dark for 24-hour periods. *Equinoctial Disruptions* Satellites are vulnerable to disruptions in the days before and after an equinox. "Sun outages" describe this disruption. In the Northern Hemisphere, sun outages occur in the days before the March equinox and after the September equinox. In the Southern Hemisphere, sun outages occur after the March equinox and before the September equinox. During an equinox, the sun is aligned directly behind satellites in geostationary orbit at the Equator. Situated directly above the subsolar point, the satellites are flooded with direct solar radiation. This solar radiation can interfere with and even stop satellites from transmitting signals. Many communications satellites orbit around the Equator, and consumers may experience slow Internet connections, radio static, or frozen television screens during equinoctial sun outages. *Extraterrestrial Equinoxes* Most planets experience equinoxes. The timing of equinoxes is determined by the planet's axial tilt and orbital characteristics. On the gas giant Saturn, for example, equinoxes are particularly dramatic. About 15 years separate the equinoxes on Saturn, and the equinoxes last about four days. Saturn's spectacular ring system orbits in the same plane as the planet's equator. Although the rings extend thousands of kilometers into space, they are actually very thin, only about a kilometer wide. During Saturn's equinoxes, the rings (and Saturn's equator) line up perfectly with the sun. Photos taken from the solar perspective reveal the rings as a razor-thin line. **The Culture of the Equinoxes** Like the solstices, equinoxes are historical markers of seasonal change. *March Equinox* the March equinox, unofficially marking the spring season, is traditionally observed as a time of rebirth and renewal. For this reason, many cultures have celebrated the March equinox as the first day of the new year. The ancient Babylonian calendar began on the first full moon after the March equinox, and today, many cultural and religious calendars continue to celebrate the new year in the spring. Perhaps the most widespread and well-known equinoctial new year is Nowruz, the first day of the year in the Persian calendar. For more than 3,000 years, Nowruz has been a religious holiday in Zoroastrianism, but today it is marked by secular celebrations throughout Eastern Europe and Central Asia. The Nowruz holiday includes mythical figures (such as Amu Nowruz, sometimes nicknamed the "Iranian Santa Claus"), traditional family gatherings, and the items of "haft-sin." Haft-sin are seven symbolic foods associated with Nowruz, all beginning with the Arabic or Persian letter *sin: sabze* (sprouts, symbolizing rebirth); *samanu* (sweet pudding, symbolizing wealth); *senjed* (dried, date-like fruits, symbolizing love); seer (garlic, symbolizing health); *seeb* (apples, symbolizing beauty); *somac* (red sumac fruit, symbolizing the color of sunrise); and *serkeh* (vinegar, symbolizing age and wisdom). Outside new year celebrations, the March equinox is celebrated on holidays all over the world. Vernal Equinox Day is a national holiday in Japan. The Jewish festival of Passover begins the night of a full moon after the March equinox. The date of Easter, one of the most important holidays in the Christian calendar, is calculated using the March equinox. *September Equinox* Fewer events mark the September equinox. Perhaps the most familiar of these are Rosh Hashanah and Yom Kippur, Judaism's "High Holy Days." Rosh Hashanah is the Jewish new year, marked around the September equinox. Rosh Hashanah is calculated as 163 days after the first day of Passover (which itself is calculated by the March equinox.) The sounding of the shofar, a ram's horn used as a trumpet for thousands of years of Jewish ritual, welcomes Rosh Hashanah. Yom Kippur, the holiest day in the Jewish calendar, falls about 10 days after Rosh Hashanah. Yom Kippur is a solemn holiday known as the "Day of Atonement." It is traditionally observed with a daylong fast and prayers for forgiveness. Most cultural events associated with the September equinox are tied to autumnal harvest festivals. Chuseok, celebrated over a three-day period in the Koreas, is one of the most familiar of these folk festivals. Sometimes nicknamed "Korean Thanksgiving," Chuseok is a celebration of family and Korea's rich agricultural heritage, where the day and night are equal in the whole world; because the earth and sun are completely facing each other.

As a result of that, September will have equal day and night in the whole world (give or take an hour in difference). God's Fairness for humans in fasting duties. (For verification https://www.sunrise-and-sunset.com). There are countries where the sun doesn't set for 5 months or more; so how they fast?? The equinox information wasn't discovered until recently!!!

So, When Is Ramadan??? Ramadan should fall approximately on 7st of Sep for one year, then on the 17th of Sep for another year, and then on the 27th of Sep for another year depend on the moon. After that, go back to the Sep 7st and so on.

With the technology we can know exactly Ramadan each year, we should have a set calendar. Its shame that we are living in the 2022 like we are living in dark ages!

THE PROPHECY AND RAMADAN

Now let us go back to Ramadan; how a guy from the desert (PBUH) knew this information; so, he fasted in SEP, or why the Quran specify Ramadan for the fasting month?? OMG!!!!!!

If we fix the Hijri year, we would fix everything!!

- Will we ignore this lively miracle!! This is why we don't have answers for, why the name of months doesn't match what they are named for???
- How about the pilgrim months???

Muharram: This is the first month in the Hijri calendar, and it means 'forbidden.' This month came about to prevent the Arabs from fighting.

Safar: Meaning 'empty,' this month was named so because pre-Islamic Arabs used to leave their homes in search of food during this month. Some sources say that this name actually derived from pre-Islamic Arabs conducting raids during this time on houses, leaving them 'empty.'

Rabi al-Awwal: The word Rabi means 'spring.' Al-awwal means 'the first', so together, this month means 'the first spring.'

Rabi al-Thani: Meaning 'the second spring,' it is also sometimes referred to as Rabi al-akhar or 'the last spring' because it refers to the end of Spring season.

Jumada al-awwal: The word Jumada means 'dry/parched'. At the time of the pre-Islamic Arabs, the land tended to be very dry during this month, either due to intense heat or sources of water being frozen due to cold temperatures.

Jumada al-thani: This has the same meaning as the previous month, but it marks the end of the land being dry, which is why it is sometimes called 'Jumada al-akhira', which means 'the end of the dry season.'

Rajab: This month is derived from the word 'Rajaba'- which means 'respect.' When Prophet Muhammad ﷺ sighted the moon of Rajab, he used to make this Dua:

Allāhumma bārik lanā fī rajaba wa sha'bāna wa balligh-nā ramaḍāna

"O Allah! Make the months of Rajab and Sha'ban blessed for us, and allow us to reach the month of Ramadan."

8. Sha'ban: This month means 'scattered' because it marks the time of year when Arab tribes would disperse to find water and new pastures.

Ramadan: Derived from the root word 'Ramad', which means 'burning' in reference to the scorching heat that characterized this month.

Shawwal: The name of this month means to carry or lift because, during this time, female camels would carry a new camel fetus and would produce less milk as a result.

Dhul Qidah: This month literally translates to "the one of sitting/truce" because all fighting ceased during this month.

Dhul Hijjah: This month is called 'the one of pilgrimage' because it is the month in which Hajj is performed.

The Sacred Months

There are 4 months in the Hijri calendar which are known as 'Al-ashhur al-Hurum' or 'The Sacred Months' – they are Muharram, Rajab, Dhul Qidah, and Dhul Hijjah. They are called such because Allah prohibited fighting and hunting during these particular months, except in cases when an individual or group is attacked first and needs to fight back in self-defense.

MONTHS ALLOCATING

To be fair to the environment and the animal, these months are prohibited for hunting. And it will make sense when Rabi is spring to come in spring. These three months of HURUM are crucial for animals' reproduction also, all animals reach their peak growth in strength in July, which happens to be Rajab and also HURUM. So, if we are rotating the HIJRI year 10 days every year, so that makes us in HIJRI older than our ages, and not constant on when the animal reproduces and the benefit of eliminating the order of not to hunt during these months. We harmed the environment and the animals in our countries more than ever and lot of important animals extinguished because of our ignorance. We now have a knowledge about earth and universe and nature more than in the days when they decided to eliminate the month to straighten the year, and I am very sure if they had this information, they would embrace it and cherish it because its Godly order and they messed with it. Due to biological facts, most of the animals who lives at land need these months to reproduce, on the other hands you can hunt from the sea all year around. Isn't God is the greatest.

إِنَّمَا ٱلنَّسِىٓءُ زِيَادَةٌ فِى ٱلْكُفْرِ ۖ يُضَلُّ بِهِ ٱلَّذِينَ كَفَرُواْ يُحِلُّونَهُۥ عَامًا وَيُحَرِّمُونَهُۥ عَامًا لِّيُوَاطِـُٔواْ عِدَّةَ مَا حَرَّمَ ٱللَّهُ فَيُحِلُّواْ مَا حَرَّمَ ٱللَّهُ ۚ زُيِّنَ لَهُمْ سُوٓءُ أَعْمَـٰلِهِمْ ۗ وَٱللَّهُ لَا يَهْدِى ٱلْقَوْمَ ٱلْكَـٰفِرِينَ ٣٧

Reallocating the sanctity of ˹these˺ months¹ is an increase in disbelief, by which the disbelievers are led ˹far˺ astray. They adjust the sanctity one year and uphold it in another, only to maintain the number of months sanctified by Allah, violating the very months Allah has made sacred. Their evil deeds have been made appealing to them. And Allah does not guide the disbelieving people.

At-Taubah 37

It's simply explaining that some disbeliever tries to use the correction of months in a way that can change the months, so they don't fight because there is no fighting in these months and changing the rules of correcting the months. The Arab used it for many years, and even before Muhamad PBUH. He never changed it.

Actually, stop correcting the months is the same as reallocating these months the disbelievers use to change it, so they don't have to fight, and those who started the HIJRI years did the same by canceling it completely. Same outcome!!!

Anything mess with the allocation of months is considered bad because the calculation for it is easy and simple. You still need to follow the moon to determine the months, but since the Hijri year shift ten days every year, you add a month every 2 years and 8 months, so it goes back on track, and it always happens after Rajab because Rajab is always in July and never change and also called Mudar due the people of Mudar.

يَٰٓأَيُّهَا ٱلَّذِينَ ءَامَنُوا۟ كُتِبَ عَلَيْكُمُ ٱلصِّيَامُ كَمَا كُتِبَ عَلَى ٱلَّذِينَ مِن قَبْلِكُمْ لَعَلَّكُمْ تَتَّقُونَ ١٨٣

"O believers! Fasting is prescribed for you—as it was for those before you¹—so perhaps you will become mindful ˹of Allah. ˺"

Al-Baqarah183

أَيَّامًا مَّعْدُودَٰتٍّ ۚ فَمَن كَانَ مِنكُم مَّرِيضًا أَوْ عَلَىٰ سَفَرٍ فَعِدَّةٌ مِّنْ أَيَّامٍ أُخَرَ ۚ وَعَلَى الَّذِينَ يُطِيقُونَهُ فِدْيَةٌ طَعَامُ مِسْكِينٍ ۖ فَمَن تَطَوَّعَ خَيْرًا فَهُوَ خَيْرٌ لَّهُ ۚ وَأَن تَصُومُوا خَيْرٌ لَّكُمْ ۖ إِن كُنتُمْ تَعْلَمُونَ ١٨٤

"˹Fast a˺ prescribed number of days.¹ But whoever of you is ill or on a journey, then ˹let them fast˺ an equal number of days ˹after Ramadan. ˺ For those who can only fast with extreme difficulty,² compensation can be made by feeding a needy person ˹for every day not fasted˺. But whoever volunteers to give more, it is better for them. And to fast is better for you, if only you knew."

Al-Baqarah184

This specified the conditions of fasting, and clearly, if you can fast hardly, you feed a needy person for the whole month instead, but if you fast, it's better for you. When Quran specifies the Fidia in the same meaning that Abraham PBUH was going to sacrifice his son Fidia. And to assure that God said if you volunteer, to fast it's better for you.

69

It's Not Hardship

So, you have options because Islam is a relief religion, not a difficult one, so you don't have to play the devil's advocate, and in order not to fast, you drive a special distance so you can break your fast, that's what we called a loop hole in the system, but actually not you still have to fast again unless you feed for the needy.

Let's say hypothetically; the Muslim population in the world is 1.7 billion people, and 10 percent very rich, 20 percent medium, and the rest of the population is needy or hardly can make it. If the fifty percent chose not to fast and they have to pay the Fidia, which they have to feed, the other Fifty percent isn't that humane and good for all, but also if they decide to fast too, that will be even better for them. They all explain how good fasting is for you, and that's why God orders us but none talk about giving and how that is good for everyone.

How is Ramadan fair worldwide as we see it now?

Where is the fairness? Just look at the data for Sep worldwide, then you will realize the fairness.

IF THEY KNEW!

وَكَذَٰلِكَ أَنزَلْنَٰهُ قُرْءَانًا عَرَبِيًّا وَصَرَّفْنَا فِيهِ مِنَ ٱلْوَعِيدِ لَعَلَّهُمْ يَتَّقُونَ أَوْ يُحْدِثُ لَهُمْ ذِكْرًا ١١٣ فَتَعَٰلَى ٱللَّهُ ٱلْمَلِكُ ٱلْحَقُّ ۗ وَلَا تَعْجَلْ بِٱلْقُرْءَانِ مِن قَبْلِ أَن يُقْضَىٰٓ إِلَيْكَ وَحْيُهُۥ ۖ وَقُل رَّبِّ زِدْنِى عِلْمًا ١١٤

"And so, we have sent it down as an Arabic Quran and varied the warnings in it, so perhaps they will shun evil or it may cause them to be mindful. Exalted is Allah, the True King! Do not rush to recite ˹a revelation of˺ the Quran ˹O Prophet˺ before it is ˹properly˺ conveyed to you,1 and pray, "My Lord! Increase me in knowledge.""

Taha113 114

We can easily recognize the Hijri year that started 17 years after the prophet's death, messed up the Arabic years, and reallocated the months; because it's done by Humans with no understanding of God's wisdom behind this matter. The Prophet PBUH knew, which is why, he never changed the months; he always fasts in September and pilgrim (Hajj) in December.

They think they did the Islam a good deed! Islam is a complete message they just have to follow so no more miracles get lost after all they are humans not prophets or messengers.

Jul-22						number of hours	Sep-22			number of hours
Longyearbyen						24 hours sun never set for four months april to aug	Longyearbyen			13 hrs it will shift by 10 days per year average from 2020 2021 2022
Oslo norway						18 hrs average	Oslo Norway			13 hrs average
Russia Moscow						16 hrs Average	Russia Moscow			12.5 hrs average
London, United Kingdom						16 hrs average	London, United Kingdom			12.5 hrs average
new york						15 hrs average	new york			12.5hrs average
shanghi, China						14 hrs Average	shanghi, China			12.5 hrs average
Mecca , Saudi Arabia						13.5 Hrs average	Mecca , Saudi Arabia			12.5 hrs average
Buenos Aires, Argentine						10 Hrs average	Buenos Aires, Argentine			12 hrs average
Australia melbourne						9.5 Hrs average	Australia melbourne			12 hrs average

Where is the fairness? Just look at the data for Sep worldwide, then you will realize the fairness. There are countries the sun doesn't set for four to five months! How will they fast, and the condition of fasting is from sunrise to sunset?

خَلَقَ ٱلْإِنسَٰنُ مِنْ عَجَلٍ ۚ سَأُوْرِيكُمْ ءَايَٰتِى فَلَا تَسْتَعْجِلُونِ ٣٧

"Humankind is made of haste. I will soon show you My signs, so do not ask Me to hasten them."

Al-Anbya37

IS THERE IS GRAVE PUNISHMENT?

The Holly Quran has all the verses emphasizing that when death happens, the time stop for the dead one, and when the resurrection happens, they will think that they just slept a day or half the day or a few hours. To wake up again for judgment day, it's almost in every Ayah specified that,

قَالُوا يَٰوَيْلَنَا مَنْ بَعَثَنَا مِن مَّرْقَدِنَا ۜ هَٰذَا مَا وَعَدَ ٱلرَّحْمَٰنُ وَصَدَقَ ٱلْمُرْسَلُونَ ٥٢

"They will cry, "Woe to us! Who has raised us up from our place of rest? This must be what the Most Compassionate warned us of; the messengers told the truth!"

Are they sleeping?

وَعُرِضُواْ عَلَىٰ رَبِّكَ صَفًّا لَّقَدْ جِئْتُمُونَا كَمَا خَلَقْنَٰكُمْ أَوَّلَ مَرَّةٍ بَلْ زَعَمْتُمْ أَلَّن نَّجْعَلَ لَكُم مَّوْعِدًا ﴿٤٨﴾

And they will be presented before your Lord in rows, [and He will say], "You have certainly come to Us just as We created you the first time. But you claimed that We would never make for you an appointment."

Al-kahaf48

Will they be presented before Lord or the two angels???

وَوُضِعَ ٱلْكِتَٰبُ فَتَرَى ٱلْمُجْرِمِينَ مُشْفِقِينَ مِمَّا فِيهِ وَيَقُولُونَ يَٰوَيْلَتَنَا مَالِ هَٰذَا ٱلْكِتَٰبِ لَا يُغَادِرُ صَغِيرَةً وَلَا كَبِيرَةً إِلَّا أَحْصَىٰهَا وَوَجَدُواْ مَا عَمِلُواْ حَاضِرًا وَلَا يَظْلِمُ رَبُّكَ أَحَدًا ﴿٤٩﴾

And the record [of deeds] will be placed [open], and you will see the criminals fearful of that within it, and they will say, "Oh, woe to us! What is this book that leaves nothing small or great except that it has enumerated it?" And they will find what they did present [before them]. And your Lord does injustice to no one.

Alkahaf 49

When is that at the grave or on Judgement Day??

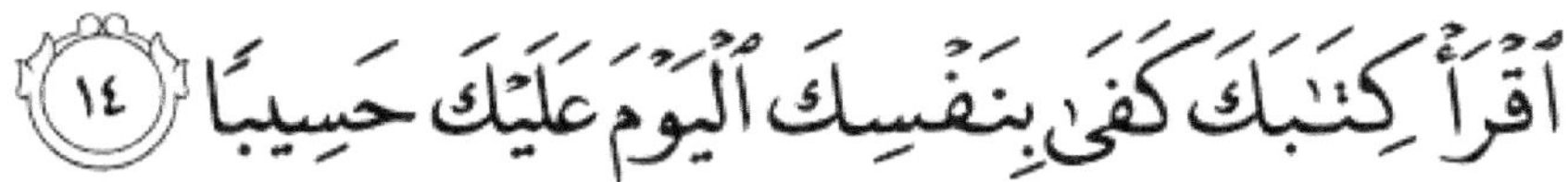

[It will be said], "Read your record. Sufficient is yourself against you this Day as accountant."

Al-Isra14

Again, if I will read my own book on judgement day, why they asked me in the grave?

"[Mention, O Muhammad], the Day We will call forth every people with their record [of deeds]. Then whoever is given his record in his right hand - those will read their records, and injustice will not be done to them, [even] as much as a thread [inside the date seed]."

Al-Isra71

"Allah will judge between you on the Day of Resurrection concerning that over which you used to differ."

Al-Hajj69

وَيَوْمَ يُعْرَضُ الَّذِينَ كَفَرُوا عَلَى النَّارِ أَلَيْسَ هَذَا بِالْحَقِّ قَالُوا بَلَى وَرَبِّنَا قَالَ فَذُوقُوا الْعَذَابَ بِمَا كُنتُمْ تَكْفُرُونَ ﴿٣٤﴾

And the Day those who disbelieved are exposed to the Fire [it will be said], "Is this not the truth?" They will say, "Yes, by our Lord." He will say, "Then taste the punishment because you used to disbelieve."

Al-Ahqaf34

وَيَوْمَ تَقُومُ السَّاعَةُ يُقْسِمُ الْمُجْرِمُونَ مَا لَبِثُوا غَيْرَ سَاعَةٍ كَذَلِكَ كَانُوا ﴿٥٥﴾ يُؤْفَكُونَ

"And the Day the Hour appears the criminals will swear they had remained but an hour. Thus, they were deluded."

Ar-room55

WOW, the criminals think they slept only one hour, felt no grave punishment, nothing?

وَأَمَّا مَنْ أُوتِيَ كِتَابَهُ بِشِمَالِهِ فَيَقُولُ يَا لَيْتَنِي لَمْ أُوتَ كِتَابِيَهْ25

But as for he who is given his record in his left hand, he will say, "Oh, I wish I had not been given my record."

Al-haaqqa25

He just found out what his punishment will be, and he wishes that he didn't know. Why? The two angels didn't tell him that in the grave?

الْيَوْمَ نَخْتِمُ عَلَى أَفْوَاهِهِمْ وَتُكَلِّمُنَا أَيْدِيهِمْ وَتَشْهَدُ أَرْجُلُهُمْ بِمَا كَانُوا يَكْسِبُونَ65

"That Day, we will seal over their mouths, and their hands will speak to Us, and their feet will testify about what they used to earn. Where this happen in the grave or at judgement day?"

Yaseen 65

Does that happen in the grave?

There is almost in each Surah proof there is no grave punishment before the resurrection, and there is no two angel asking people questions, only God is the judge on judgement day. All the proof that we need in Infront of our eyes and still believe in one hadeeth can blow all this proof??? When will we go back to the miracle that God gave us (QURAN).

The Islam religion has been a subject of many attacks to deteriorate Muslims from right and wrong. The only path is going to be God's book who is protected by God, and no one could ever change that fact although they tried so many times and they failed, so they try that with Hadeeth, publishing lies about our prophet PBUH.

إِنَّا نَحْنُ نَزَّلْنَا الذِّكْرَ وَإِنَّا لَهُ لَحَافِظُونَ9

"Indeed, it is We who sent down the Qur'an and indeed, we will be its guardian."

Al-Hijr9

وَمَا أَرْسَلْنَا قَبْلَكَ إِلَّا رِجَالًا نُوحِي إِلَيْهِمْ فَاسْأَلُوا أَهْلَ الذِّكْرِ إِنْ كُنْتُمْ لَا تَعْلَمُونَ43

"And We sent not before you, [O Muhammad], except men to whom We revealed [the message], so ask the people of the message if you do not know."

An-nahl43

وَهَٰذَا ذِكْرٌ مُبَارَكٌ أَنْزَلْنَاهُ ۚ أَفَأَنْتُمْ لَهُ مُنْكِرُونَ ٥٠

"And this ˹Quran˺ is a blessed reminder which We have revealed. Will you ˹pagans˺ then deny it?"

Al-Anbya50

It's an obvious and clear message that we should follow the Quran, and any Hadith that doesn't match the Quran it's a lie. How can we know that, if we don't read the Quran?? If the men of the cloth read the Quran, they will not allow the rumors to spread and will not allow the people to believe such a lie, and create the lies about two angels, Munker and Nakeer (how they came up with the names) who will judge you in the grave and punish you instead of judgment day after the resurrection. It will be known to all Muslims, this lie, and they believe it more than Quran (أستغفر الله) I seek forgiveness from Allah.

In Quran, All the answers we need, and you have some people questioning you, you can't read the Quran and understand it, and there is nothing in Quran that tell you how to pray? Or how and how??

Before I answer that, I would like to explain two kinds of Hadith

- **Action Hadith**
- **Verbal Hadith**

Action Hadith is the action of the prophet that was witnessed by millions of people and kept on going to this day.

Verbal Hadith basically can be true or can be a lie. (Prophet has many Friday's speeches how come we don't have just one, and in that one, the final one is not fully right because it's different between sunaa and Shiitt,) and how is this hadith about one person telling another and then another person that he heard the prophet say that but none of the others heard that??? Why is there no hadeeth during the ERA of the first four khulafaa after the prophet??? Many, many questions about Hadith, but why go into that if we have the Hadeeth of GOD (Allah), the Holly Quran????

Studies prove that any words, when it travels between more than two people things, will be either added or deducted, and it will be taken out of context.

The only Ayah I heard that supports their Hadith about grave punishment is

فَكَيْفَ إِذَا تَوَفَّتْهُمُ ٱلْمَلَٰئِكَةُ يَضْرِبُونَ وُجُوهَهُمْ وَأَدْبَٰرَهُمْ ٢٧

"Then how ˹horrible˺ will it be when the angels take their souls, beating their faces and backs!"

Muhammad27

And this Ayah talking about during death time, not after, and its nothing to suggest that is the grave punishment and the two angels because it's obvious it was during a fight and more than one angel involved.

One of the reasons we are discussing this is not to tell the people don't worry about the grave punishments because there is none. What we want, is everyone to read the Quran many times so they will be aware of bad Hadith, instead, you scare people with the grave punishment, isn't better for them to be scared of eternity in hell as punishment at judgment day, and quick question how come Satan (Shaitan) doesn't get grave punishment and he is the responsible for most of the disbelief? He supposes to be the first one to get punished. The awareness of bad Hadith is a must, so no one can get us far from Quran or brain wash with different propaganda that can destroy Islam within.

On top of common things among Muslims; if you ask any Muslim who takes a soul, the answer is Azrael!

ٱلَّذِينَ تَتَوَفَّاهُمُ ٱلْمَلَٰئِكَةُ طَيِّبِينَ ۙ يَقُولُونَ سَلَٰمٌ عَلَيْكُمُ ٱدْخُلُوا ٱلْجَنَّةَ بِمَا كُنتُمْ تَعْمَلُونَ ٣٢

Those whose souls the angels take while they are virtuous, saying ⸢to them⸣, "Peace be upon you! Enter Paradise for what you used to do."

An-Nahl32

ٱلَّذِينَ تَتَوَفَّاهُمُ ٱلْمَلَٰئِكَةُ ظَالِمِىٓ أَنفُسِهِمْ ۖ فَأَلْقَوُا ٱلسَّلَمَ مَا كُنَّا نَعْمَلُ مِن سُوٓءٍ ۚ بَلَىٰٓ إِنَّ ٱللَّهَ عَلِيمٌۢ بِمَا كُنتُمْ تَعْمَلُونَ ٢٨

"Those whose souls the angels seize while they wrong themselves will then offer ⸢full⸣ submission ⸢and say falsely,⸣ "We did not do any evil." ⸢The angels will say,⸣ "No! Surely Allah fully knows what you used to do."

An-nahl28

Where the Azrael name is mentioned in Quran, it's not one angel who collects the souls!!!!!

قُلْ يَتَوَفَّىٰكُم مَّلَكُ ٱلْمَوْتِ ٱلَّذِى وُكِّلَ بِكُمْ ثُمَّ إِلَىٰ رَبِّكُمْ تُرْجَعُونَ ١١

Say, ⸢O Prophet,⸣ "Your soul will be taken by the Angel of Death, who is in charge of you. Then to your Lord, you will ⸢all⸣ be returned."

As-Sajdah (11)

Just to shed light on names, it could be right could be wrong, but it's totally not important to know; since God didn't specify it. Also, to show how rumors spread and start to manipulate the religion if we start to get away from Quran and follow just Hadith, any Hadith that goes against Quran, we shouldn't mention it, we shouldn't even repeat it.

I would like to finish with two more ayahs, although there is a lot of proof almost in each surah, as I mentioned before.

وَقَالُوا لِجُلُودِهِمْ لِمَ شَهِدتُّمْ عَلَيْنَا ۖ قَالُوا أَنطَقَنَا اللَّهُ الَّذِى أَنطَقَ كُلَّ شَىْءٍ وَهُوَ خَلَقَكُمْ أَوَّلَ مَرَّةٍ وَإِلَيْهِ تُرْجَعُونَ ٢١

They will ask their skin ˹furiously, ˺ "Why have you testified against us?" It will say, "We have been made to speak by Allah, who causes all things to speak. He ˹is the One Who˺ created you the first time, and to Him you were bound to return."

Fussilat21

وَمَا كُنتُمْ تَسْتَتِرُونَ أَن يَشْهَدَ عَلَيْكُمْ سَمْعُكُمْ وَلَا أَبْصَارُكُمْ وَلَا جُلُودُكُمْ وَلَكِن ظَنَنتُمْ أَنَّ اللَّهَ لَا يَعْلَمُ كَثِيرًا مِّمَّا تَعْمَلُونَ ٢٢

"You did not ˹bother to˺ hide yourselves from your ears, eyes, and skin to prevent them from testifying against you. Rather, you assumed that Allah did not know much of what you used to do."

Fussilat22

After everything has been said here, will you still think of Grave punishment? Isn't it time to start going back to Quran? If they lie to us about this, what else do they lie to us about? Why does the Hadith get to be glorified on God's words, Quran??

إِنَّكَ لَا تُسْمِعُ ٱلْمَوْتَىٰ وَلَا تُسْمِعُ ٱلصُّمَّ ٱلدُّعَاءَ إِذَا وَلَّوْاْ مُدْبِرِينَ ٨٠

"You certainly cannot make the dead hear ˹the truth˺. Nor can you make the deaf hear the call when they turn their backs and walk away."

An-Naml80

يَوْمَئِذٍ يَصْدُرُ ٱلنَّاسُ أَشْتَاتًا لِّيُرَوْاْ أَعْمَٰلَهُمْ ٦

On that Day people will proceed in separate groups¹ to be shown ˹the consequences of˺ their deeds.

Az-Zalzalah 6.

People have faith in GOD and love his prophet, but I get the feeling, that; men of clothes doesn't want that. All what they want is to diverted them from the straight path and to make it complicated for them, so; they either give up or don't care anymore. Look what happened to our Islamic world. The streets are dirty, the poverty sky rocketing, the bad things are sky rocketing and everyone hate everyone. All of that ignorance is manmade and goes back to the men in clothes.

83

TIME AND SLEEP

Sleep and death are similar to GOD, and GOD decide who wakes up or not, the time belongs to GOD, and when a person dies, his time stops, so when the human resurrects again, they will think they were sleeping, and they just woke up although it could be many years since their sleep or death.

اَللّٰهُ يَتَوَفَّى ٱلْأَنفُسَ حِينَ مَوْتِهَا وَٱلَّتِى لَمْ تَمُتْ فِى مَنَامِهَا ۖ فَيُمْسِكُ ٱلَّتِى قَضَىٰ عَلَيْهَا ٱلْمَوْتَ وَيُرْسِلُ ٱلْأُخْرَىٰ إِلَىٰ أَجَلٍ مُّسَمًّى ۚ إِنَّ فِى ذَٰلِكَ لَءَايَٰتٍ لِّقَوْمٍ يَتَفَكَّرُونَ ٤٢

"It is' Allah 'Who' calls back the souls 'of people' upon their death as well as 'the souls' of the living during their sleep. Then He keeps those for whom He has ordained death, and releases the others until 'their' appointed time. Surely in this are signs for people who reflect."

Azzumar42

وَتَحْسَبُهُمْ أَيْقَاظًا وَهُمْ رُقُودٌ ۚ وَنُقَلِّبُهُمْ ذَاتَ ٱلْيَمِينِ وَذَاتَ ٱلشِّمَالِ ۖ وَكَلْبُهُم بَٰسِطٌ ذِرَاعَيْهِ بِٱلْوَصِيدِ ۚ لَوِ ٱطَّلَعْتَ عَلَيْهِمْ لَوَلَّيْتَ مِنْهُمْ فِرَارًا وَلَمُلِئْتَ مِنْهُمْ رُعْبًا ١٨ وَكَذَٰلِكَ بَعَثْنَٰهُمْ لِيَتَسَآءَلُوا۟ بَيْنَهُمْ ۚ قَالَ قَآئِلٌ مِّنْهُمْ كَمْ لَبِثْتُمْ ۖ قَالُوا۟ لَبِثْنَا يَوْمًا أَوْ بَعْضَ يَوْمٍ ۚ قَالُوا۟ رَبُّكُمْ أَعْلَمُ بِمَا لَبِثْتُمْ فَٱبْعَثُوٓا۟ أَحَدَكُم بِوَرِقِكُمْ هَٰذِهِۦ إِلَى ٱلْمَدِينَةِ فَلْيَنظُرْ أَيُّهَا أَزْكَىٰ طَعَامًا فَلْيَأْتِكُم بِرِزْقٍ مِّنْهُ وَلْيَتَلَطَّفْ وَلَا يُشْعِرَنَّ بِكُمْ أَحَدًا ١٩

"And you would have thought they were awake,1 though they were asleep. We turned them over, to the right and left, while their dog stretched his forelegs at the entrance. Had you looked at them, you would have certainly fled away from them, filled with horror. And so We awakened them so that they might question one another. One of them exclaimed, "How long have you remained ˹asleep˺?" Some replied, "Perhaps a day, or part of a day." They said ˹to one another˺, "Your Lord knows best how long you have remained. So send one of you with these silver coins of yours to the city, and let him find which food is the purest, and then bring you provisions from it. Let him be ˹exceptionally˺ cautious, and do not let him give you away."

Al-Kahf 18, 19

أَوْ كَٱلَّذِى مَرَّ عَلَىٰ قَرْيَةٍ وَهِىَ خَاوِيَةٌ عَلَىٰ عُرُوشِهَا قَالَ أَنَّىٰ يُحْىِۦ هَـٰذِهِ ٱللَّهُ بَعْدَ مَوْتِهَا ۖ فَأَمَاتَهُ ٱللَّهُ مِائَةَ عَامٍ ثُمَّ بَعَثَهُ ۖ قَالَ كَمْ لَبِثْتَ ۖ قَالَ لَبِثْتُ يَوْمًا أَوْ بَعْضَ يَوْمٍ قَالَ بَل لَّبِثْتَ مِائَةَ عَامٍ فَٱنظُرْ إِلَىٰ طَعَامِكَ وَشَرَابِكَ لَمْ يَتَسَنَّهْ ۖ وَٱنظُرْ إِلَىٰ حِمَارِكَ وَلِنَجْعَلَكَ ءَايَةً لِّلنَّاسِ ۖ وَٱنظُرْ إِلَى ٱلْعِظَامِ كَيْفَ نُنشِزُهَا ثُمَّ نَكْسُوهَا لَحْمًا فَلَمَّا تَبَيَّنَ لَهُ قَالَ أَعْلَمُ أَنَّ ٱللَّهَ عَلَىٰ كُلِّ شَىْءٍ قَدِيرٌ ٢٥٩

"Or ˹are you not aware of˺ the one who passed by a city which was in ruins. He wondered, "How could Allah bring this back to life after its destruction?" So Allah caused him to die for a hundred years then brought him back to life. Allah asked, "How long have you remained ˹in this state˺?" He replied, "Perhaps a day or part of a day." Allah said, "No! You have remained here for a hundred years! Just look at your food and drink—they have not spoiled. ˹But now˺ look at ˹the remains of˺ your donkey! And

˹so˺ We have made you into a sign for humanity. And look at the bones ˹of the donkey˺, how We bring them together then clothe them with flesh!"1 When this was made clear to him, he declared, "˹Now˺ I know that Allah is Most Capable of everything."

Al-Baqara 259

In both, we see the time concept stopped for them, when GOD woke them up, they thought they had slept for a few hours only.

And with all the proof we displayed here, we found that there is no Grave punishment, and that should be the least of your worries; if the meaning behind this Hadith is to scare humans, you should scare them from the eternity in Hell, which by far is greater.

Lies are the key to destroy the whole thing, and the easy way to have people believe, tell a lie and say that the prophet said that. Really the only way we can spot a lie is by comparing it to Quran; if it's matched, its good Hadith, if it goes totally against Quran, here you go, you spotted the lie. How a messenger can go against his GOD?

Unfortunately, most Muslims know Hadith more than Quran. They never read the Quran, and if they read the Quran, they are not listening. The Quran in many Islamic countries became a sign of death, if you go by houses and you hear the Quran loud, immediately you will know there is death happening in this house!

لِّيُنذِرَ مَن كَانَ حَيًّا وَيَحِقَّ ٱلْقَوْلُ عَلَى ٱلْكَـٰفِرِينَ ٧٠

"To warn whoever is ˹truly˺ alive and fulfil the decree ˹of torment˺ against the disbelievers."

Yaseen70

Is Jesus Coming Back? How about Al-Mahdi?

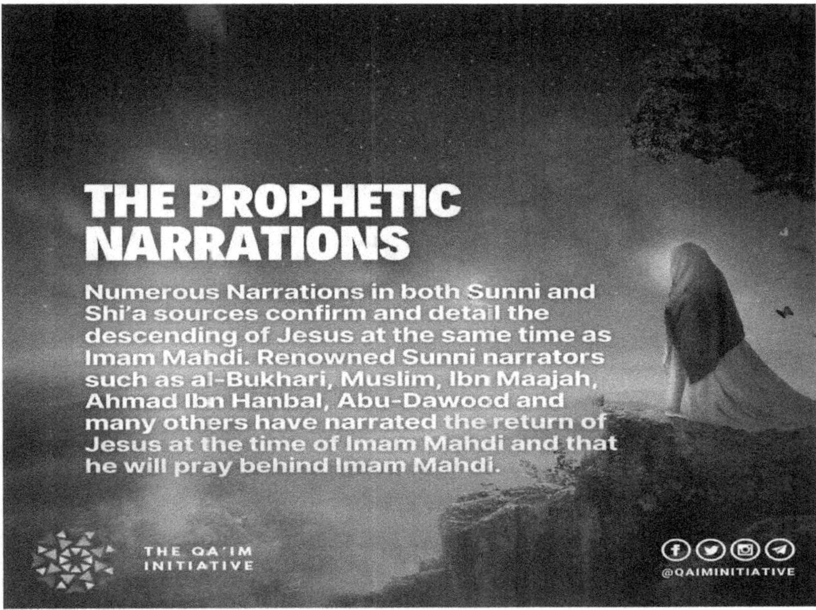

Another belief that has been going on for many years, actually till now.

If you ask any Muslim, he or she would tell you yes, Jesus is Coming Back, and there is an antichrist and the Mahdi; that's what the Quran denies absolutely.

إِنَّ مَثَلَ عِيسَىٰ عِندَ ٱللَّهِ كَمَثَلِ ءَادَمَ ۖ خَلَقَهُۥ مِن تُرَابٍ ثُمَّ قَالَ لَهُۥ كُن فَيَكُونُ ٥٩

Indeed, the example of Jesus in the sight of Allah is like that of Adam. He created him from dust, then said to him, "Be!" And he was!

Al-Imran 59

Is Adam coming back too?? They are both created by God, one from mud, no father or mother, and one from mother; only. Will that make Adam the God since he doesn't have a father or mother?

يَـٰٓأُخْتَ هَـٰرُونَ مَا كَانَ أَبُوكِ ٱمْرَأَ سَوْءٍ وَمَا كَانَتْ أُمُّكِ بَغِيًّا ٢٨ فَأَشَارَتْ إِلَيْهِ ۖ قَالُوا۟ كَيْفَ نُكَلِّمُ مَن كَانَ فِى ٱلْمَهْدِ صَبِيًّا ٢٩ قَالَ إِنِّى عَبْدُ ٱللَّهِ ءَاتَٮٰنِىَ ٱلْكِتَـٰبَ وَجَعَلَنِى نَبِيًّا ٣٠ وَجَعَلَنِى مُبَارَكًا أَيْنَ مَا كُنتُ وَأَوْصَـٰنِى بِٱلصَّلَوٰةِ وَٱلزَّكَوٰةِ مَا دُمْتُ حَيًّا ٣١ وَبَرًّۢا بِوَٰلِدَتِى وَلَمْ يَجْعَلْنِى جَبَّارًا شَقِيًّا ٣٢ وَٱلسَّلَـٰمُ عَلَىَّ يَوْمَ وُلِدتُّ وَيَوْمَ أَمُوتُ وَيَوْمَ أُبْعَثُ حَيًّا ٣٣ ذَٰلِكَ عِيسَى ٱبْنُ مَرْيَمَ ۚ قَوْلَ ٱلْحَقِّ ٱلَّذِى فِيهِ يَمْتَرُونَ ٣٤

O sister of Aaron![1] Your father was not an indecent man, nor was your mother unchaste." So, she pointed to the baby. They exclaimed, "How can we talk to someone who is an infant in the cradle?" ˹Jesus˺ declared, "I am truly a servant of Allah. He has destined me to be given the Scripture and to be a prophet. He has made me a blessing wherever I go and bid me establish prayer and give alms tax as long as I live, and to be kind to my mother. He has not made me arrogant or defiant. Peace be upon me the day I was born, the day I die, and the day I will be raised back to life!" That is Jesus, son of Mary. ˹And this is˺ a word of truth about which they dispute.

Maryam28 29 30 31 32 33 34

88

If Jesus says that Peace be upon me the day I was born (and he born) the day I die (and God take him and raise him), and the day I will be raised back to life (will he be resurrected on day different than our resurrection day?? Does he have two resurrection days and the same thing for John (Yehia PBUH)

John (Yehia) PBUH, GOD, said the same thing about him, will he come back also?

John (Yehia PBUH and Jesus PBUH both have miraculous birth, Jesus PBUH was born from a mother and no father, John (Yehia BPUH) was born from a parent very old and the mom couldn't ever have a baby.

يَٰيَحْيَىٰ خُذِ ٱلْكِتَٰبَ بِقُوَّةٍ ۖ وَءَاتَيْنَٰهُ ٱلْحُكْمَ صَبِيًّا ١٢ وَحَنَانًا مِّن لَّدُنَّا وَزَكَوٰةً وَكَانَ تَقِيًّا ١٣ وَبَرًّۢا بِوَٰلِدَيْهِ وَلَمْ يَكُن جَبَّارًا عَصِيًّا ١٤ وَسَلَٰمٌ عَلَيْهِ يَوْمَ وُلِدَ وَيَوْمَ يَمُوتُ وَيَوْمَ يُبْعَثُ حَيًّا ١٥

ˊIt was later said, ˋ "O John! Hold firmly to the Scriptures." And We granted him wisdom while ˋhe was stillˊ a child, as well as purity and compassion from Us. And he was God-fearing and kind to his parents. He was neither arrogant nor disobedient. Peace be upon him the day he was born, and the day of his death, and the day he will be raised back to life!

Maryam 12 13 14 15

إِذْ قَالَ ٱللَّهُ يَٰعِيسَىٰ إِنِّى مُتَوَفِّيكَ وَرَافِعُكَ إِلَىَّ وَمُطَهِّرُكَ مِنَ ٱلَّذِينَ كَفَرُوا۟ وَجَاعِلُ ٱلَّذِينَ ٱتَّبَعُوكَ فَوْقَ ٱلَّذِينَ كَفَرُوٓا۟ إِلَىٰ يَوْمِ ٱلْقِيَٰمَةِ ۖ ثُمَّ إِلَىَّ مَرْجِعُكُمْ فَأَحْكُمُ بَيْنَكُمْ فِيمَا كُنتُمْ فِيهِ تَخْتَلِفُونَ ٥٥

˹Remember˺ when Allah said, "O Jesus! I will take you1 and raise you up to Myself. I will deliver you from those who disbelieve and elevate your followers above the disbelievers until the Day of Judgment. Then to Me, you will ˹all˺ return, and I will settle all your disputes.

Aal-Imran 55

مَا قُلْتُ لَهُمْ إِلَّا مَا أَمَرْتَنِى بِهِ أَنِ اعْبُدُوا اللَّهَ رَبِّى وَرَبَّكُمْ وَكُنْتُ عَلَيْهِمْ شَهِيدًا مَا دُمْتُ فِيهِمْ فَلَمَّا تَوَفَّيْتَنِى كُنْتَ أَنْتَ الرَّقِيبَ عَلَيْهِمْ وَأَنْتَ عَلَى كُلِّ شَىْءٍ شَهِيدٌ ١١٧

I never told them anything except what You ordered me to say: "Worship Allah—my Lord and your Lord!" And I was witness over them as long as I remained among them. But when You took me,1 You were the witness over them—and You are a Witness over all things.

al-maeda117

So, Jesus Died?

حُرِّمَتْ عَلَيْكُمُ الْمَيْتَةُ وَالدَّمُ وَلَحْمُ الْخِنْزِيرِ وَمَا أُهِلَّ لِغَيْرِ اللَّهِ بِهِ وَالْمُنْخَنِقَةُ وَالْمَوْقُوذَةُ وَالْمُتَرَدِّيَةُ وَالنَّطِيحَةُ وَمَا أَكَلَ السَّبُعُ إِلَّا مَا ذَكَّيْتُمْ وَمَا ذُبِحَ عَلَى النُّصُبِ وَأَنْ تَسْتَقْسِمُوا بِالْأَزْلَامِ ۚ ذَلِكُمْ فِسْقٌ ۗ الْيَوْمَ يَئِسَ الَّذِينَ كَفَرُوا مِنْ دِينِكُمْ فَلَا تَخْشَوْهُمْ وَاخْشَوْنِ ۚ الْيَوْمَ أَكْمَلْتُ لَكُمْ دِينَكُمْ وَأَتْمَمْتُ عَلَيْكُمْ نِعْمَتِى وَرَضِيتُ لَكُمُ الْإِسْلَامَ دِينًا ۚ فَمَنِ اضْطُرَّ فِى مَخْمَصَةٍ غَيْرَ مُتَجَانِفٍ لِإِثْمٍ ۙ فَإِنَّ اللَّهَ غَفُورٌ رَحِيمٌ ٣

Forbidden to you are carrion, blood, and swine; what is slaughtered in the name of any other than Allah; what is killed by strangling, beating, a fall, or by being gored to death; what is partly eaten by a predator unless you slaughter it; and what is sacrificed on altars. You are also forbidden to draw lots for decisions.[1] This is all evil. Today the disbelievers have given up all hope of ˹undermining˺ your faith. So do not fear them; fear Me! Today I have perfected your faith for you, completed My favor upon you, and chosen Islam as your way. But whoever is compelled by extreme hunger—not intending to sin—then surely Allah is All-Forgiving, Most Merciful.

Al-maeda3

God has completed the message, and Muhamad PBUH fulfilled his duty, so what else could someone can come up with? Even suggesting that it is destroying the religion and blow for the Holy book.

مَّا كَانَ مُحَمَّدٌ أَبَآ أَحَدٍ مِّن رِّجَالِكُمْ وَلَٰكِن رَّسُولَ ٱللَّهِ وَخَاتَمَ ٱلنَّبِيِّـۧنَ ۗ وَكَانَ ٱللَّهُ بِكُلِّ شَىْءٍ عَلِيمًا ٤٠

Muhammad is not the father of any of your men,[1] but is the Messenger of Allah and the seal of the prophets. And Allah has ˹perfect˺ knowledge of all things.

Al-Ahzab 40

So, with all that has been said, we find that what GOD said about John (Yehia) PBUH what Jesus PBUH has said exactly the same thing when he just born. What that means is he is coming back too, also, Adam PBUH is the same as Jesus PBUH; is he coming back too?

91

Isn't Mohamad PBUH the last prophet?? Isn't the message complete? So, what is the point for any one whether to show up or not? Is he going to bring something new different than what the prophet already brought??

WHY?

Judaism believe that Jesus PBUH has yet to come, and they are still waiting for him. That means there will be animosity with the Christian, especially after Islam admits the prophecy of Jesus and Merry the virgin. The only way to make peace is to convince both parties that he will come back, and that is how the story started, it was so easy for Christian when the body was not in the cave, and for Muslims it was easier by just saying, that Muhamad PBUH said that! As we see that they couldn't change a word in Quran, but they succeeded in convincing everyone that you can't understand the Quran and you need to depend on the Hadith where they can feed the people their Propaganda.

To believe such a thing is considered blowing to the Quran and Islam; because it's the opposite what the Quran came with. It's like to say the Quran and the Message are incomplete, and someone will come later to correct it!

Talking about or even suggesting that a prophet or any man will come is trying to blow up the Quran and the religion. The Idea behind that, it gets the Muslims farther away from the miracle book Quran. As long as Muslims not reading the most important book in their life, you can make them believe anything. It's a devilish plan to direct the Muslim concentration on Hadith and books by this person or that with all respect; and remove the Quran from their minds and hearts.

لَا إِكْرَاهَ فِى ٱلدِّينِ ۖ قَد تَّبَيَّنَ ٱلرُّشْدُ مِنَ ٱلْغَىِّ ۚ فَمَن يَكْفُرْ بِٱلطَّٰغُوتِ وَيُؤْمِن بِٱللَّهِ فَقَدِ ٱسْتَمْسَكَ بِٱلْعُرْوَةِ ٱلْوُثْقَىٰ لَا ٱنفِصَامَ لَهَا ۗ وَٱللَّهُ سَمِيعٌ عَلِيمٌ ٢٥٦

"Let there be no compulsion in religion, for the truth stands out clearly from falsehood.¹ So whoever renounces false gods and believes in Allah has certainly grasped the firmest, unfailing hand-hold. And Allah is All-Hearing, All-Knowing."

Al-Baqarah256

سَأَصْرِفُ عَنْ ءَايَٰتِىَ ٱلَّذِينَ يَتَكَبَّرُونَ فِى ٱلْأَرْضِ بِغَيْرِ ٱلْحَقِّ وَإِن يَرَوْا۟ كُلَّ ءَايَةٍ لَّا يُؤْمِنُوا۟ بِهَا وَإِن يَرَوْا۟ سَبِيلَ ٱلرُّشْدِ لَا يَتَّخِذُوهُ سَبِيلًا وَإِن يَرَوْا۟ سَبِيلَ ٱلْغَىِّ يَتَّخِذُوهُ سَبِيلًا ۚ ذَٰلِكَ بِأَنَّهُمْ كَذَّبُوا۟ بِـَٔايَٰتِنَا وَكَانُوا۟ عَنْهَا غَٰفِلِينَ ١٤٦

"I will turn away from My signs those who act unjustly with arrogance in the land. And even if they were to see every sign, they still would not believe in them. If they see the Right Path, they will not take it. But if they see a crooked path, they will follow it. This is because they denied Our signs and were heedless of them."

Al-A'raf146

قُلْ أُوحِىَ إِلَىَّ أَنَّهُ ٱسْتَمَعَ نَفَرٌ مِّنَ ٱلْجِنِّ فَقَالُوٓا۟ إِنَّا سَمِعْنَا قُرْءَانًا عَجَبًا ١

"Say, ˹O Prophet,˺ "It has been revealed to me that a group of jinn listened ˹to the Quran,˺ and said ˹to their fellow jinn˺: 'Indeed, we have heard a wondrous recitation."

Al-Jinn1

يَهْدِىٓ إِلَى ٱلرُّشْدِ فَـَٔامَنَّا بِهِۦ ۖ وَلَن نُّشْرِكَ بِرَبِّنَآ أَحَدًا ٢

"It leads to Right Guidance so we believed in it, and we will never associate anyone with our Lord ˹in worship˺."

Al-Jinn2

We have to be careful of what we believe in or not, and with what we hear when it comes to GOD. The message is complete and no more profits to come or anyone else, just ask yourself why they should come? To spread the justice or to be fair to the people, my question where they were all these years? Where is the fairness to come for some not to others? There is no point at all. Its only lies even in the Christianity they mis interrupted that Jesus PBUH will come back, and what meant is he coming back in resurrection day same as the Quran mentioned. The same resurrection day for all the people and that what he told his decibels. And since his decibels died and he never returned it's the proof that his return will be resurrection day.

See below:

Before Jesus left this earth, He said He would return. During His Olivet Discourse, the Lord told His disciples that everyone one day would "see the Son of Man coming on the clouds of heaven, with power and great glory" (Matthew 24:30). The night of His arrest, Jesus promised, "I will come back and take you to be with me that you also may be where I am" (John 14:3). And as He stood trial before the high priest, Jesus said, "You will see the Son of Man sitting at the right hand of the Mighty One and coming on the clouds of heaven" (Mark 14:62). We have the promises, but we are still waiting. Jesus has not returned yet.

There is also an assurance from the angels that Jesus would return some day. After Jesus ascended into heaven, as His disciples were still gazing up into the sky, two angels comforted the disciples with these words: "This same Jesus, who has been taken from you into heaven, will come back in the same way you have seen him go into heaven" (Acts 1:11). Later, John sees a vision of Jesus Christ telling him, "Look, I am coming soon!" (Revelation 22:7). Still, Jesus has not returned. Where is He, and what's taking Him so long?

https://www.gotquestions.org/why-hasnt-Jesus-returned-yet.html

WHAT IS THE WILL IN ISLAM??

كُتِبَ عَلَيْكُمْ إِذَا حَضَرَ أَحَدَكُمُ ٱلْمَوْتُ إِن تَرَكَ خَيْرًا ٱلْوَصِيَّةُ لِلْوَٰلِدَيْنِ وَٱلْأَقْرَبِينَ بِٱلْمَعْرُوفِ ۖ حَقًّا عَلَى ٱلْمُتَّقِينَ ١٨٠

"It is prescribed that when death approaches any of you—if they leave something of value—a will should be made in favor of parents and immediate family with fairness.[1] ⸢This is⸣ an obligation on those who are mindful ⸢of Allah⸣."

albaqara180

So, we have to write Will??

فَمَنۢ بَدَّلَهُۥ بَعْدَ مَا سَمِعَهُۥ فَإِنَّمَآ إِثْمُهُۥ عَلَى ٱلَّذِينَ يُبَدِّلُونَهُۥٓ ۚ إِنَّ ٱللَّهَ سَمِيعٌ عَلِيمٌ ١٨١

"But whoever changes the will after hearing it,[1] the blame will only be on those who made the change. Indeed, Allah is All-Hearing, All-Knowing."

Al-Baqarah 181

يَـٰٓأَيُّهَا ٱلَّذِينَ ءَامَنُوا۟ شَهَـٰدَةُ بَيْنِكُمْ إِذَا حَضَرَ أَحَدَكُمُ ٱلْمَوْتُ حِينَ ٱلْوَصِيَّةِ ٱثْنَانِ ذَوَا عَدْلٍ مِّنكُمْ أَوْ ءَاخَرَانِ مِنْ غَيْرِكُمْ إِنْ أَنتُمْ ضَرَبْتُمْ فِى ٱلْأَرْضِ فَأَصَـٰبَتْكُم مُّصِيبَةُ ٱلْمَوْتِ ۚ تَحْبِسُونَهُمَا مِنۢ بَعْدِ ٱلصَّلَوٰةِ فَيُقْسِمَانِ بِٱللَّهِ إِنِ ٱرْتَبْتُمْ لَا نَشْتَرِى بِهِۦ ثَمَنًا وَلَوْ كَانَ ذَا قُرْبَىٰ ۙ وَلَا نَكْتُمُ شَهَـٰدَةَ ٱللَّهِ إِنَّآ إِذًا لَّمِنَ ٱلْـَٔاثِمِينَ ١٠٦

"O believers! When death approaches any of you, call upon two just Muslim men to witness as you make a bequest; otherwise, two non-Muslims if you are afflicted with death while on a journey.[1] If you doubt ˹their testimony˺, keep them after prayer and let them testify under oath ˹saying˺, "By Allah! We would never sell our testimony for any price, even in favour of a close relative, nor withhold the testimony of Allah. Otherwise, we would surely be sinful.""

Almaeda106

يُوصِيكُمُ ٱللَّهُ فِىٓ أَوْلَـٰدِكُمْ ۖ لِلذَّكَرِ مِثْلُ حَظِّ ٱلْأُنثَيَيْنِ ۚ فَإِن كُنَّ نِسَآءً فَوْقَ ٱثْنَتَيْنِ فَلَهُنَّ ثُلُثَا مَا تَرَكَ ۖ وَإِن كَانَتْ وَٰحِدَةً فَلَهَا ٱلنِّصْفُ ۚ وَلِأَبَوَيْهِ لِكُلِّ وَٰحِدٍ مِّنْهُمَا ٱلسُّدُسُ مِمَّا تَرَكَ إِن كَانَ لَهُۥ وَلَدٌ ۚ فَإِن لَّمْ يَكُن لَّهُۥ وَلَدٌ وَوَرِثَهُۥٓ أَبَوَاهُ فَلِأُمِّهِ ٱلثُّلُثُ ۚ فَإِن كَانَ لَهُۥٓ إِخْوَةٌ فَلِأُمِّهِ ٱلسُّدُسُ ۚ مِنۢ بَعْدِ وَصِيَّةٍ يُوصِى بِهَآ أَوْ دَيْنٍ ۗ ءَابَآؤُكُمْ وَأَبْنَآؤُكُمْ لَا تَدْرُونَ أَيُّهُمْ أَقْرَبُ لَكُمْ نَفْعًا ۚ فَرِيضَةً مِّنَ ٱللَّهِ ۗ إِنَّ ٱللَّهَ كَانَ عَلِيمًا حَكِيمًا ١١

"Allah commands you regarding your children: the share of the male will be twice that of the female.[1] If you leave only two ˹or more˺ females, their share is two-thirds of the estate. But if there is only one female, her share will be one-half. Each parent is entitled to one-sixth if you leave offspring.[2] But if you are childless and your parents are the only heirs, then your mother will receive one-third.[3] But if you leave siblings, then your mother will receive one-sixth[4]—after the fulfilment of bequests and debts.[5] ˹Be fair to˺ your parents and children, as you do not ˹fully˺ know who is more beneficial to you.[6] ˹This is˺ an obligation from Allah. Surely Allah is All-Knowing, All-Wise."

An-Nissa 11

وَلَكُمْ نِصْفُ مَا تَرَكَ أَزْوَٰجُكُمْ إِن لَّمْ يَكُن لَّهُنَّ وَلَدٌ ۚ فَإِن كَانَ لَهُنَّ وَلَدٌ فَلَكُمُ ٱلرُّبُعُ مِمَّا تَرَكْنَ ۚ مِنۢ بَعْدِ وَصِيَّةٍ يُوصِينَ بِهَآ أَوْ دَيْنٍ ۚ وَلَهُنَّ ٱلرُّبُعُ مِمَّا تَرَكْتُمْ إِن لَّمْ يَكُن لَّكُمْ وَلَدٌ ۚ فَإِن كَانَ لَكُمْ وَلَدٌ فَلَهُنَّ ٱلثُّمُنُ مِمَّا تَرَكْتُم ۚ مِّنۢ بَعْدِ وَصِيَّةٍ تُوصُونَ بِهَآ أَوْ دَيْنٍ ۗ وَإِن كَانَ رَجُلٌ يُورَثُ كَلَـٰلَةً أَوِ ٱمْرَأَةٌ وَلَهُۥٓ أَخٌ أَوْ أُخْتٌ فَلِكُلِّ وَٰحِدٍ مِّنْهُمَا ٱلسُّدُسُ ۚ فَإِن كَانُوٓا۟ أَكْثَرَ مِن ذَٰلِكَ فَهُمْ شُرَكَآءُ فِى ٱلثُّلُثِ ۚ مِنۢ بَعْدِ وَصِيَّةٍ يُوصَىٰ بِهَآ أَوْ دَيْنٍ غَيْرَ مُضَآرٍّ ۚ وَصِيَّةً مِّنَ ٱللَّهِ ۗ وَٱللَّهُ عَلِيمٌ حَلِيمٌ ١٢

"You will inherit half of what your wives leave if they are childless. But if they have children, then ˹your share is˺ one-fourth of the estate—after the fulfilment of bequests and debts. And your wives will inherit one-fourth of what you leave if you are childless. But if you have children, then your wives will receive one-eighth of your estate—after the fulfilment of bequests and debts. And if a man or a woman leaves neither parents nor children but only a brother or a sister ˹from their mother's side˺, they will each inherit one-sixth, but if they are more than one, they ˹all˺ will share one-third of the estate[1]—after the fulfilment of bequests and debts without harm ˹to the heirs˺.[2] ˹This is˺ a commandment from Allah. And Allah is All-Knowing, Most Forbearing."

An-nissa 12

Why do the men in cloth consider the will is for a third what you own only???

What is the proof??

Why God emphasizing that do this after the will and debt???

They depend on this weak hadith:

حَدَّثَنَا قُتَيْبَةُ، حَدَّثَنَا جَرِيرٌ، عَنْ عَطَاءِ بْنِ السَّائِبِ، عَنْ أَبِي عَبْدِ الرَّحْمَنِ السُّلَمِيّ، عَنْ سَعْدِ بْنِ مَالِكٍ، قَالَ عَادَنِي رَسُولُ اللَّهِ صلى الله عليه وسلم وَأَنَا مَرِيضٌ فَقَالَ " أَوْصَيْتَ " . قُلْتُ نَعَمْ . قَالَ " بِكَمْ " . قُلْتُ بِمَالِي كُلِّهِ فِي سَبِيلِ اللَّهِ . قَالَ " فَمَا تَرَكْتَ لِوَلَدِكَ " . قُلْتُ هُمْ أَغْنِيَاءُ بِخَيْرٍ . قَالَ " أَوْصِ بِالْعُشْرِ " . فَمَا زِلْتُ أُنَاقِصُهُ حَتَّى قَالَ " أَوْصِ بِالثُّلُثِ وَالثُّلُثُ كَثِيرٌ " . قَالَ أَبُو عَبْدِ الرَّحْمَنِ وَنَحْنُ نَسْتَحِبُّ أَنْ يَنْقُصَ مِنَ الثُّلُثِ لِقَوْلِ رَسُولِ اللَّهِ صلى الله عليه وسلم " وَالثُّلُثُ كَثِيرٌ " . قَالَ وَفِي الْبَابِ عَنِ ابْنِ عَبَّاسٍ . قَالَ أَبُو عِيسَى حَدِيثُ سَعْدٍ حَدِيثٌ حَسَنٌ

صَحِيحٌ وَقَدْ رُوِيَ عَنْهُ مِنْ غَيْرِ وَجْهٍ وَقَدْ رُوِيَ عَنْهُ " وَالثُّلُثُ كَبِيرٌ " .
وَالْعَمَلُ عَلَى هَذَا عِنْدَ أَهْلِ الْعِلْمِ لَا يَرَوْنَ أَنْ يُوصِيَ الرَّجُلُ بِأَكْثَرَ مِنَ
الثُّلُثِ وَيَسْتَحِبُّونَ أَنْ يَنْقُصَ مِنَ الثُّلُثِ . قَالَ سُفْيَانُ الثَّوْرِيُّ كَانُوا
يَسْتَحِبُّونَ فِي الْوَصِيَّةِ الْخُمُسَ دُونَ الرُّبُعِ وَالرُّبُعَ دُونَ الثُّلُثِ وَمَنْ
أَوْصَى بِالثُّلُثِ فَلَمْ يَتْرُكْ شَيْئًا وَلَا يَجُوزُ لَهُ إِلاَّ الثُّلُثُ .

Sa'd bin Malik said: "The Messenger of Allah came to visit me while I was sick. He said: 'Do you have a will?' I said: 'Yes.' He said: 'For how much?' I said: 'All of my wealth, for the cause of Allah.' He said: 'What did you leave for your children?'" He (Sa'd) said: "They are rich in goodness.' He said: 'Will a tenth.'" He (Sa'd) said: "He (pbuh) continued decreasing it until he said: 'Will a third, and a third is too great.'" (One of the narrators:) Abdur-Rahman said: "We considered it recommended that it be less than a third, since the Messenger of Allah said: 'And a third is too great.'"

Jami` at-Tirmidhi 975

https://sunnah.com/tirmidhi:975.

Based on that they decided you only can write third of you own, how they got that conclusion I don't know!

Debt and Will in the same degree its either or.

For example, if I have 1000 dollars in the assets and I have debt of 1000 dollars, so there is nothing left to inherit! So, the rule of the third doesn't imply?? And since the rule doesn't imply to debt, it doesn't imply the will! Because God ties them together.

But why God specifies the shares and how to be distributed?? Good question!

How many people write their will before they die? Not a lot, so the rule of distribution will imply to them!

How many people have wealth gain after they wrote the will?

And the excess of wealth outside the will falls under the rule of distribution. But also, on the other hand, God gave us guidance and directed us on how we distribute our wealth in the will, and so we be fair to everyone from our immediate family.

The guidance of Muslims to encourage them to write a will based on fairness and God's guidance that should be a priority for men of clothes, not to hope that they don't have a Will and get their hands on the rest.

For example, if a man has only a daughter and he didn't write a Will, the daughter will fall under the law of distribution, and the rest of the money will go to the Islamic organization, but what if He wrote a Will?? Why are you still denying the right for a human to give his only child what he worked hard for?? Under what law? Islam is all about fairness and logic.

I read something about Islam, not logic, and that is what Hadith said (We see people wiping over the upper and lower parts of the khuffayn, *so what is the ruling of this wiping and what is the ruling of their prayers?*

Their prayers and *wudhu* are correct, but they should be informed that wiping over the lower part of the *khuffayn* is not from the *sunnah*. So in the *sunnah* is the *hadith* of 'Ali ibn Abi Talib *radiallahu 'anhu* who said, "If the religion were according to opinion then the underside of the *khuffayn* would have been wiped, but I have seen the Messenger of Allah *sallallahu 'alayhi wa sallam* wiping over the upper part of the *khuffayn*." And this indicates that only the upper part of the *khuffayn* is legislated to be wiped.

https://sunnahonline.com/library/fiqh-and-sunnah/278-rulings-regarding-the-wiping-over-the-socks-for-purification

Again, since they couldn't change the Quran, they wanted to pass on nonsense,

يَـٰٓأَيُّهَا ٱلَّذِينَ ءَامَنُوٓاْ إِذَا قُمْتُمْ إِلَى ٱلصَّلَوٰةِ فَٱغْسِلُواْ وُجُوهَكُمْ وَأَيْدِيَكُمْ إِلَى ٱلْمَرَافِقِ وَٱمْسَحُواْ بِرُءُوسِكُمْ وَأَرْجُلَكُمْ إِلَى ٱلْكَعْبَيْنِ ۚ وَإِن كُنتُمْ جُنُبًا فَٱطَّهَّرُواْ ۚ وَإِن كُنتُم مَّرْضَىٰٓ أَوْ عَلَىٰ سَفَرٍ أَوْ جَآءَ أَحَدٌ مِّنكُم مِّنَ ٱلْغَآئِطِ أَوْ لَـٰمَسْتُمُ ٱلنِّسَآءَ فَلَمْ تَجِدُواْ مَآءً فَتَيَمَّمُواْ صَعِيدًا طَيِّبًا فَٱمْسَحُواْ بِوُجُوهِكُمْ وَأَيْدِيكُم مِّنْهُ ۚ مَا يُرِيدُ ٱللَّهُ لِيَجْعَلَ عَلَيْكُم مِّنْ حَرَجٍ وَلَـٰكِن يُرِيدُ لِيُطَهِّرَكُمْ وَلِيُتِمَّ نِعْمَتَهُ عَلَيْكُمْ لَعَلَّكُمْ تَشْكُرُونَ ٦

"O, believers! When you rise up for prayer, wash your faces and your hands up to the elbows, wipe your heads and wash your feet to the ankles. And if you are in a state of ˹full˺ impurity,[1] then take a full bath. But if you are ill, on a journey, or have relieved yourselves, or have been intimate with your wives and cannot find water, then purify yourselves with clean earth by wiping your faces and hands.[2] It is not Allah's Will to burden you, but to purify you and complete His favor upon you, so perhaps you will be grateful."

Al-Ma'idah6

God, when order us to clean before prayer, started with washing hands and face but since he doesn't want us to wash the head only to wipe and that should be before washing sequences to finish washing with the feet. It's clear either or for the feet wiping or washing the word feet not any covers on them such as socks or no *khuffayn*, but again they couldn't change the Quran; they changed things in the Hadith.

And from a cleaning point, why not wash your feet? Why you make things difficult when God made them easy?

It's not opinion? It's facts, it's logic. Let us stop spreading the lies about our prophet PBUH.

سَنُرِيهِمْ ءَايَـٰتِنَا فِى ٱلْـَٔافَاقِ وَفِىٓ أَنفُسِهِمْ حَتَّىٰ يَتَبَيَّنَ لَهُمْ أَنَّهُ ٱلْحَقُّ ۗ أَوَلَمْ يَكْفِ بِرَبِّكَ أَنَّهُ عَلَىٰ كُلِّ شَىْءٍ شَهِيدٌ ٥٣

"We will show them Our signs in the universe and within themselves until it becomes clear to them that this ˹Quran˺ is the truth. Is it not enough that your Lord is a Witness over all things?"

Fussilat 53

God will show us the meaning of his word in ourselves and in the creatures, God created, and in everything till we realize that the Quran is the truth. God wants to question things to learn and advance and improve ourselves.

قُلْ سِيرُوا۟ فِى ٱلْأَرْضِ ثُمَّ ٱنظُرُوا۟ كَيْفَ كَانَ عَـٰقِبَةُ ٱلْمُكَذِّبِينَ ١١

Say, "Travel throughout the land and see the fate of the deniers."

Al-An'am1

Its science, its logic its faith. Stop belittling the Islam nation with stuff even ignorant will not accept. We should be the best nation that GOD chose between nations.

IS THE LIQUOR FORBIDDEN (HARAM)?

The liquor has been mentioned only three times in Quran directly and one time indirectly. And if we are shedding some light on the matter is not to encourage drinking, but just to distinguish between forbidden Haram and what is bad for you but not forbidden. And to show the GOD wisdom behind everything GOD forbid or not.

The Haram (Forbidden) is an order from God to think, commit, say its Halal, or to add to the Haram or to take from the Haram, and with that said and done, the God Almighty gave a lean way if you forced to do it, God is forgiving.

يَـٰٓأَيُّهَا ٱلنَّبِىُّ لِمَ تُحَرِّمُ مَآ أَحَلَّ ٱللَّهُ لَكَ ۖ تَبْتَغِى مَرْضَاتَ أَزْوَٰجِكَ ۚ وَٱللَّهُ غَفُورٌ رَّحِيمٌ ١

"O Prophet! Why do you prohibit ˹yourself˺ from what Allah has made lawful to you, seeking to please your wives? And Allah is All-Forgiving, Most Merciful."

Al-Tahrim 1

إِنَّمَا حَرَّمَ عَلَيْكُمُ ٱلْمَيْتَةَ وَٱلدَّمَ وَلَحْمَ ٱلْخِنزِيرِ وَمَآ أُهِلَّ بِهِۦ لِغَيْرِ ٱللَّهِ ۖ فَمَنِ ٱضْطُرَّ غَيْرَ بَاغٍ وَلَا عَادٍ فَلَآ إِثْمَ عَلَيْهِ ۚ إِنَّ ٱللَّهَ غَفُورٌ رَّحِيمٌ ١٧٣

"He has only forbidden you ˹to eat˺ carrion, blood, swine,¹ and what is slaughtered in the name of any other than Allah. But if someone is compelled by necessity—neither driven by desire nor exceeding immediate need—they will not be sinful. Surely Allah is All-Forgiving, Most Merciful. So, as we see Only God can say this Haram or Halal and God specify that in Quran."

Al-Baqara 178

Some people go by Hadith, and they say this person said it's Haram or this Person said it's Halal, let's agree on one thing, this matter only for God; no one can add or deduct. The Almighty is not afraid to forbid the liquor such as GOD forbids the blood and pork and etc. Also, Quran is not a maze you should go to this verse abut in this verse or GOD said in this verse something close to that. Seriously! But even if you go to many verses, you will find that GOD forbid the abuse of liquor and to get drunk and same as GOD forbids if you are married four women you are forbid to marry the fifth, but GOD didn't forbid women. God limited the women and limited the consumption of alcohol, after all God promise the believers with both in heave lot of women and lot of liquor as rivers.

Again, our debate is not to encourage drinking it's to prove to the world ISLAM is not hypocrite religion, The GOD Almighty is the wise not to let such thing occur to his message, because if GOD forbid liquor even if you are sick, you can't touch or have it in any medications.

LIQUOR IN QURAN

1.

يَـٰٓأَيُّهَا ٱلَّذِينَ ءَامَنُوا۟ لَا تَقْرَبُوا۟ ٱلصَّلَوٰةَ وَأَنتُمْ سُكَـٰرَىٰ حَتَّىٰ تَعْلَمُوا۟ مَا تَقُولُونَ وَلَا جُنُبًا إِلَّا عَابِرِى سَبِيلٍ حَتَّىٰ تَغْتَسِلُوا۟ۚ وَإِن كُنتُم مَّرْضَىٰٓ أَوْ عَلَىٰ سَفَرٍ أَوْ جَآءَ أَحَدٌ مِّنكُم مِّنَ ٱلْغَآئِطِ أَوْ لَـٰمَسْتُمُ ٱلنِّسَآءَ فَلَمْ تَجِدُوا۟ مَآءً فَتَيَمَّمُوا۟ صَعِيدًا طَيِّبًا فَٱمْسَحُوا۟ بِوُجُوهِكُمْ وَأَيْدِيكُمْۗ إِنَّ ٱللَّهَ كَانَ عَفُوًّا غَفُورًا ٤٣

"O believers! Do not approach prayer while intoxicated[1] until you are aware of what you say, nor in a state of ˹full˺ impurity[2]—unless you merely pass through ˹the mosque˺—until you have bathed. But if you are ill, on a journey, or have relieved yourselves, or been intimate with your wives and cannot find water, then purify yourselves with clean earth, wiping your faces and hands.[3] And Allah is Ever-Pardoning, All-Forgiving."

An-Nissa 1

2.

يَسْـَٔلُونَكَ عَنِ ٱلْخَمْرِ وَٱلْمَيْسِرِۖ قُلْ فِيهِمَآ إِثْمٌ كَبِيرٌ وَمَنَـٰفِعُ لِلنَّاسِ وَإِثْمُهُمَآ أَكْبَرُ مِن نَّفْعِهِمَاۗ وَيَسْـَٔلُونَكَ مَاذَا يُنفِقُونَ قُلِ ٱلْعَفْوَۗ كَذَٰلِكَ يُبَيِّنُ ٱللَّهُ لَكُمُ ٱلْـَٔايَـٰتِ لَعَلَّكُمْ تَتَفَكَّرُونَ ٢١٩

"They ask you ˹O Prophet˺ about intoxicants and gambling. Say, "There is great evil in both, as well as some benefit for people—but the evil outweighs the benefit."[1] They ˹also˺ ask you ˹O

108

Prophet˺ what they should donate. Say, "Whatever you can spare." This is how Allah makes His revelations clear to you ˹believers˺, so perhaps you may reflect."

Al-Baqaraa 2

3.

يَـٰٓأَيُّهَا ٱلَّذِينَ ءَامَنُوٓا۟ إِنَّمَا ٱلْخَمْرُ وَٱلْمَيْسِرُ وَٱلْأَنصَابُ وَٱلْأَزْلَـٰمُ رِجْسٌ مِّنْ عَمَلِ ٱلشَّيْطَـٰنِ فَٱجْتَنِبُوهُ لَعَلَّكُمْ تُفْلِحُونَ ٩٠

"O believers! Intoxicants, gambling, idols, and drawing lots for decisions¹ are all evil of Satan's handiwork. So, shun them so you may be successful."

Almaeda 90

إِنَّمَا يُرِيدُ ٱلشَّيْطَـٰنُ أَن يُوقِعَ بَيْنَكُمُ ٱلْعَدَٰوَةَ وَٱلْبَغْضَآءَ فِى ٱلْخَمْرِ وَٱلْمَيْسِرِ وَيَصُدَّكُمْ عَن ذِكْرِ ٱللَّهِ وَعَنِ ٱلصَّلَوٰةِ ۖ فَهَلْ أَنتُم مُّنتَهُونَ ٩١

"Satan's plan is to stir up hostility and hatred between you with intoxicants and gambling and to prevent you from remembering Allah and praying. Will you not then abstain?"

Almaeda91

4.

وَإِنَّ لَكُمْ فِى ٱلْأَنْعَـٰمِ لَعِبْرَةً ۖ نُّسْقِيكُم مِّمَّا فِى بُطُونِهِ مِنۢ بَيْنِ فَرْثٍ وَدَمٍ لَّبَنًا خَالِصًا سَآئِغًا لِّلشَّـٰرِبِينَ ٦٦

"And there is certainly a lesson for you in cattle: We give you to drink of what is in their bellies, from between digested food and blood: pure milk, pleasant to drink."

Annahl 66

وَمِن ثَمَرَٰتِ ٱلنَّخِيلِ وَٱلْأَعْنَٰبِ تَتَّخِذُونَ مِنْهُ سَكَرًا وَرِزْقًا حَسَنًا ۗ إِنَّ فِى ذَٰلِكَ لَءَايَةً لِّقَوْمٍ يَعْقِلُونَ ٦٧

"And from the fruits of palm trees and grapevines you derive intoxicants[1] as well as wholesome provision. Surely in this is a sign for those who understand."

Annahl67

Again, we never see where it's Haram, it is bad; and it must be avoided, but it's not Haram. And there is a huge difference, it's most likely to limit the consumption of it or stay away from consumption.

The men in clothes are eminent about the forbidden of liquor, but it's ok to consume it as a medicine when they are sick! Because as we all know, the liquor goes into many medicines, and GOD will never forbid something that doesn't make sense to forbid, he is Almighty the Wise, does that make any sense? It's bad yes, and there is a benefit to it; yes, try to stay away from it, absolutely yes. But it's not forbidden (Haram).

There are so many medications that require alcohol in them, so is it ok for that? But when you say its Haram, you can't consume these medications?

God Almighty, who created us and sent the Quran, is better to know not to forbid something that could be a beneficial in a way to humanity.

Scholar Dr. Mohamad Chahrour shed light on this subject and detailed it from Quran, and the criticisms came from Imam based on Hadith, listen to the comparison between both where Dr. Chahrour says God says, and the Imam say hadith from this guy or Hadith from that guy said. Please listen to both how they argue the matter; you will see that anyone will argue with you on a basis that has never proven or on any say other than what God said; then, there is a problem and special propaganda.

https://www.youtube.com/watch?v=EVENWrWQ3cE

They use the Hadith to brainwash the new generation to direct them to achieve their agenda by using religion for their own reasons, not as faith.

If some will say God said, you can't argue by Ibn Dawood or Ibn Masood or human say, just be careful what this argument is about and never compare what God said to anything else. You believe what GOD said and support it, not by blowing it out of context and depending on other translations. Quran is easy to read, and God sent the message for humans to read and understand it. Not just for men in clothes.

The use of alcohol in a wide range of medications, and to clear the wound or due to covid in many hand-sanitizing products.

THE FORBIDDEN IN QURAN

QURANIC VERSES ABOUT FORBIDDEN

The Topic Forbidden حَرَّمَ mentioned almost in 40 Verses in Quran.

٨٥ ثُمَّ أَنْتُمْ هَؤُلَاءِ تَقْتُلُونَ أَنْفُسَكُمْ وَتُخْرِجُونَ فَرِيقًا مِنْكُمْ مِنْ دِيَارِهِمْ تَظَاهَرُونَ عَلَيْهِمْ بِالْإِثْمِ وَالْعُدْوَانِ وَإِنْ يَأْتُوكُمْ أُسَارَى تُفَادُوهُمْ وَهُوَ مُحَرَّمٌ عَلَيْكُمْ إِخْرَاجُهُمْ أَفَتُؤْمِنُونَ بِبَعْضِ الْكِتَابِ وَتَكْفُرُونَ بِبَعْضٍ فَمَا جَزَاءُ مَنْ يَفْعَلُ ذَلِكَ مِنْكُمْ إِلَّا خِزْيٌ فِي الْحَيَاةِ الدُّنْيَا وَيَوْمَ الْقِيَامَةِ يُرَدُّونَ إِلَى أَشَدِّ الْعَذَابِ وَمَا اللَّهُ بِغَافِلٍ عَمَّا تَعْمَلُونَ

85 Then, you are those [same ones who are] killing one another and evicting a party of your people from their homes, cooperating against them in sin and aggression. And if they come to you as captives, you ransom them, although their eviction was forbidden to you. So, do you believe in part of the Scripture and disbelieve in part? Then what is the recompense for those who do that among you except disgrace in worldly life; and on the Day of Resurrection, they will be sent back to the severest of punishment. And Allah is not unaware of what you do.

(2:85) Albaqara 85

١٧٣ إِنَّمَا حَرَّمَ عَلَيْكُمُ الْمَيْتَةَ وَالدَّمَ وَلَحْمَ الْخِنْزِيرِ وَمَا أُهِلَّ بِهِ لِغَيْرِ اللهِ فَمَنِ اضْطُرَّ غَيْرَ بَاغٍ وَلَا عَادٍ فَلَا إِثْمَ عَلَيْهِ إِنَّ اللهَ غَفُورٌ رَحِيمٌ

173 He has only forbidden to you dead animals, blood, the flesh of swine, and that which has been dedicated to other than Allah. But whoever is forced [by necessity], neither desiring [it] nor transgressing [its limit], there is no sin upon him. Indeed, Allah is Forgiving and Merciful.

2:173 Albaqara 173

٢٧٥ الَّذِينَ يَأْكُلُونَ الرِّبَا لَا يَقُومُونَ إِلَّا كَمَا يَقُومُ الَّذِي يَتَخَبَّطُهُ الشَّيْطَانُ مِنَ الْمَسِّ ذَٰلِكَ بِأَنَّهُمْ قَالُوا إِنَّمَا الْبَيْعُ مِثْلُ الرِّبَا وَأَحَلَّ اللهُ الْبَيْعَ وَحَرَّمَ الرِّبَا فَمَنْ جَاءَهُ مَوْعِظَةٌ مِنْ رَبِّهِ فَانْتَهَى فَلَهُ مَا سَلَفَ وَأَمْرُهُ إِلَى اللهِ وَمَنْ عَادَ فَأُولَٰئِكَ أَصْحَابُ النَّارِ هُمْ فِيهَا خَالِدُونَ

275 Those who consume interest cannot stand [on the Day of Resurrection] except as one stands who is being beaten by Satan into insanity. That is because they say, "Trade is [just] like interest." But Allah has permitted trade and has forbidden interest. So, whoever has received an admonition from his Lord and desists may have what is past, and his affair rests with Allah. But whoever returns to [dealing in interest or usury] – those are the companions of the <u>Fire</u>; they will abide eternally therein.

2:275: Albaqarah 275

٥٠ وَمُصَدِّقًا لِمَا بَيْنَ يَدَيَّ مِنَ التَّوْرَاةِ وَلِأُحِلَّ لَكُم بَعْضَ الَّذِي حُرِّمَ عَلَيْكُمْ ۚ وَجِئْتُكُم بِآيَةٍ مِّن رَّبِّكُمْ فَاتَّقُوا اللَّهَ وَأَطِيعُونِ

50 And [I have come] confirming what was before me of the Torah and to make lawful for you some of what was forbidden to you. And I have come to you with a sign from your Lord, so fear Allah and obey me.

(3:50) Al Imran 50

٩٣ كُلُّ الطَّعَامِ كَانَ حِلًّا لِّبَنِي إِسْرَائِيلَ إِلَّا مَا حَرَّمَ إِسْرَائِيلُ عَلَىٰ نَفْسِهِ مِن قَبْلِ أَن تُنَزَّلَ التَّوْرَاةُ ۗ قُلْ فَأْتُوا بِالتَّوْرَاةِ فَاتْلُوهَا إِن كُنتُمْ صَادِقِينَ

93 All food was lawful to the Children of Israel except what Israel had made unlawful to himself before the Torah was revealed. Say, [O Muhammad], "So bring the Torah and recite it, if you should be truthful.

(3:93) Al Imran93

٢٣ حُرِّمَتْ عَلَيْكُمْ أُمَّهَاتُكُمْ وَبَنَاتُكُمْ وَأَخَوَاتُكُمْ وَعَمَّاتُكُمْ وَخَالَاتُكُمْ وَبَنَاتُ الْأَخِ وَبَنَاتُ الْأُخْتِ وَأُمَّهَاتُكُمُ اللَّاتِي أَرْضَعْنَكُمْ وَأَخَوَاتُكُم مِّنَ الرَّضَاعَةِ وَأُمَّهَاتُ نِسَائِكُمْ وَرَبَائِبُكُمُ اللَّاتِي فِي حُجُورِكُم مِّن نِّسَائِكُمُ اللَّاتِي دَخَلْتُم بِهِنَّ فَإِن لَّمْ تَكُونُوا دَخَلْتُم بِهِنَّ فَلَا جُنَاحَ عَلَيْكُمْ وَحَلَائِلُ أَبْنَائِكُمُ الَّذِينَ مِنْ أَصْلَابِكُمْ وَأَن تَجْمَعُوا بَيْنَ الْأُخْتَيْنِ إِلَّا مَا قَدْ سَلَفَ ۗ إِنَّ اللَّهَ كَانَ غَفُورًا رَّحِيمًا

23 Prohibited to you [for marriage] are your mothers, your daughters, your sisters, your father's sisters, your mother's sisters,

114

your brother's daughters, your sister's daughters, your [milk] mothers who nursed you, your sisters through nursing, your wives' mothers, and your step-daughters under your guardianship [born] of your wives unto whom you have gone in. But if you have not gone in unto them, there is no sin upon you. And [also prohibited are] the wives of your sons who are from your [own] loins, and that you take [in marriage] two sisters simultaneously, except for what has already occurred. Indeed, Allah is ever Forgiving and Merciful.

(4:23) An-nissa 23

١٦٠ فَبِظُلْمٍ مِنَ الَّذِينَ هَادُوا حَرَّمْنَا عَلَيْهِمْ طَيِّبَاتٍ أُحِلَّتْ لَهُمْ وَبِصَدِّهِمْ عَنْ سَبِيلِ اللهِ كَثِيرًا

160 For wrongdoing on the part of the Jews, we made unlawful for them [certain] good foods which had been lawful to them, and for their averting from the way of Allah many [people].

(4:160) An-nissa

٣ حُرِّمَتْ عَلَيْكُمُ الْمَيْتَةُ وَالدَّمُ وَلَحْمُ الْخِنْزِيرِ وَمَا أُهِلَّ لِغَيْرِ اللهِ بِهِ وَالْمُنْخَنِقَةُ وَالْمَوْقُوذَةُ وَالْمُتَرَدِّيَةُ وَالنَّطِيحَةُ وَمَا أَكَلَ السَّبُعُ إِلَّا مَا ذَكَّيْتُمْ وَمَا ذُبِحَ عَلَى النُّصُبِ وَأَنْ تَسْتَقْسِمُوا بِالْأَزْلَامِ ذَلِكُمْ فِسْقٌ الْيَوْمَ يَئِسَ الَّذِينَ كَفَرُوا مِنْ دِينِكُمْ فَلَا تَخْشَوْهُمْ وَاخْشَوْنِ الْيَوْمَ أَكْمَلْتُ لَكُمْ دِينَكُمْ وَأَتْمَمْتُ عَلَيْكُمْ نِعْمَتِي وَرَضِيتُ لَكُمُ الْإِسْلَامَ دِينًا فَمَنِ اضْطُرَّ فِي مَخْمَصَةٍ غَيْرَ مُتَجَانِفٍ لِإِثْمٍ فَإِنَّ اللهَ غَفُورٌ رَحِيمٌ

3 Prohibited to you are dead animals, blood, the flesh of swine, and that which has been dedicated to other than Allah, and [those animals] killed by strangling or by a violent blow or by a head-long

fall or by the goring of horns, and those from which a wild animal has eaten, except what you [are able to] slaughter [before its death], and those which are sacrificed on stone altars, and [prohibited is] that you seek decision through divining arrows. That is grave disobedience. This day those who disbelieve have despaired of [defeating] your religion; so, fear them not, but fear Me. This day I have perfected for you your religion and completed My favor upon you and have approved for you Islam as religion. But whoever is forced by severe hunger with no inclination to sin – then indeed, Allah is Forgiving and Merciful.

(5:3) AlMaeda3

٢٦ قَالَ فَإِنَّهَا مُحَرَّمَةٌ عَلَيْهِمْ أَرْبَعِينَ سَنَةً يَتِيهُونَ فِي الْأَرْضِ فَلَا تَأْسَ عَلَى الْقَوْمِ الْفَاسِقِينَ

26 [Allah] said, "Then indeed, it is forbidden to them for forty years [in which] they will wander throughout the land. So do not grieve over the defiantly disobedient people.

(5:26) Almaeda 26

٨٧ يَا أَيُّهَا الَّذِينَ آمَنُوا لَا تُحَرِّمُوا طَيِّبَاتِ مَا أَحَلَّ اللَّهُ لَكُمْ وَلَا تَعْتَدُوا إِنَّ اللَّهَ لَا يُحِبُّ الْمُعْتَدِينَ

87 O you who have believed, do not prohibit the good things which Allah has made lawful to you and do not transgress. Indeed, Allah does not like transgressors.

(5:87) Almaeda 87

٩٦ أُحِلَّ لَكُمْ صَيْدُ الْبَحْرِ وَطَعَامُهُ مَتَاعًا لَكُمْ وَلِلسَّيَّارَةِ ۖ وَحُرِّمَ عَلَيْكُمْ صَيْدُ الْبَرِّ مَا دُمْتُمْ حُرُمًا ۗ وَاتَّقُوا اللَّهَ الَّذِي إِلَيْهِ تُحْشَرُونَ

96 Lawful to you is game from the sea and its food as provision for you and the travelers, but forbidden to you is game from the land as long as you are in the state of ihram. And fear Allah to whom you will be gathered.

(5:96) Almaeda 96

١١٩ وَمَا لَكُمْ أَلَّا تَأْكُلُوا مِمَّا ذُكِرَ اسْمُ اللَّهِ عَلَيْهِ وَقَدْ فَصَّلَ لَكُمْ مَا حَرَّمَ عَلَيْكُمْ إِلَّا مَا اضْطُرِرْتُمْ إِلَيْهِ ۗ وَإِنَّ كَثِيرًا لَيُضِلُّونَ بِأَهْوَائِهِمْ بِغَيْرِ عِلْمٍ ۗ إِنَّ رَبَّكَ هُوَ أَعْلَمُ بِالْمُعْتَدِينَ

119 And why should you not eat of that upon which the name of Allah has been mentioned while He has explained in detail to you that He has forbidden you, excepting that to which you are compelled. And indeed, do many lead [others] astray through their [own] inclinations without knowledge. Indeed, your Lord – He is most knowing of the transgressors.

(6:119) Al-Anaam

١٣٨ وَقَالُوا هَٰذِهِ أَنْعَامٌ وَحَرْثٌ حِجْرٌ لَا يَطْعَمُهَا إِلَّا مَنْ نَشَاءُ بِزَعْمِهِمْ وَأَنْعَامٌ حُرِّمَتْ ظُهُورُهَا وَأَنْعَامٌ لَا يَذْكُرُونَ اسْمَ اللَّهِ عَلَيْهَا افْتِرَاءً عَلَيْهِ ۚ سَيَجْزِيهِمْ بِمَا كَانُوا يَفْتَرُونَ

138 And they say, "These animals and crops are forbidden; no one may eat from them except whom we will," by their claim. And

117

there are those [camels] whose backs are forbidden [by them] and those upon which the name of Allah is not mentioned – [all of this] an invention of untruth about Him. He will punish them for what they were inventing.

(6:138) AlAnaam 138

١٣٩ وَقَالُوا مَا فِي بُطُونِ هَٰذِهِ الْأَنْعَامِ خَالِصَةٌ لِّذُكُورِنَا وَمُحَرَّمٌ عَلَىٰ أَزْوَاجِنَا ۖ وَإِن يَكُن مَّيْتَةً فَهُمْ فِيهِ شُرَكَاءُ ۚ سَيَجْزِيهِمْ وَصْفَهُمْ ۚ إِنَّهُ حَكِيمٌ عَلِيمٌ

139 And they say, "What is in the bellies of these animals is exclusively for our males and forbidden to our females. But if it is [born] dead, then all of them have shares therein." He will punish them for their description. Indeed, He is Wise and Knowing.

(6:139) AlAnaam139

١٤٠ قَدْ خَسِرَ الَّذِينَ قَتَلُوا أَوْلَادَهُمْ سَفَهًا بِغَيْرِ عِلْمٍ وَحَرَّمُوا مَا رَزَقَهُمُ اللَّهُ افْتِرَاءً عَلَى اللَّهِ ۚ قَدْ ضَلُّوا وَمَا كَانُوا مُهْتَدِينَ

140 Those will have lost who killed their children in foolishness without knowledge and prohibited what Allah had provided for them, inventing untruth about Allah. They have gone astray and were not [rightly] guided.

(6:140) Alanaam 140

١٤٣ ثَمَانِيَةَ أَزْوَاجٍ مِنَ الضَّأْنِ اثْنَيْنِ وَمِنَ الْمَعْزِ اثْنَيْنِ قُلْ آلذَّكَرَيْنِ حَرَّمَ أَمِ الْأُنْثَيَيْنِ أَمَّا اشْتَمَلَتْ عَلَيْهِ أَرْحَامُ الْأُنْثَيَيْنِ نَبِّئُونِي بِعِلْمٍ إِنْ كُنْتُمْ صَادِقِينَ

143 [They are] eight mates – of the sheep, two and of the goats, two. Say, "Is it the two males He has forbidden or the two females or that which the wombs of the two females contain? Inform me with knowledge, if you should be truthful.

(6:143) Alanaam 143

١٤٤ وَمِنَ الْإِبِلِ اثْنَيْنِ وَمِنَ الْبَقَرِ اثْنَيْنِ قُلْ آلذَّكَرَيْنِ حَرَّمَ أَمِ الْأُنْثَيَيْنِ أَمَّا اشْتَمَلَتْ عَلَيْهِ أَرْحَامُ الْأُنْثَيَيْنِ أَمْ كُنْتُمْ شُهَدَاءَ إِذْ وَصَّاكُمُ اللهُ بِهَذَا فَمَنْ أَظْلَمُ مِمَّنِ افْتَرَى عَلَى اللهِ كَذِبًا لِيُضِلَّ النَّاسَ بِغَيْرِ عِلْمٍ إِنَّ اللهَ لَا يَهْدِي الْقَوْمَ الظَّالِمِينَ

144 And of the camels, two and of the cattle, two. Say, "Is it the two males He has forbidden or the two females or that which the wombs of the two females contain? Or were you witnesses when Allah charged you with this? Then who is more unjust than one who invents a lie about Allah to mislead the people by [something] other than knowledge? Indeed, Allah does not guide the wrongdoing people.

(6:144) Alanaam 144

١٤٥ قُلْ لَا أَجِدُ فِي مَا أُوحِيَ إِلَيَّ مُحَرَّمًا عَلَى طَاعِمٍ يَطْعَمُهُ إِلَّا أَنْ يَكُونَ مَيْتَةً أَوْ دَمًا مَسْفُوحًا أَوْ لَحْمَ خِنْزِيرٍ فَإِنَّهُ رِجْسٌ أَوْ فِسْقًا أُهِلَّ لِغَيْرِ اللهِ بِهِ فَمَنِ اضْطُرَّ غَيْرَ بَاغٍ وَلَا عَادٍ فَإِنَّ رَبَّكَ غَفُورٌ رَحِيمٌ

119

145 Say, "I do not find within that which was revealed to me
[anything] forbidden to one who would eat it unless it be a dead
animal or blood spilled out or the flesh of swine – for indeed, it
is impure – or it be [that slaughtered in] disobedience, dedicated
to other than Allah. But whoever is forced [by necessity], neither
desiring [it] nor transgressing [its limit], then indeed, your Lord is
Forgiving and Merciful.

(6:145) Alanaam 145

١٤٦ وَعَلَى الَّذِينَ هَادُوا حَرَّمْنَا كُلَّ ذِي ظُفُرٍ ۖ وَمِنَ الْبَقَرِ وَالْغَنَمِ حَرَّمْنَا عَلَيْهِمْ
شُحُومَهُمَا إِلَّا مَا حَمَلَتْ ظُهُورُهُمَا أَوِ الْحَوَايَا أَوْ مَا اخْتَلَطَ بِعَظْمٍ ۚ ذَٰلِكَ جَزَيْنَاهُمْ
بِبَغْيِهِمْ ۖ وَإِنَّا لَصَادِقُونَ

146 And to those who are Jews We prohibited every animal of
uncloven hoof; and of the cattle and the sheep We prohibited to
them their fat, except what adheres to their backs or the entrails
or what is joined with bone. [By] that We repaid them for
their injustice. And indeed, we are truthful.

(6:146) Al-Anaam 146

١٤٨ سَيَقُولُ الَّذِينَ أَشْرَكُوا لَوْ شَاءَ اللَّهُ مَا أَشْرَكْنَا وَلَا آبَاؤُنَا وَلَا حَرَّمْنَا مِنْ شَيْءٍ
كَذَٰلِكَ كَذَّبَ الَّذِينَ مِنْ قَبْلِهِمْ حَتَّىٰ ذَاقُوا بَأْسَنَا ۗ قُلْ هَلْ عِنْدَكُمْ مِنْ عِلْمٍ فَتُخْرِجُوهُ
لَنَا ۖ إِنْ تَتَّبِعُونَ إِلَّا الظَّنَّ وَإِنْ أَنْتُمْ إِلَّا تَخْرُصُونَ

148 Those who associated with Allah will say, "If Allah had willed,
we would not have associated [anything] and neither would our
fathers, nor would we have prohibited anything." Likewise, did
those before deny until they tasted Our punishment. Say, "Do

you have any knowledge that you can produce for us? You follow
not except assumption, and you are not but falsifying.

(6:148) AlAnaam 148

قُلْ هَلُمَّ شُهَدَاءَكُمُ الَّذِينَ يَشْهَدُونَ أَنَّ اللَّهَ حَرَّمَ هَذَا فَإِنْ شَهِدُوا فَلَا تَشْهَدْ ١٥٠
مَعَهُمْ وَلَا تَتَّبِعْ أَهْوَاءَ الَّذِينَ كَذَّبُوا بِآيَاتِنَا وَالَّذِينَ لَا يُؤْمِنُونَ بِالْآخِرَةِ وَهُمْ
بِرَبِّهِمْ يَعْدِلُونَ

150 Say, [O Muhammad], "Bring forward your witnesses who will
testify that Allah has prohibited this." And if they testify, do not
testify with them. And do not follow the desires of those who deny
Our verses and those who do not believe in the Hereafter, while
they equate [others] with their Lord.

(6:150) AlAnaam 150

قُلْ تَعَالَوْا أَتْلُ مَا حَرَّمَ رَبُّكُمْ عَلَيْكُمْ أَلَّا تُشْرِكُوا بِهِ شَيْئًا وَبِالْوَالِدَيْنِ إِحْسَانًا ١٥١
وَلَا تَقْتُلُوا أَوْلَادَكُمْ مِنْ إِمْلَاقٍ نَحْنُ نَرْزُقُكُمْ وَإِيَّاهُمْ وَلَا تَقْرَبُوا الْفَوَاحِشَ مَا
ظَهَرَ مِنْهَا وَمَا بَطَنَ وَلَا تَقْتُلُوا النَّفْسَ الَّتِي حَرَّمَ اللَّهُ إِلَّا بِالْحَقِّ ذَلِكُمْ وَصَّاكُمْ بِهِ
لَعَلَّكُمْ تَعْقِلُونَ

151 Say, "Come, I will recite what your Lord has prohibited to
you. [He commands] that you not associate anything with Him,
and to parents, good treatment, and do not kill your children out
of poverty; We will provide for you and them. And do not
approach immoralities – what is apparent of them and what is
concealed. And do not kill the soul which Allah has forbidden [to

121

be killed] except by [legal] right. This has He instructed you that
you may use reason.

(6:151) AlAnaam 151

٣٢ قُلْ مَنْ حَرَّمَ زِينَةَ اللهِ الَّتِي أَخْرَجَ لِعِبَادِهِ وَالطَّيِّبَاتِ مِنَ الرِّزْقِ ۚ قُلْ هِيَ لِلَّذِينَ
آمَنُوا فِي الْحَيَاةِ الدُّنْيَا خَالِصَةً يَوْمَ الْقِيَامَةِ ۗ كَذَلِكَ نُفَصِّلُ الْآيَاتِ لِقَوْمٍ يَعْلَمُونَ

32 Say, "Who has forbidden the adornment of Allah which He
has produced for His servants and the good [lawful] things of
provision?" Say, "They are for those who believe during the
worldly life [but] exclusively for them on the Day of
Resurrection." Thus, do We detail the verses for a people who
know.

(7:32) AlAaraf32

٣٣ قُلْ إِنَّمَا حَرَّمَ رَبِّيَ الْفَوَاحِشَ مَا ظَهَرَ مِنْهَا وَمَا بَطَنَ وَالْإِثْمَ وَالْبَغْيَ بِغَيْرِ
الْحَقِّ وَأَنْ تُشْرِكُوا بِاللهِ مَا لَمْ يُنَزِّلْ بِهِ سُلْطَانًا وَأَنْ تَقُولُوا عَلَى اللهِ مَا لَا
تَعْلَمُونَ

33 Say, "My Lord has only forbidden immoralities – what is
apparent of them and what is concealed – and sin, and oppression
without right, and that you associate with Allah that for which He
has not sent down authority, and that you say about Allah that
which you do not know.

(7:33) AlAaraf33

١٥٧ الَّذِينَ يَتَّبِعُونَ الرَّسُولَ النَّبِيَّ الْأُمِّيَّ الَّذِي يَجِدُونَهُ مَكْتُوبًا عِنْدَهُمْ فِي التَّوْرَاةِ وَالْإِنْجِيلِ يَأْمُرُهُمْ بِالْمَعْرُوفِ وَيَنْهَاهُمْ عَنِ الْمُنْكَرِ وَيُحِلُّ لَهُمُ الطَّيِّبَاتِ وَيُحَرِّمُ عَلَيْهِمُ الْخَبَائِثَ وَيَضَعُ عَنْهُمْ إِصْرَهُمْ وَالْأَغْلَالَ الَّتِي كَانَتْ عَلَيْهِمْ ۚ فَالَّذِينَ آمَنُوا بِهِ وَعَزَّرُوهُ وَنَصَرُوهُ وَاتَّبَعُوا النُّورَ الَّذِي أُنْزِلَ مَعَهُ ۙ أُولَٰئِكَ هُمُ الْمُفْلِحُونَ

157 Those who follow the Messenger, the unlettered prophet, whom they find written in what they have of the Torah and the Gospel, who enjoins upon them what is right and forbids them what is wrong and makes lawful for them the good things and prohibits for them the evil and relieves them of their burden and the shackles which were upon them. So they who have believed in him, honored him, supported him and followed the light which was sent down with him – it is those who will be the successful.

(7:157) AlAaraf 157

٣٧ إِنَّمَا النَّسِيءُ زِيَادَةٌ فِي الْكُفْرِ ۖ يُضَلُّ بِهِ الَّذِينَ كَفَرُوا يُحِلُّونَهُ عَامًا وَيُحَرِّمُونَهُ عَامًا لِيُوَاطِئُوا عِدَّةَ مَا حَرَّمَ اللَّهُ فَيُحِلُّوا مَا حَرَّمَ اللَّهُ ۚ زُيِّنَ لَهُمْ سُوءُ أَعْمَالِهِمْ ۗ وَاللَّهُ لَا يَهْدِي الْقَوْمَ الْكَافِرِينَ

37 Indeed, the postponing [of restriction within sacred months] is an increase in disbelief by which those who have disbelieved are led [further] astray. They make it lawful one year and unlawful another year to correspond to the number made unlawful by Allah and [thus] make lawful what Allah has made unlawful. Made pleasing to them is the evil of their deeds; and Allah does not guide the disbelieving people.

(9:37) At-Taubah37

٥٩ قُلْ أَرَأَيْتُمْ مَا أَنْزَلَ اللهُ لَكُمْ مِنْ رِزْقٍ فَجَعَلْتُمْ مِنْهُ حَرَامًا وَحَلَالًا قُلْ آللَّهُ أَذِنَ لَكُمْ ۖ أَمْ عَلَى اللهِ تَفْتَرُونَ

59 Say, "Have you seen what Allah has sent down to you of provision of which you have made [some] lawful and [some] unlawful?" Say, "Has Allah permitted you [to do so], or do you invent [something] about Allah?

(10:59) Yunis 59

٣٥ قَالَ الَّذِينَ أَشْرَكُوا لَوْ شَاءَ اللهُ مَا عَبَدْنَا مِنْ دُونِهِ مِنْ شَيْءٍ نَحْنُ وَلَا آبَاؤُنَا وَلَا حَرَّمْنَا مِنْ دُونِهِ مِنْ شَيْءٍ ۚ كَذَلِكَ فَعَلَ الَّذِينَ مِنْ قَبْلِهِمْ ۚ فَهَلْ عَلَى الرُّسُلِ إِلَّا الْبَلَاغُ الْمُبِينُ

35 And those who associate others with Allah say, "If Allah had willed, we would not have worshipped anything other than Him, neither we nor our fathers, nor would we have forbidden anything through other than Him." Thus, did those do before them. So is there upon the messengers except [the duty of] clear notification?

(16:35) An-Nahl 35

١١٥ إِنَّمَا حَرَّمَ عَلَيْكُمُ الْمَيْتَةَ وَالدَّمَ وَلَحْمَ الْخِنْزِيرِ وَمَا أُهِلَّ لِغَيْرِ اللهِ بِهِ ۖ فَمَنِ اضْطُرَّ غَيْرَ بَاغٍ وَلَا عَادٍ فَإِنَّ اللهَ غَفُورٌ رَحِيمٌ

115 He has only forbidden to you dead animals, blood, the flesh of swine, and that which has been dedicated to other than Allah. But whoever is forced [by necessity], neither desiring [it] nor

transgressing [its limit] – then indeed, Allah is Forgiving and Merciful.

(16:115) An-Nahl115

١١٦ وَلَا تَقُولُوا لِمَا تَصِفُ أَلْسِنَتُكُمُ الْكَذِبَ هَٰذَا حَلَالٌ وَهَٰذَا حَرَامٌ لِتَفْتَرُوا عَلَى اللَّهِ الْكَذِبَ ۚ إِنَّ الَّذِينَ يَفْتَرُونَ عَلَى اللَّهِ الْكَذِبَ لَا يُفْلِحُونَ

116 And do not say about what your tongues assert of untruth, "This is lawful and this is unlawful," to invent falsehood about Allah. Indeed, those who invent falsehood about Allah will not success.

(16:116) An-Nahl 116

١١٨ وَعَلَى الَّذِينَ هَادُوا حَرَّمْنَا مَا قَصَصْنَا عَلَيْكَ مِنْ قَبْلُ ۖ وَمَا ظَلَمْنَاهُمْ وَلَٰكِنْ كَانُوا أَنْفُسَهُمْ يَظْلِمُونَ

118 And to those who are Jews We have prohibited that which We related to you before. And We did not wrong them [thereby], but they were wronging themselves.

(16:118) An-Nahl 118

٣٣ وَلَا تَقْتُلُوا النَّفْسَ الَّتِي حَرَّمَ اللَّهُ إِلَّا بِالْحَقِّ ۗ وَمَنْ قُتِلَ مَظْلُومًا فَقَدْ جَعَلْنَا لِوَلِيِّهِ سُلْطَانًا فَلَا يُسْرِفْ فِي الْقَتْلِ ۖ إِنَّهُ كَانَ مَنْصُورًا

33 And do not kill the soul which Allah has forbidden, except by right. And whoever is killed unjustly – We have given his heir

125

authority, but let him not exceed limits in [the matter of] taking
life. Indeed, he has been supported [by the law].

(17:33) Al-Israa 33

٣ الزَّانِي لَا يَنْكِحُ إِلَّا زَانِيَةً أَوْ مُشْرِكَةً وَالزَّانِيَةُ لَا يَنْكِحُهَا إِلَّا زَانٍ أَوْ مُشْرِكٌ ۚ وَحُرِّمَ ذَٰلِكَ عَلَى الْمُؤْمِنِينَ

3 The fornicator does not marry except a [female] fornicator or
polytheist, and none marries her except a fornicator or a
polytheist, and that has been made unlawful to the believers.

(24:3) Annur 3

٦٨ وَالَّذِينَ لَا يَدْعُونَ مَعَ اللَّهِ إِلَٰهًا آخَرَ وَلَا يَقْتُلُونَ النَّفْسَ الَّتِي حَرَّمَ اللَّهُ إِلَّا بِالْحَقِّ وَلَا يَزْنُونَ ۚ وَمَنْ يَفْعَلْ ذَٰلِكَ يَلْقَ أَثَامًا

68 And those who do not invoke with Allah another deity or kill
the soul which Allah has forbidden [to be killed], except by right,
and do not commit unlawful sexual intercourse. And whoever
should do that will meet a penalty.

(25:68) Al Furqan 68

١ يَا أَيُّهَا النَّبِيُّ لِمَ تُحَرِّمُ مَا أَحَلَّ اللَّهُ لَكَ ۖ تَبْتَغِي مَرْضَاتَ أَزْوَاجِكَ ۚ وَاللَّهُ غَفُورٌ رَحِيمٌ

1 O Prophet, why do you prohibit [yourself from] what Allah has made lawful for you, seeking the approval of your wives? And Allah is Forgiving and Merciful.

(66:1) Al-Tahreem 1

The liquor is not one of the forbidden, its bad thing to abuse or it's better to avoid it. No one can compare the forbidden to something is not forbidden, its two completely different things.

WHO IS GOING TO HEAVEN AND WHO IS GOING TO HELL?

© Can Stock Photo - csp29794027

قُلِ اللَّهُمَّ فَاطِرَ السَّمَٰوَٰتِ وَالْأَرْضِ عَٰلِمَ الْغَيْبِ وَالشَّهَٰدَةِ أَنتَ تَحْكُمُ بَيْنَ عِبَادِكَ فِى مَا كَانُوا فِيهِ يَخْتَلِفُونَ ٤٦

Say, ˹O Prophet,˺ "O Allah—Originator of the heavens and the earth, Knower of the seen and unseen! You will judge between Your servants regarding their differences."

Az-Zumar

إِنَّ الَّذِينَ ءَامَنُوا وَالَّذِينَ هَادُوا وَالصَّٰبِـِٔينَ وَالنَّصَٰرَىٰ وَالْمَجُوسَ وَالَّذِينَ أَشْرَكُوا إِنَّ اللَّهَ يَفْصِلُ بَيْنَهُمْ يَوْمَ الْقِيَٰمَةِ ۚ إِنَّ اللَّهَ عَلَىٰ كُلِّ شَىْءٍ شَهِيدٌ ١٧

"Indeed, the believers, Jews, Sabians,1 Christians, Magi,2 and the polytheists—Allah will judge between them ˹all˺ on Judgment Day. Surely Allah is a Witness over all things."

Al-Hajj

وَأَنزَلْنَا إِلَيْكَ ٱلْكِتَـٰبَ بِٱلْحَقِّ مُصَدِّقًا لِّمَا بَيْنَ يَدَيْهِ مِنَ ٱلْكِتَـٰبِ وَمُهَيْمِنًا عَلَيْهِ ۖ فَٱحْكُم بَيْنَهُم بِمَآ أَنزَلَ ٱللَّهُ ۖ وَلَا تَتَّبِعْ أَهْوَآءَهُمْ عَمَّا جَآءَكَ مِنَ ٱلْحَقِّ ۚ لِكُلٍّ جَعَلْنَا مِنكُمْ شِرْعَةً وَمِنْهَاجًا ۚ وَلَوْ شَآءَ ٱللَّهُ لَجَعَلَكُمْ أُمَّةً وَٰحِدَةً وَلَـٰكِن لِّيَبْلُوَكُمْ فِى مَآ ءَاتَىٰكُمْ ۖ فَٱسْتَبِقُوا۟ ٱلْخَيْرَٰتِ ۚ إِلَى ٱللَّهِ مَرْجِعُكُمْ جَمِيعًا فَيُنَبِّئُكُم بِمَا كُنتُمْ فِيهِ تَخْتَلِفُونَ ٤٨

"We have revealed to you ˹O Prophet˺ this Book with the truth, as a confirmation of previous Scriptures and a supreme authority on them. So, judge between them by what Allah has revealed, and do not follow their desires over the truth that has come to you. To each of you We have ordained a code of law and a way of life. If Allah had willed, He would have made you one community, but His Will is to test you with what He has given ˹each of˺ you. So, compete with one another in doing good. To Allah you will all return, then He will inform you ˹of the truth˺ regarding your differences."

يَـٰٓأَيُّهَا ٱلَّذِينَ ءَامَنُوا۟ عَلَيْكُمْ أَنفُسَكُمْ ۖ لَا يَضُرُّكُم مَّن ضَلَّ إِذَا ٱهْتَدَيْتُمْ ۚ إِلَى ٱللَّهِ مَرْجِعُكُمْ جَمِيعًا فَيُنَبِّئُكُم بِمَا كُنتُمْ تَعْمَلُونَ ١٠٥

"O believers! You are accountable only for yourselves.¹ It will not harm you if someone chooses to deviate—as long as you are "rightly" guided. To Allah you will all return, and He will inform you of what you used to do."

Al-Maeda105

إِلَيْهِ مَرْجِعُكُمْ جَمِيعًا ۖ وَعْدَ اللَّهِ حَقًّا ۚ إِنَّهُ يَبْدَؤُا۟ الْخَلْقَ ثُمَّ يُعِيدُهُ لِيَجْزِىَ الَّذِينَ ءَامَنُوا۟ وَعَمِلُوا۟ الصَّٰلِحَٰتِ بِالْقِسْطِ ۚ وَالَّذِينَ كَفَرُوا۟ لَهُمْ شَرَابٌ مِّنْ حَمِيمٍ وَعَذَابٌ أَلِيمٌ بِمَا كَانُوا۟ يَكْفُرُونَ ٤

"To Him is your return all together. Allah's promise is "always" true. Indeed, He originates the creation then resurrects it so that He may justly reward those who believe and do good. But those who disbelieve will have a boiling drink and a painful punishment for their disbelief."

Yunis 4

إِنَّ الَّذِينَ ءَامَنُوا۟ وَالَّذِينَ هَادُوا۟ وَالنَّصَٰرَىٰ وَالصَّٰبِئِينَ مَنْ ءَامَنَ بِاللَّهِ وَالْيَوْمِ الْءَاخِرِ وَعَمِلَ صَٰلِحًا فَلَهُمْ أَجْرُهُمْ عِندَ رَبِّهِمْ وَلَا خَوْفٌ عَلَيْهِمْ وَلَا هُمْ يَحْزَنُونَ ٦٢

"Indeed, the believers, Jews, Christians, and Sabians[1]—whoever "truly" believes in Allah and the Last Day and does good will have their reward with their Lord. And there will be no fear for them, nor will they grieve."

Al-Baqara62

إِنَّ ٱلَّذِينَ ءَامَنُواْ وَٱلَّذِينَ هَادُواْ وَٱلصَّٰبِٔونَ وَٱلنَّصَٰرَىٰ مَنْ ءَامَنَ بِٱللَّهِ وَٱلْيَوْمِ ٱلْءَاخِرِ وَعَمِلَ صَٰلِحًا فَلَا خَوْفٌ عَلَيْهِمْ وَلَا هُمْ يَحْزَنُونَ ٦٩

"Indeed, the believers, Jews, Sabians[1] and Christians—whoever ˹truly˺ believes in Allah and the Last Day and does good, there will be no fear for them, nor will they grieve."

Al-Maeda 69

إِنَّ ٱلَّذِينَ ءَامَنُواْ وَٱلَّذِينَ هَادُواْ وَٱلصَّٰبِئِينَ وَٱلنَّصَٰرَىٰ وَٱلْمَجُوسَ وَٱلَّذِينَ أَشْرَكُوٓاْ إِنَّ ٱللَّهَ يَفْصِلُ بَيْنَهُمْ يَوْمَ ٱلْقِيَٰمَةِ ۚ إِنَّ ٱللَّهَ عَلَىٰ كُلِّ شَىْءٍ شَهِيدٌ ١٧

"Indeed, the believers, Jews, Sabians,[1] Christians, Magi,[2] and the polytheists—Allah will judge between them ˹all˺ on Judgment Day. Surely Allah is a Witness over all things."

Al-Hajj17

It's clear that God is the Judge; now the message is complete, and the choice is clear for everyone. Unfortunately, these days everyone wants to be the judge, and everyone is right! The men's clothes keep attacking each other's beliefs to the point that they want their death!! It's insane to change the message of love and peace.

Islam Is Not A Cult

Muslims around the world are divided into many cults. And all cults think they only going to heaven. They appointed themselves as the judge to the point that Muslims from different cults are considered infidels, and it's ok to kill them or fight them or disassociate with them. Is that Islam? Are that what God asks us to do?

The mysterious part is that all the Hadeeth start to pop up in the Golden Era of Islam from Al-Bukhari. Just a quick question, what is the reason behind it? How come, for years, no one did that? And again, what is the benefit behind it since it goes against Quran?

Title	Imam al-Bukhari *Amir al-Mu'minin fi al-Hadith*
Personal	
Born	21 July 810 C.E. 13th Shawwal 194 A.H. Bukhara, Abbasid Caliphate
Died	1 September 870 (aged 60) C.E. 1 Shawwal 256 A.H.

	Khartank, Samarkand, Abbasid Caliphate
Resting place	Khartank (Samarkand, Uzbekistan)
Religion	Islam
Era	Islamic Golden Age (Abbasid era)

And then we took a big dive into the darkness and ignorance and to some people that Al-Bukhari is untouchable, you can't even say anything about him at all otherwise you are infidel, his words more important than Quran1! When will Muslims wake up? The Impact of Hadith is greatly dangerous to Islam.

The hadith had a profound and controversial influence on *tafsir* (commentaries of the Quran). The earliest commentary of the Quran, known as Tafsir Ibn Abbas is sometimes attributed to the companion Ibn Abbas.

The hadith were used in forming the basis of *Sharia* (the religious law system forming part of the Islamic tradition) and *fiqh* (Islamic jurisprudence). The hadith are at the root of why there is no single *fiqh* system but rather a collection of parallel systems within Islam.

Much of early Islamic history available today is also based on the hadith, although it has been challenged for its lack of basis in primary source material and the internal contradictions of the secondary material available.[citation needed]

أَفَلَا يَتَدَبَّرُونَ ٱلْقُرْءَانَ ۚ وَلَوْ كَانَ مِنْ عِندِ غَيْرِ ٱللَّهِ لَوَجَدُوا۟ فِيهِ ٱخْتِلَٰفًا كَثِيرًا ٨٢

"Do they not then reflect on the Quran? Had it been from anyone other than Allah, they would have certainly found in it many inconsistencies."

An-Nisa82

أَفَلَا يَتَدَبَّرُونَ ٱلْقُرْءَانَ أَمْ عَلَىٰ قُلُوبٍ أَقْفَالُهَآ ٢٤

"Do they not then reflect on the Quran? Or are there locks upon their hearts?"

Muhammad24

It's almost in each beginning of Surah that God emphasizes how glorious this book (Quran) is and how miraculous it is, and yet we don't read it or think about understanding it. Why? Because we have Hadith!! Many scholars, especially in the languages, started to detach themselves from the original idea and took deep dive into the Quran, and that's what we expect our leaders to do but unfortunately, to most, it is not easy to come out and say we want to correct our thoughts and we want to go back to the book, they fear the people and they should fear the God.

ذَٰلِكَ ٱلْكِتَٰبُ لَا رَيْبَ ۛ فِيهِ ۛ هُدًى لِّلْمُتَّقِينَ ٢

"This is the Book! There is no doubt about it¹—a guide for those mindful ˹of Allah,˺"

كِتَـٰبٌ أُنزِلَ إِلَيْكَ فَلَا يَكُن فِى صَدْرِكَ حَرَجٌ مِّنْهُ لِتُنذِرَ بِهِۦ وَذِكْرَىٰ لِلْمُؤْمِنِينَ ٢

"˹This is˺ a Book sent down to you ˹O Prophet˺—do not let anxiety into your heart regarding it—so with it you may warn ˹the disbelievers˺, and as a reminder to the believers."

Al-An'am2

الٓر ۚ كِتَـٰبٌ أُحْكِمَتْ ءَايَـٰتُهُۥ ثُمَّ فُصِّلَتْ مِن لَّدُنْ حَكِيمٍ خَبِيرٍ

"Alif-Lãm-Ra. ˹This is˺ a Book whose verses are well perfected and then fully explained. ˹It is˺ from the One ˹Who is˺ All-Wise, All-Aware."

Al-Anfal1

الٓر ۚ تِلْكَ ءَايَـٰتُ ٱلْكِتَـٰبِ ٱلْمُبِينِ ١

"Alif-Lãm-Ra. These are the verses of the clear Book."

Yusuf 1

إِنَّا أَنزَلْنَـٰهُ قُرْءَٰنًا عَرَبِيًّا لَّعَلَّكُمْ تَعْقِلُونَ ٢

"Indeed, we have sent it down as an Arabic Quran[1] so that you may understand."

Yusuf 2

الٓمٓرۚ تِلْكَ ءَايَٰتُ ٱلْكِتَٰبِۗ وَٱلَّذِىٓ أُنزِلَ إِلَيْكَ مِن رَّبِّكَ ٱلْحَقُّ وَلَٰكِنَّ أَكْثَرَ ٱلنَّاسِ لَا يُؤْمِنُونَ ١

"Alif-Lām-Mīm-Ra. These are the verses of the Book. What has been revealed to you ʿO Prophetʾ from your Lord is the truth, but most people do not believe."

Ar-Raad 1

الٓرۚ كِتَٰبٌ أَنزَلْنَٰهُ إِلَيْكَ لِتُخْرِجَ ٱلنَّاسَ مِنَ ٱلظُّلُمَٰتِ إِلَى ٱلنُّورِ بِإِذْنِ رَبِّهِمْ إِلَىٰ صِرَٰطِ ٱلْعَزِيزِ ٱلْحَمِيدِ ١

"Alif-Lām-Ra. ʿThis isʾ a Book which We have revealed to you ʿO Prophetʾ so that you may lead people out of darkness and into light, by the Will of their Lord, to the Path of the Almighty, the Praiseworthy."

Ibrahim 1

الٓرۚ تِلْكَ ءَايَٰتُ ٱلْكِتَٰبِ وَقُرْءَانٍ مُّبِينٍ ١

"Alif-Lām-Ra. These are the verses of the Book; the clear Quran."

ٱلْحَمْدُ لِلَّهِ ٱلَّذِى أَنزَلَ عَلَىٰ عَبْدِهِ ٱلْكِتَٰبَ وَلَمْ يَجْعَل لَّهُ عِوَجَا ۱

"All praise is for Allah Who has revealed the Book to His servant,[1] allowing no crookedness in it."

Al-Kahf1

مَآ أَنزَلْنَا عَلَيْكَ ٱلْقُرْءَانَ لِتَشْقَىٰ ۲

"We have not revealed the Quran to you ˹O Prophet˺ to cause you distress."

TaHa2

تَبَارَكَ ٱلَّذِى نَزَّلَ ٱلْفُرْقَانَ عَلَىٰ عَبْدِهِ لِيَكُونَ لِلْعَٰلَمِينَ نَذِيرًا ۱

"Blessed is the One Who sent down the Standard[1] to His servant,[2] so that he may be a warner to the whole world."

Al-Furkan 1

تِلْكَ ءَايَٰتُ ٱلْكِتَٰبِ ٱلْمُبِينِ ۲

"These are the verses of the clear Book."

Ash-shura2

طسٓ ۚ تِلْكَ ءَايَٰتُ ٱلْقُرْءَانِ وَكِتَابٍ مُّبِينٍ ١

"Ṭâ-Sîn. These are the verses of the Quran; the clear Book."

Anaml 1

تَنزِيلُ ٱلْكِتَٰبِ لَا رَيْبَ فِيهِ مِن رَّبِّ ٱلْعَٰلَمِينَ ٢

"The revelation of this Book is—beyond doubt—from the Lord of all worlds."

As-sajdah 2

وَٱلْقُرْءَانِ ٱلْحَكِيمِ ٢

"By the Quran, rich in wisdom!"

I can go on and on to prove how the Holly Quran is the message that is miraculous, and God glorifies it through the whole book. The question is since when did we start to depend on Hadith and leave the Quran behind? And why?

HOW ABOUT REQUESTS TO OTHER THAN GOD?

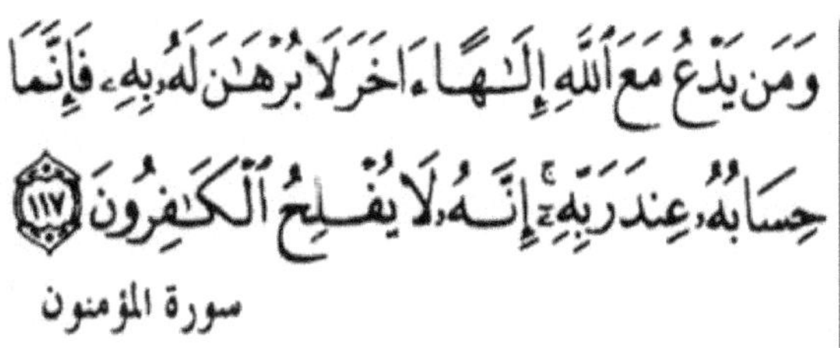

It's amazing that we are living in the 21ˢᵗ Century, and yet there are people who visit the graves and ask dead people for things in life or ask statue or ask other than GOD. The thought that there is a human or thing that can give them what they asking is really claiming partners to GOD.

"The revelation of this Book is from Allah—the Almighty, All-Wise. Indeed, we have sent down the Book to you ˹O Prophet˺ in truth, so worship Allah ˹alone˺, being sincerely devoted to Him. Indeed, sincere devotion is due ˹only˺ to Allah. As for those who take other lords besides Him, ˹saying,˺ "We worship them

139

only so they may bring us closer to Allah," surely Allah will judge between all¹ regarding what they differed about. Allah certainly does not guide whoever persists in lying and disbelief."

Az-Zummar1 2 3

أَمِ ٱتَّخَذُوا۟ مِن دُونِ ٱللَّهِ شُفَعَآءَ ۚ قُلْ أَوَلَوْ كَانُوا۟ لَا يَمْلِكُونَ شَيْئًا وَلَا يَعْقِلُونَ ٤٣

Or have they taken others besides Allah as intercessors? Say, ˹O Prophet, ˺ "˹Would they do so, ˺ even though those ˹idols˺ have neither authority nor intelligence?"

Az-Zumar43

قُل لِّلَّهِ ٱلشَّفَـٰعَةُ جَمِيعًا ۖ لَّهُۥ مُلْكُ ٱلسَّمَـٰوَٰتِ وَٱلْأَرْضِ ۖ ثُمَّ إِلَيْهِ تُرْجَعُونَ ٤٤

Say, "All intercession belongs to Allah ˹alone˺. To Him belongs the kingdom of the heavens and the earth. Then to Him you will ˹all˺ be returned."

Az-Zumar44

It's so astonishing that when you ask people why you don't ask GOD directly, they don't have answers! That is what they found their fathers doing. One of the hardest things in life ever is trying to change the mentality of a person that got brainwashed for many years. Every human, the minute they are born, has been given a name, identity, and religion. Then the human will keep defending a belief that is not his for rest of his life.

وَإِذَا ذُكِرَ ٱللَّهُ وَحْدَهُ ٱشْمَأَزَّتْ قُلُوبُ ٱلَّذِينَ لَا يُؤْمِنُونَ بِٱلْآخِرَةِ ۖ وَإِذَا ذُكِرَ ٱلَّذِينَ مِن دُونِهِ إِذَا هُمْ يَسْتَبْشِرُونَ ٤٥

"Yet when Allah alone is mentioned, the hearts of those who disbelieve in the Hereafter are filled with disgust. But as soon as those ˹gods˺ other than Him are mentioned, they are filled with joy."

Az-Zumar45

وَلَا يَمْلِكُ ٱلَّذِينَ يَدْعُونَ مِن دُونِهِ ٱلشَّفَٰعَةَ إِلَّا مَن شَهِدَ بِٱلْحَقِّ وَهُمْ يَعْلَمُونَ ٨٦

"˹But˺ those ˹objects of worship˺ they invoke besides Him have no power to intercede, except those who testify to the truth knowingly."

Az-Zukhruf86

وَلَئِن سَأَلْتَهُم مَّنْ خَلَقَهُمْ لَيَقُولُنَّ ٱللَّهُ ۖ فَأَنَّىٰ يُؤْفَكُونَ ٨٧

"If you ask them ˹O Prophet˺ who created them, they will certainly say, "Allah!" How can they then be deluded ˹from the truth? ˺"

Az-Zukhruf87

يَدْعُواْ مِن دُونِ ٱللَّهِ مَا لَا يَضُرُّهُ وَمَا لَا يَنفَعُهُ ۚ ذَٰلِكَ هُوَ ٱلضَّلَٰلُ ٱلْبَعِيدُ ١٢

141

"They call besides Allah what can neither harm nor benefit them.
That is ˹truly˺ the farthest one can stray."

Al-Hajj12

يَدْعُواْ لَمَن ضَرُّهُۥ أَقْرَبُ مِن نَّفْعِهِۦ ۚ لَبِئْسَ ٱلْمَوْلَىٰ وَلَبِئْسَ ٱلْعَشِيرُ ١٣

"They invoke those whose worship leads to harm, not benefit.
What an evil patron and what an evil associate!"

Al-Hajj13

يَٰٓأَيُّهَا ٱلنَّاسُ ضُرِبَ مَثَلٌ فَٱسْتَمِعُواْ لَهُۥٓ ۚ إِنَّ ٱلَّذِينَ تَدْعُونَ مِن دُونِ ٱللَّهِ لَن يَخْلُقُواْ ذُبَابًا وَلَوِ ٱجْتَمَعُواْ لَهُۥ ۖ وَإِن يَسْلُبْهُمُ ٱلذُّبَابُ شَيْئًا لَّا يَسْتَنقِذُوهُ مِنْهُ ۚ ضَعُفَ ٱلطَّالِبُ وَٱلْمَطْلُوبُ ٧٣

"O humanity! A lesson is set forth, so listen to it ˹carefully˺: those
˹idols˺ you invoke besides Allah can never create ˹so much as˺ a
fly, even if they ˹all˺ were to come together for that. And if a fly
were to snatch anything away from them, they cannot ˹even˺
retrieve it from the fly. How powerless are those who invoke and
those invoked!"

Al-Hajj73

وَمِنَ ٱلنَّاسِ مَن يَتَّخِذُ مِن دُونِ ٱللَّهِ أَندَادًا يُحِبُّونَهُمْ كَحُبِّ ٱللَّهِ ۗ وَٱلَّذِينَ ءَامَنُوٓا أَشَدُّ حُبًّا لِلَّهِ ۗ وَلَوْ يَرَى ٱلَّذِينَ ظَلَمُوٓا إِذْ يَرَوْنَ ٱلْعَذَابَ أَنَّ ٱلْقُوَّةَ لِلَّهِ جَمِيعًا وَأَنَّ ٱللَّهَ شَدِيدُ ٱلْعَذَابِ ١٦٥

"Still there are some who take others as Allah's equal—they love them as they should love Allah—but the ˹true˺ believers love Allah even more. If only the wrongdoers could see the ˹horrible˺ punishment ˹awaiting them˺, they would certainly realize that all power belongs to Allah and that Allah is indeed severe in punishment."

Al-Baqarah165

وَقَالَ رَبُّكُمُ ٱدْعُونِيٓ أَسْتَجِبْ لَكُمْ ۚ إِنَّ ٱلَّذِينَ يَسْتَكْبِرُونَ عَنْ عِبَادَتِى سَيَدْخُلُونَ جَهَنَّمَ دَاخِرِينَ ٦٠

"Your Lord has proclaimed, "Call upon Me, I will respond to you. Surely those who are too proud to worship Me will enter Hell, fully humbled.""

Ghafir60

وَإِذَا سَأَلَكَ عِبَادِى عَنِّى فَإِنِّى قَرِيبٌ ۖ أُجِيبُ دَعْوَةَ ٱلدَّاعِ إِذَا دَعَانِ ۖ فَلْيَسْتَجِيبُوا لِى وَلْيُؤْمِنُوا بِى لَعَلَّهُمْ يَرْشُدُونَ ١٨٦

"When My servants ask you ˹O Prophet˺ about Me: I am truly nearby. I respond to one's prayer when they call upon Me. So let them respond ˹with obedience˺ to Me and believe in Me, perhaps they will be guided ˹to the Right Way. ˺"

Al-Baqarah186

With all the evidence in the Quran that God Almighty allows you to ask directly but unfortunately, for a lot of humans, they want to request from people, dead people!! When the Muslims will realize that all humans are alike and all servant of God. God is the only supreme power who can forgive us or punish us, make us wealthy or make us poor, make us healthy or make us sick. God only has the will for everything and not the servant (us).

ٱسْتَغْفِرْ لَهُمْ أَوْ لَا تَسْتَغْفِرْ لَهُمْ إِن تَسْتَغْفِرْ لَهُمْ سَبْعِينَ مَرَّةً فَلَن يَغْفِرَ ٱللَّهُ لَهُمْ ذَلِكَ بِأَنَّهُمْ كَفَرُواْ بِٱللَّهِ وَرَسُولِهِ ۗ وَٱللَّهُ لَا يَهْدِى ٱلْقَوْمَ ٱلْفَٰسِقِينَ ٨٠

"˹It does not matter˺ whether you ˹O Prophet˺ pray for them to be forgiven or not. Even if you pray for their forgiveness seventy times, Allah will never forgive them. That is because they have lost faith in Allah and His Messenger. And Allah does not guide the rebellious people."

At-Tawbah80

قُلْ إِنَّمَآ أَنَا۠ بَشَرٌ مِّثْلُكُمْ يُوحَىٰٓ إِلَىَّ أَنَّمَآ إِلَٰهُكُمْ إِلَٰهٌ وَٰحِدٌ ۖ فَمَن كَانَ يَرْجُواْ لِقَآءَ رَبِّهِ فَلْيَعْمَلْ عَمَلًا صَٰلِحًا وَلَا يُشْرِكْ بِعِبَادَةِ رَبِّهِ أَحَدًا ١١٠

"Say, ˹O Prophet, ˺ "I am only a man like you, ˹but˺ it has been revealed to me that your God is only One God. So, whoever

144

hopes for the meeting with their Lord, let them do good deeds and associate none in the worship of their Lord."

Al-Kahf110

قُلْ إِنَّمَآ أَنَا بَشَرٌ مِّثْلُكُمْ يُوحَىٰ إِلَىَّ أَنَّمَآ إِلَٰهُكُمْ إِلَٰهٌ وَٰحِدٌ فَٱسْتَقِيمُوٓا۟ إِلَيْهِ وَٱسْتَغْفِرُوهُ وَوَيْلٌ لِّلْمُشْرِكِينَ ٦

Say, ˹O Prophet, ˺ "I am only a man like you, ˹but˺ it has been revealed to me that your God is only One God. So, take the Straight Way towards Him, and seek His forgiveness. And woe to the polytheists."

Fussilat6

وَمَا مُحَمَّدٌ إِلَّا رَسُولٌ قَدْ خَلَتْ مِن قَبْلِهِ ٱلرُّسُلُ ۚ أَفَإِي۟ن مَّاتَ أَوْ قُتِلَ ٱنقَلَبْتُمْ عَلَىٰٓ أَعْقَٰبِكُمْ وَمَن يَنقَلِبْ عَلَىٰ عَقِبَيْهِ فَلَن يَضُرَّ ٱللَّهَ شَيْـًٔا ۗ وَسَيَجْزِى ٱللَّهُ ٱلشَّٰكِرِينَ ١٤٤

"Muhammad is no more than a messenger; other messengers have gone before him. If he were to die or to be killed, would you regress into disbelief? Those who do so will not harm Allah whatsoever. And Allah will reward those who are grateful."

Al 'Imran144

لَهُ دَعْوَةُ ٱلْحَقِّ ۚ وَٱلَّذِينَ يَدْعُونَ مِن دُونِهِ لَا يَسْتَجِيبُونَ لَهُم بِشَيْءٍ إِلَّا كَبَٰسِطِ كَفَّيْهِ إِلَى ٱلْمَآءِ لِيَبْلُغَ فَاهُ وَمَا هُوَ بِبَٰلِغِهِ ۚ وَمَا دُعَآءُ ٱلْكَٰفِرِينَ إِلَّا فِى ضَلَٰلٍ ١٤

"Calling upon Him ˹alone˺ is the truth. But those ˹idols˺ the pagans invoke besides Him ˹can˺ never respond to them in any way. ˹It is˺ just like someone who stretches out their hands to water, ˹asking it˺ to reach their mouths, but it can never do so. The calls of the disbelievers are only in vain."

Ar-Ra'd14

Who The Prophets And Messengers Ask For Help?

All the prophets and messengers always called onto God asking forgiveness or help, and yet we find Muslims asking people or calling upon humans for help or forgiveness! Isn't Quran clear on that?

It's the curse of Hadith, made people believe the most contradicting ridiculous thing and ignore the Holly Quran, sending humanity back to the dark ages. Aren't we worshiping God? So why ask else? Do we have faith in God? Why call upon else? You walk in an Islamic country where all Muslims cussing and cursing at God, and it's normal, but can anyone dare to curse or cuss at their leader, Imam, or men of cloths!

What misery! We get mad when the west drew Muhamad PBUH, but we ignore that we drew him in the ugliest way throughout the Hadith. Check hadith about the women period? Bukhari and Muslim. It's in utmost disrespect for Prophet PBUH; there is no way a Muslim wrote that!

Also, don't forget to read the section where if a fly fell in your food or drink, you must sink the fly in your food because in one wing is poison and in the other medicine!! HUH!! How in the hell this got to be a Hadith? Where are all the men of clothes from this ridicule? And you don't want the west to draw bad pictures about our beloved Prophet? Why are we sinking in ignorance? It's 21 century!

هُنَالِكَ دَعَا زَكَرِيَّا رَبَّهُ ۖ قَالَ رَبِّ هَبْ لِى مِن لَّدُنكَ ذُرِّيَّةً طَيِّبَةً ۖ إِنَّكَ سَمِيعُ ٱلدُّعَاءِ ٣٨

Then and there, Zachariah prayed to his Lord, saying, "My Lord! Grant me—by your grace—righteous offspring. You are certainly the Hearer of ˹all˺ prayers."

Ali 'Imran38

وَنُوحًا إِذْ نَادَىٰ مِن قَبْلُ فَٱسْتَجَبْنَا لَهُ فَنَجَّيْنَـٰهُ وَأَهْلَهُ مِنَ ٱلْكَرْبِ ٱلْعَظِيمِ ٧٦

"And ˹remember˺ when Noah had cried out to Us earlier, so We responded to him and delivered him and his family¹ from the great distress."

Al-Anbya76

وَأَيُّوبَ إِذْ نَادَىٰ رَبَّهُ أَنِّى مَسَّنِىَ ٱلضُّرُّ وَأَنتَ أَرْحَمُ ٱلرَّٰحِمِينَ ۞ ٨٣

And ˹remember˺ when Job cried out to his Lord, "I have been touched with adversity,¹ and You are the Most Merciful of the merciful."

Al-Anbya83

وَذَا ٱلنُّونِ إذ ذَهَبَ مُغَاضِبًا فَظَنَّ أَن لَّن نَّقْدِرَ عَلَيْهِ فَنَادَىٰ فِى ٱلظُّلُمَـٰتِ أَن لَّآ إِلَـٰهَ
إِلَّآ أَنتَ سُبْحَـٰنَكَ إِنِّى كُنتُ مِنَ ٱلظَّـٰلِمِينَ ٨٧

And ˹remember˺ when the Man of the Whale stormed off ˹from his city˺ in a rage, thinking We would not restrain him.[1] Then in the ˹veils of˺ darkness[2] he cried out, "There is no god ˹worthy of worship˺ except You. Glory be to You! I have certainly done wrong."

Al-Anbya87

THE SIGNS OF THE END DAY?

Another lie we grew up living with is the signs of the end day, and the stories what could happen and what will happen. It's really brainwash for ignorance. What I am shocked by is why? Where are all our scientists and thinkers? Why are they afraid? Is the man of clothes partner in this crime? Is their job just to get paid? The faith has nothing to do with it; they just sold their souls?

وَإِنَّ مِنْهُمْ لَفَرِيقًا يَلْوُنَ أَلْسِنَتَهُم بِالْكِتَبِ لِتَحْسَبُوهُ مِنَ الْكِتَبِ وَمَا هُوَ مِنَ الْكِتَبِ وَيَقُولُونَ هُوَ مِنْ عِندِ اللَّهِ وَمَا هُوَ مِنْ عِندِ اللَّهِ وَيَقُولُونَ عَلَى اللَّهِ الْكَذِبَ وَهُمْ يَعْلَمُونَ ٧٨

"There are some among them who distort the Book with their tongues to make you think this ˹distortion˺ is from the Book—but it is not what the Book says. They say, "It is from Allah"—but it is not from Allah. And ˹so˺ they attribute lies to Allah knowingly."

Al 'Imran78

وَمَا قَدَرُوا۟ ٱللَّهَ حَقَّ قَدْرِهِۦ إِذْ قَالُوا۟ مَآ أَنزَلَ ٱللَّهُ عَلَىٰ بَشَرٍ مِّن شَىْءٍ ۗ قُلْ مَنْ أَنزَلَ ٱلْكِتَٰبَ ٱلَّذِى جَآءَ بِهِۦ مُوسَىٰ نُورًا وَهُدًى لِّلنَّاسِ ۖ تَجْعَلُونَهُۥ قَرَاطِيسَ تُبْدُونَهَا وَتُخْفُونَ كَثِيرًا ۖ وَعُلِّمْتُم مَّا لَمْ تَعْلَمُوٓا۟ أَنتُمْ وَلَآ ءَابَآؤُكُمْ ۖ قُلِ ٱللَّهُ ۖ ثُمَّ ذَرْهُمْ فِى خَوْضِهِمْ يَلْعَبُونَ ٩١

"And they[1] have not shown Allah His proper reverence when they said, "Allah has revealed nothing to any human being." Say, ˹O Prophet, ˺ "Who then revealed the Book brought forth by Moses as a light and guidance for people, which you split into separate sheets—revealing some and hiding much? You have been taught ˹through this Quran˺ what neither you nor your forefathers knew." Say, ˹O Prophet, ˺ "Allah ˹revealed it˺!" Then leave them to amuse themselves with falsehood."

Al-An'am91

وَهَٰذَا كِتَٰبٌ أَنزَلْنَٰهُ مُبَارَكٌ مُّصَدِّقُ ٱلَّذِى بَيْنَ يَدَيْهِ وَلِتُنذِرَ أُمَّ ٱلْقُرَىٰ وَمَنْ حَوْلَهَا وَٱلَّذِينَ يُؤْمِنُونَ بِٱلْءَاخِرَةِ يُؤْمِنُونَ بِهِۦ ۖ وَهُمْ عَلَىٰ صَلَاتِهِمْ يُحَافِظُونَ ٩٢

"This is a blessed Book which We have revealed—confirming what came before it—so you may warn the mother of Cities[1] and

151

everyone around it. Those who believe in the Hereafter ˹truly˺ believe in it and guard their prayers."

Al-An'am92

وَمَنْ أَظْلَمُ مِمَّنِ ٱفْتَرَىٰ عَلَى ٱللَّهِ كَذِبًا أَوْ قَالَ أُوحِىَ إِلَىَّ وَلَمْ يُوحَ إِلَيْهِ شَىْءٌ وَمَن قَالَ سَأُنزِلُ مِثْلَ مَآ أَنزَلَ ٱللَّهُ ۗ وَلَوْ تَرَىٰ إِذِ ٱلظَّٰلِمُونَ فِى غَمَرَٰتِ ٱلْمَوْتِ وَٱلْمَلَٰٓئِكَةُ بَاسِطُوٓا۟ أَيْدِيهِمْ أَخْرِجُوٓا۟ أَنفُسَكُمُ ۖ ٱلْيَوْمَ تُجْزَوْنَ عَذَابَ ٱلْهُونِ بِمَا كُنتُمْ تَقُولُونَ عَلَى ٱللَّهِ غَيْرَ ٱلْحَقِّ وَكُنتُمْ عَنْ ءَايَٰتِهِۦ تَسْتَكْبِرُونَ ٩٣

Who does more wrong than the one who fabricates lies against Allah or claims, "I have received revelations!"—although nothing was revealed to them—or the one who says, "I can reveal the like of Allah's revelations!"? If you ˹O Prophet˺ could only see the wrongdoers in the throes of death while the angels are stretching out their hands ˹saying˺, "Give up your souls! Today you will be rewarded with the torment of disgrace for telling lies about Allah and for being arrogant towards His revelations!"

Al-An'am93

152

RUMORS

So, let us go back to the end day, with all the stories that we heard, and it's still going around in the Muslim world. That Jesus will come back and antichrist too with miraculous power also the Mahdi, and lot of other nonsense stories; that goes against the Quran teaching and create ignorance state and keep Muslims busy in hopeless and endless fiction stories.

يَسْـَٔلُونَكَ عَنِ ٱلسَّاعَةِ أَيَّانَ مُرْسَىٰهَا ۖ قُلْ إِنَّمَا عِلْمُهَا عِندَ رَبِّى ۖ لَا يُجَلِّيهَا لِوَقْتِهَآ إِلَّا هُوَ ۚ ثَقُلَتْ فِى ٱلسَّمَـٰوَٰتِ وَٱلْأَرْضِ ۚ لَا تَأْتِيكُمْ إِلَّا بَغْتَةً ۗ يَسْـَٔلُونَكَ كَأَنَّكَ حَفِىٌّ عَنْهَا ۖ قُلْ إِنَّمَا عِلْمُهَا عِندَ ٱللَّهِ وَلَـٰكِنَّ أَكْثَرَ ٱلنَّاسِ لَا يَعْلَمُونَ ١٨٧

They ask you ˹O Prophet˺ regarding the Hour, "When will it be?" Say, "That knowledge is only with my Lord. He alone will reveal it when the time comes. It is too tremendous for the heavens and the earth and will only take you by surprise." They ask you as if you had full knowledge of it. Say, "That knowledge is only with Allah, but most people do not know."

Al-A'raf 187

That knowledge is only with God!

وَمَا خَلَقْنَا ٱلسَّمَـٰوَٰتِ وَٱلْأَرْضَ وَمَا بَيْنَهُمَآ إِلَّا بِٱلْحَقِّ ۗ وَإِنَّ ٱلسَّاعَةَ لَـَٔاتِيَةٌ فَٱصْفَحِ ٱلصَّفْحَ ٱلْجَمِيلَ ٨٥

"We have not created the heavens and the earth and everything in between except for a purpose. And the Hour is certain to come, so forgive graciously."

Al-Hijr 85

وَلِلَّهِ غَيْبُ ٱلسَّمَـٰوَٰتِ وَٱلْأَرْضِ ۚ وَمَآ أَمْرُ ٱلسَّاعَةِ إِلَّا كَلَمْحِ ٱلْبَصَرِ أَوْ هُوَ أَقْرَبُ ۚ إِنَّ ٱللَّهَ عَلَىٰ كُلِّ شَىْءٍ قَدِيرٌ ٧٧

"To Allah ˹alone˺ belongs ˹the knowledge of˺ the unseen in the heavens and the earth. Bringing about the Hour would only take the blink of an eye, or even less. Surely Allah is Most Capable of everything."

An-Nahl 77

It only takes the blink of an eye!

إِنَّ ٱللَّهَ عِندَهُ عِلْمُ ٱلسَّاعَةِ وَيُنَزِّلُ ٱلْغَيْثَ وَيَعْلَمُ مَا فِى ٱلْأَرْحَامِ ۖ وَمَا تَدْرِى نَفْسٌ مَّاذَا تَكْسِبُ غَدًا ۖ وَمَا تَدْرِى نَفْسٌ بِأَىِّ أَرْضٍ تَمُوتُ ۚ إِنَّ ٱللَّهَ عَلِيمٌ خَبِيرٌ ٣٤

"Indeed, Allah ˹alone˺ has the knowledge of the Hour. He sends down the rain,[1] and knows what is in the wombs.[2] No soul knows what it will earn for tomorrow, and no soul knows in what land it will die. Surely Allah is All-Knowing, All-Aware."

Are you still in doubt? Do you think anyone other than God has the knowledge or can tell the signs or know the future?

Any say goes against God say id fabricated. The argument should be equivalent between the two opponents? Who is equivalent to GOD? No one, so what God said always come first and unequivocal to any human, not even the prophet.

IS IT SUNNAH'S GOD OR SUNNAH'S MESSENGER?

وَأَطِيعُواْ ٱللَّهَ وَرَسُولَهُ وَلَا تَنَـٰزَعُواْ فَتَفْشَلُواْ وَتَذْهَبَ رِيحُكُمْ وَٱصْبِرُواْ إِنَّ ٱللَّهَ مَعَ
ٱلصَّـٰبِرِينَ (الانفال)٤٦

"Obey Allah and His Messenger and do not dispute with one another, or you would be discouraged and weakened. Persevere! Surely Allah is with those who persevere."

46Al-Anfal

Allah is always with those who are truly patient. And obey God's command through the Messenger.

يَسْـَٔلُونَكَ عَنِ ٱلْأَنفَالِ قُلِ ٱلْأَنفَالُ لِلَّهِ وَٱلرَّسُولِ فَٱتَّقُواْ ٱللَّهَ وَأَصْلِحُواْ ذَاتَ بَيْنِكُمْ
وَأَطِيعُواْ ٱللَّهَ وَرَسُولَهُ إِن كُنتُم مُّؤْمِنِينَ (الانفال) ١

They ask you ʿO Prophetʾ regarding the spoils of war. Say, "Their distribution is decided by Allah and His Messenger. So be mindful of Allah, settle your affairs, and obey Allah and His Messenger if you are ʿtrueʾ believers."

1Al-Anfal

Fear God. And obey God through the Messenger in Anfal.

ءَأَشْفَقْتُمْ أَن تُقَدِّمُوا بَيْنَ يَدَىْ نَجْوَىكُمْ صَدَقَتٍ ۚ فَإِذْ لَمْ تَفْعَلُوا وَتَابَ اللَّهُ عَلَيْكُمْ فَأَقِيمُوا الصَّلَوٰةَ وَءَاتُوا الزَّكَوٰةَ وَأَطِيعُوا اللَّهَ وَرَسُولَهُ ۚ وَاللَّهُ خَبِيرٌ بِمَا تَعْمَلُونَ (المجادلة)١٣

Are you afraid of spending in charity before your private consultations ˈwith himˈ? Since you are unable to do so, and Allah has turned to you in mercy, then ˈcontinue toˈ establish prayer, pay alms-tax, and obey Allah and His Messenger. And Allah is All-Aware of what you do.

13Al-Mujadila

God is -aware of what you do. Obey God in alms and good deeds through the Messenger.

ذَلِكَ بِأَنَّهُمْ شَاقُّوا اللَّهَ وَرَسُولَهُ ۚ وَمَن يُشَاقِقِ اللَّهَ وَرَسُولَهُ فَإِنَّ اللَّهَ شَدِيدُ الْعِقَابِ (الانفال)١٣

This is because they defied Allah and His Messenger. And whoever defies Allah and His Messenger, then ˈknow thatˈ Allah is surely severe in punishment.

13Al-Anfal

God is severe in punishment; any one opposes the command of God through the opposing of the Messenger delivering the message.

وَلَوْ أَنَّهُمْ رَضُوا مَا ءَاتَىٰهُمُ اللَّهُ وَرَسُولُهُ وَقَالُوا حَسْبُنَا اللَّهُ سَيُؤْتِينَا اللَّهُ مِن فَضْلِهِ وَرَسُولُهُ إِنَّا إِلَى اللَّهِ رَاغِبُونَ ٥٩(التوبة)

If only they had been contenting with what Allah and His
Messenger had given them and said, "Allah is sufficient for us!
Allah will grant us out of His bounty, and so will His Messenger.
To Allah 'alone' we turn with hope."

59At-Tawbah

And they said God and His Messenger suffice us; God will give
us of His bounty. Just if they were satisfied with what God gave
them through the Messenger.

قُلْ يَـٰٓأَيُّهَا ٱلنَّاسُ إِنِّى رَسُولُ ٱللَّهِ إِلَيْكُمْ جَمِيعًا ٱلَّذِى لَهُ مُلْكُ ٱلسَّمَـٰوَٰتِ وَٱلْأَرْضِ لَا إِلَـٰهَ
إِلَّا هُوَ يُحْىِۦ وَيُمِيتُ فَـَٔامِنُواْ بِٱللَّهِ وَرَسُولِهِ ٱلنَّبِىِّ ٱلْأُمِّىِّ ٱلَّذِى يُؤْمِنُ بِٱللَّهِ وَكَلِمَـٰتِهِۦ
وَٱتَّبِعُوهُ لَعَلَّكُمْ تَهْتَدُونَ (الأعراف)١٥٨

Say, 'O Prophet, ' "O humanity! I am Allah's Messenger to you
all. To Him 'alone' belongs the kingdom of the heavens and the
earth. There is no god 'worthy of worship' except Him. He gives
life and causes death." So, believe in Allah and His Messenger,
the unlettered Prophet, who believes in Allah and His revelations.
And follow him, so you may be 'rightly' guided.

158Al-A'raf

وَمَا كَانَ لِمُؤْمِنٍ وَلَا مُؤْمِنَةٍ إِذَا قَضَى ٱللَّهُ وَرَسُولُهُۥ أَمْرًا أَن يَكُونَ لَهُمُ ٱلْخِيَرَةُ مِنْ
أَمْرِهِمْ وَمَن يَعْصِ ٱللَّهَ وَرَسُولَهُۥ فَقَدْ ضَلَّ ضَلَـٰلًا مُّبِينًا (الأحزاب)٣٦

158

"It is not for a believing man or woman—when Allah and His Messenger decree a matter—to have any other choice in that matter.1 Indeed, whoever disobeys Allah and His Messenger has clearly gone ˹far˺ astray."

36 Al-Ahzab

God has decreed an order through His Messenger.

وَإِذْ تَقُولُ لِلَّذِى أَنْعَمَ ٱللَّهُ عَلَيْهِ وَأَنْعَمْتَ عَلَيْهِ أَمْسِكْ عَلَيْكَ زَوْجَكَ وَٱتَّقِ ٱللَّهَ وَتُخْفِى فِى نَفْسِكَ مَا ٱللَّهُ مُبْدِيهِ وَتَخْشَى ٱلنَّاسَ وَٱللَّهُ أَحَقُّ أَن تَخْشَـٰهُ ۖ فَلَمَّا قَضَىٰ زَيْدٌ مِنْهَا وَطَرًا زَوَّجْنَـٰكَهَا لِكَىْ لَا يَكُونَ عَلَى ٱلْمُؤْمِنِينَ حَرَجٌ فِىٓ أَزْوَٰجِ أَدْعِيَآئِهِمْ إِذَا قَضَوْا۟ مِنْهُنَّ وَطَرًا ۚ وَكَانَ أَمْرُ ٱللَّهِ مَفْعُولًا (الأحزاب)٣٧

"And ˹remember, O Prophet,˺ when you said to the one[1] for whom Allah has done a favor and you ˹too˺ have done a favour,[2] "Keep your wife and fear Allah," while concealing within yourself what Allah was going to reveal. And ˹so˺ you were considering the people, whereas Allah was more worthy of your consideration. So, when Zaid totally lost interest in ˹keeping˺ his wife, we gave her to you in marriage, so that there would be no blame on the believers for marrying the ex-wives of their adopted sons after their divorce. And Allah's command is totally binding.

37 Al-Ahzab

Here God differentiated by what God blessed him with and what the Messenger bestowed upon him. Where the Prophet raised him. But God is more right to fear. God is revealing.

159

مَّا كَانَ عَلَى ٱلنَّبِيِّ مِنْ حَرَجٍ فِيمَا فَرَضَ ٱللَّهُ لَهُ ۖ سُنَّةَ ٱللَّهِ فِى ٱلَّذِينَ خَلَوْا۟ مِن قَبْلُ ۚ وَكَانَ أَمْرُ ٱللَّهِ قَدَرًا مَّقْدُورًا (الأحزاب)٣٨

"There is no blame on the Prophet for doing what Allah has ordained for him. That has been the way of Allah with those ˹prophets˺ who had gone before. And Allah's command has been firmly decreed."

38Al-Ahzab

God's law and way. God's command.

وَأَذَٰنٌ مِّنَ ٱللَّهِ وَرَسُولِهِ إِلَى ٱلنَّاسِ يَوْمَ ٱلْحَجِّ ٱلْأَكْبَرِ أَنَّ ٱللَّهَ بَرِىٓءٌ مِّنَ ٱلْمُشْرِكِينَ ۙ وَرَسُولُهُ ۚ فَإِن تُبْتُمْ فَهُوَ خَيْرٌ لَّكُمْ ۖ وَإِن تَوَلَّيْتُمْ فَٱعْلَمُوٓا۟ أَنَّكُمْ غَيْرُ مُعْجِزِى ٱللَّهِ ۗ وَبَشِّرِ ٱلَّذِينَ كَفَرُوا۟ بِعَذَابٍ أَلِيمٍ (التوبة)٣

"A declaration from Allah and His Messenger ˹is made˺ to all people on the day of the greater pilgrimage1 that Allah and His Messenger are free of the polytheists. So if you ˹pagans˺ repent, it will be better for you. But if you turn away, then know that you will have no escape from Allah. And give good news ˹O Prophet˺ to the disbelievers of a painful punishment."

3At-Tawbah

They can't escape GOD. And authorized the people to the pilgrimage through the Messenger.

160

وَلَمَّا رَءَا ٱلْمُؤْمِنُونَ ٱلْأَحْزَابَ قَالُوا هَٰذَا مَا وَعَدَنَا ٱللَّهُ وَرَسُولُهُ وَصَدَقَ ٱللَّهُ وَرَسُولُهُ وَمَا زَادَهُمْ إِلَّا إِيمَٰنًا وَتَسْلِيمًا (الأحزاب)٢٢

"When the believers saw the enemy alliance, they said, "This is what Allah and His Messenger had promised us. The promise of Allah and His Messenger has come true." And this only increased them in faith and submission.

22Al-Ahzab

وَأَطِيعُوا ٱللَّهَ وَأَطِيعُوا ٱلرَّسُولَ فَإِن تَوَلَّيْتُمْ فَإِنَّمَا عَلَىٰ رَسُولِنَا ٱلْبَلَٰغُ ٱلْمُبِينُ (التغابن)١٢

"Obey Allah and obey the Messenger! But if you turn away, then Our Messenger's duty is only to deliver ˹the message˺ clearly."

12At-Taghabun

What is Messenger's duty but to deliver the message

۞ يَٰٓأَيُّهَا ٱلرَّسُولُ بَلِّغْ مَا أُنزِلَ إِلَيْكَ مِن رَّبِّكَ وَإِن لَّمْ تَفْعَلْ فَمَا بَلَّغْتَ رِسَالَتَهُ وَٱللَّهُ يَعْصِمُكَ مِنَ ٱلنَّاسِ إِنَّ ٱللَّهَ لَا يَهْدِى ٱلْقَوْمَ ٱلْكَٰفِرِينَ (المائدة)٦٧

"O Messenger! Convey everything revealed to you from your Lord. If you do not, then you have not delivered His message. Allah will ˹certainly˺ protect you from the people. Indeed, Allah does not guide the people who disbelieve."

67Al-Ma'idah

O Messenger, convey what has been sent down to you from your Lord.

وَٱلَّذِينَ يُؤْمِنُونَ بِمَا أُنزِلَ إِلَيْكَ وَمَا أُنزِلَ مِن قَبْلِكَ وَبِٱلْءَاخِرَةِ هُمْ يُوقِنُونَ (البقرة) ٤

"And who believe in what has been revealed to you ˹O Prophet˺ and what was revealed before you, and have sure faith in the Hereafter."

4Al-Baqarah

What has been sent down to you?

وَأَنِ ٱحْكُم بَيْنَهُم بِمَا أُنزَلَ ٱللَّهُ وَلَا تَتَّبِعْ أَهْوَاءَهُمْ وَٱحْذَرْهُمْ أَن يَفْتِنُوكَ عَنْ بَعْضِ مَا أُنزَلَ ٱللَّهُ إِلَيْكَ فَإِن تَوَلَّوْا فَٱعْلَمْ أَنَّمَا يُرِيدُ ٱللَّهُ أَن يُصِيبَهُم بِبَعْضِ ذُنُوبِهِمْ وَإِنَّ كَثِيرًا مِّنَ ٱلنَّاسِ لَفَسِقُونَ (المائدة) ٤٩

"And judge between them ˹O Prophet˺ by what Allah has revealed, and do not follow their desires. And beware, so they do not lure you away from some of what Allah has revealed to you. If they turn away ˹from Allah's judgment˺, then know that it is Allah's Will to repay them for some of their sins, and that many people are indeed rebellious."

49Al-Ma'idah

And judge by what God has sent down.

لَكِنِ ٱلرَّٰسِخُونَ فِى ٱلْعِلْمِ مِنْهُمْ وَٱلْمُؤْمِنُونَ يُؤْمِنُونَ بِمَآ أُنزِلَ إِلَيْكَ وَمَآ أُنزِلَ مِن قَبْلِكَ ۚ
وَٱلْمُقِيمِينَ ٱلصَّلَوٰةَ ۚ وَٱلْمُؤْتُونَ ٱلزَّكَوٰةَ وَٱلْمُؤْمِنُونَ بِٱللَّهِ وَٱلْيَوْمِ ٱلْءَاخِرِ أُو۟لَٰٓئِكَ
سَنُؤْتِيهِمْ أَجْرًا عَظِيمًا (النساء)١٦٢

"But those of them well-grounded in knowledge, the faithful ʿwhoʾ believe in what has been revealed to you ʿO Prophetʾ and what was revealed before you—ʿespeciallyʾ those who establish prayer—and those who pay alms-tax and believe in Allah and the Last Day, to these ʿpeopleʾ We will grant a great reward."

162An-Nisa

سُنَّةَ ٱللَّهِ ٱلَّتِى قَدْ خَلَتْ مِن قَبْلُ ۖ وَلَن تَجِدَ لِسُنَّةِ ٱللَّهِ تَبْدِيلًا (الفتح)٢٣

"ʿThis isʾ Allah's way, already long established ʿin the pastʾ. And you will find no change in Allah's way."

23Al-Fath

And you will find no change in Allah's way.

سُنَّةَ مَن قَدْ أَرْسَلْنَا قَبْلَكَ مِن رُّسُلِنَا ۖ وَلَا تَجِدُ لِسُنَّتِنَا تَحْوِيلًا (الاسراء)٧٧

"ʿThis has beenʾ Our way with the messengers We sent before you. And you will never find any change in Our way."

77Al-Isra

And you will never find any change in Our way.

مَّا كَانَ عَلَى ٱلنَّبِيِّ مِنْ حَرَجٍ فِيمَا فَرَضَ ٱللَّهُ لَهُ سُنَّةَ ٱللَّهِ فِى ٱلَّذِينَ خَلَوْا۟ مِن قَبْلُ وَكَانَ أَمْرُ ٱللَّهِ قَدَرًا مَّقْدُورًا (الأحزاب)٣٨

"There is no blame on the Prophet for doing what Allah has ordained for him. That has been the way of Allah with those ˹prophets˺ who had gone before. And Allah's command has been firmly decreed."

38Al-Ahzab

إِنَّ ٱلَّذِينَ لَا يُؤْمِنُونَ بِـَٔايَـٰتِ ٱللَّهِ لَا يَهْدِيهِمُ ٱللَّهُ وَلَهُمْ عَذَابٌ أَلِيمٌ (النحل)١٠٤

Surely those who do not believe in Allah's revelations will never be guided by Allah, and they will suffer a painful punishment.

104An-Nahl

وَمَا ٱخْتَلَفْتُمْ فِيهِ مِن شَىْءٍ فَحُكْمُهُ إِلَى ٱللَّهِ ذَٰلِكُمُ ٱللَّهُ رَبِّى عَلَيْهِ تَوَكَّلْتُ وَإِلَيْهِ أُنِيبُ (الشورى)١٠

˹Say to the believers, O Prophet,˺ "Whatever you may differ about, its judgment rests with Allah. That is Allah—my Lord. In Him I put my trust, and to Him I ˹always˺ turn."

10Ash-Shuraa

Judgment rests with God.

فَلِذَٰلِكَ فَٱدْعُ ۖ وَٱسْتَقِمْ كَمَا أُمِرْتَ ۖ وَلَا تَتَّبِعْ أَهْوَآءَهُمْ ۖ وَقُلْ ءَامَنتُ بِمَآ أَنزَلَ ٱللَّهُ مِن كِتَٰبٍ ۖ وَأُمِرْتُ لِأَعْدِلَ بَيْنَكُمُ ۖ ٱللَّهُ رَبُّنَا وَرَبُّكُمْ ۖ لَنَآ أَعْمَٰلُنَا وَلَكُمْ أَعْمَٰلُكُمْ ۖ لَا حُجَّةَ بَيْنَنَا وَبَيْنَكُمُ ۖ ٱللَّهُ يَجْمَعُ بَيْنَنَا ۖ وَإِلَيْهِ ٱلْمَصِيرُ (الشورى) ١٥

Because of that, you ˹O Prophet˺ will invite ˹all˺. Be steadfast as you are commanded, and do not follow their desires. And say, "I believe in every Scripture Allah has revealed. And I am commanded to judge fairly among you. Allah is our Lord and your Lord. We will be accountable for our deeds and you for yours. There is no ˹need for˺ contention between us. Allah will gather us together ˹for judgment˺. And to Him is the final return."

15Ash-Shuraa

So, call people and say: I believe in what God has revealed of the Book, and I am commanded to judge with justice.

ٱللَّهُ ٱلَّذِىٓ أَنزَلَ ٱلْكِتَٰبَ بِٱلْحَقِّ وَٱلْمِيزَانَ ۗ وَمَا يُدْرِيكَ لَعَلَّ ٱلسَّاعَةَ قَرِيبٌ (الشورى) ١٧

"It is Allah Who has revealed the Book with the truth and the balance ˹of justice˺. You never know, perhaps the Hour is near."

17Ash-Shuraa

We see many verses from Quran that God commanded us to obey and to obey the Messenger by the divine command that God revealed, which is the message. How can we know God's command or promise if the Messenger did not inform us of it? But we have to distinguish between the command from God and not from the Messenger because in obedience, God assembled in his book by saying God and His Messenger, but God did not combine what was revealed or what he ruled. If the judgment and the laws and the rule for God alone. The Noble Messenger has delivered the message, and we have to obey God and the Messenger, but the Messenger cannot enact, legislate, or rule on any subject outside of God's law. Because the rule is only for God, and it is God's Sunnah, you will not find God's Sunnah to be transformed. Therefore, whoever believes that the Messenger has a Sunnah must refer to the Book of God because in that, there is an association with God. The Noble Messenger fulfilled the trust, conveyed the message, and struggled in the nation the best jihad, so do not attribute to him the Sunnah and rulings because they belong to God alone, and we must obey the Messenger with the message that he conveyed, which is the Noble Qur'an. This is an intrusive act; its outward appearance is good, and its interior is disbelief and disobedience.

وَجَعَلُوا لَهُ مِنْ عِبَادِهِ جُزْءًا ۚ إِنَّ ٱلْإِنسَٰنَ لَكَفُورٌ مُّبِينٌ (الزخرف) ١٥

"Still the pagans have made some of His creation out to be a part of Him.1 Indeed, humankind is clearly ungrateful."

15Az-Zukhruf

There is not one of God's servants who shares God's judgment, revelation, and enactment of laws, no matter how high his rank. So, we have to pay close attention to this issue. The prophet Muhammad PBUH organized the legislation but did not legislate. The Sunnah were not prescribed by him, but rather he indicated the Sunnah. He guided us to the true worship of God.

أَفَلَا يَتَدَبَّرُونَ ٱلْقُرْءَانَ أَمْ عَلَىٰ قُلُوبٍ أَقْفَالُهَا (محمد) ٢٤

"Do they not then reflect on the Quran? Or are there locks upon their hearts?"

24Muhammad

أَفَلَا يَتَدَبَّرُونَ ٱلْقُرْءَانَ ۚ وَلَوْ كَانَ مِنْ عِندِ غَيْرِ ٱللَّهِ لَوَجَدُوا۟ فِيهِ ٱخْتِلَٰفًا كَثِيرًا (النساء ٨٢)

Do they not then reflect on the Quran? Had it been from anyone other than Allah, they would have certainly found in it many inconsistencies.

82An-Nisa

CONCLUSION AND THOUGHTS

The intention of this book is to shed light on an important subject. Islam got hijacked a long time ago. This book is not the only one talking about that! There is a lot of scholars, and free thinkers who shed some light on similar subjects as long as I and a lot of people have questions on many subjects, why the men of clothes and the leaders of many Islamic foundations don't get together and discuss this matter and help the public to change and correct the path for Muslims back to Islam. By doing so, the whole world will know Islam is not terrorist religion and prevent any organization from manipulating the minds of teens to commit terrorist acts. The actions of the bad apples don't constitute the rest of the apples are bad or the container of the apples.

لَا إِكْرَاهَ فِى ٱلدِّينِ ۖ قَد تَّبَيَّنَ ٱلرُّشْدُ مِنَ ٱلْغَيِّ ۚ فَمَن يَكْفُرْ بِٱلطَّٰغُوتِ وَيُؤْمِنۢ بِٱللَّهِ فَقَدِ ٱسْتَمْسَكَ بِٱلْعُرْوَةِ ٱلْوُثْقَىٰ لَا ٱنفِصَامَ لَهَا ۗ وَٱللَّهُ سَمِيعٌ عَلِيمٌ ٢٥٦

"Let there be no compulsion in religion, for the truth stands out clearly from falsehood.¹ So whoever renounces false gods and believes in Allah has certainly grasped the firmest, unfailing hand-hold. And Allah is All-Hearing, All-Knowing."

Al-Baqarah 256

حُرِّمَتْ عَلَيْكُمُ ٱلْمَيْتَةُ وَٱلدَّمُ وَلَحْمُ ٱلْخِنزِيرِ وَمَا أُهِلَّ لِغَيْرِ ٱللَّهِ بِهِۦ وَٱلْمُنْخَنِقَةُ وَٱلْمَوْقُوذَةُ وَٱلْمُتَرَدِّيَةُ وَٱلنَّطِيحَةُ وَمَا أَكَلَ ٱلسَّبُعُ إِلَّا مَا ذَكَّيْتُمْ وَمَا ذُبِحَ عَلَى ٱلنُّصُبِ وَأَن تَسْتَقْسِمُوا بِٱلْأَزْلَٰمِ ۚ ذَٰلِكُمْ فِسْقٌ ۗ ٱلْيَوْمَ يَئِسَ ٱلَّذِينَ كَفَرُوا مِن دِينِكُمْ فَلَا تَخْشَوْهُمْ وَٱخْشَوْنِ ۚ ٱلْيَوْمَ أَكْمَلْتُ لَكُمْ دِينَكُمْ وَأَتْمَمْتُ عَلَيْكُمْ نِعْمَتِى وَرَضِيتُ لَكُمُ ٱلْإِسْلَٰمَ دِينًا ۚ فَمَنِ ٱضْطُرَّ فِى مَخْمَصَةٍ غَيْرَ مُتَجَانِفٍ لِّإِثْمٍ ۙ فَإِنَّ ٱللَّهَ غَفُورٌ رَّحِيمٌ ٣

"Forbidden to you are carrion, blood, and swine; what is slaughtered in the name of any other than Allah; what is killed by strangling, beating, a fall, or by being gored to death; what is partly eaten by a predator unless you slaughter it; and what is sacrificed on altars. You are also forbidden to draw lots for decisions.[1] This is all evil. Today the disbelievers have given up all hope of ˹undermining˺ your faith. So do not fear them; fear Me! Today I have perfected your faith for you, completed My favor upon you, and chosen Islam as your way. But whoever is compelled by extreme hunger—not intending to sin—then surely Allah is All-Forgiving, Most Merciful."

Al-Maeda 3

The message is complete, and it's up to everyone whether they believe it or not. The beauty of Islam is that it's a religion of faith. If you have faith, you will not find excuses or look for a loophole in the religion, so you don't fulfill your obligations. Do you think God doesn't know that?

يَسْتَخْفُونَ مِنَ ٱلنَّاسِ وَلَا يَسْتَخْفُونَ مِنَ ٱللَّهِ وَهُوَ مَعَهُمْ إِذْ يُبَيِّتُونَ مَا لَا يَرْضَىٰ مِنَ ٱلْقَوْلِ ۚ وَكَانَ ٱللَّهُ بِمَا يَعْمَلُونَ مُحِيطًا ١٠٨

"They try to hide ˹their deception˺ from people, but they can never hide it from Allah—in Whose presence they plot by night what is displeasing to Him. And Allah is Fully Aware of what they do."

An-Nisa108

هَٰٓأَنتُمۡ هَٰٓؤُلَآءِ جَٰدَلۡتُمۡ عَنۡهُمۡ فِى ٱلۡحَيَوٰةِ ٱلدُّنۡيَا فَمَن يُجَٰدِلُ ٱللَّهَ عَنۡهُمۡ يَوۡمَ ٱلۡقِيَٰمَةِ أَم مَّن يَكُونُ عَلَيۡهِمۡ وَكِيلًا ١٠٩

"Here you are! You ˹believers˺ are advocating for them in this life, but who will ˹dare to˺ advocate for them before Allah on the Day of Judgment? Or who will come to their defenses?"

An-Nisa109

We are invoking everyone to start reading Quran, start learning the religion, start to love God the Creator almighty, and don't leave room for anyone to change the truth about Islam. Don't allow anyone to tell you I heard this from that on that and about that, really, it's like the prophet was whispering only to this person; and its surfaced after 200 years, seriously!

Start thinking for yourself; you are not ignorant, and they not smarter than you. Everyone comes up with Hadith compared to Quran if its match is good, but if it goes against Quran, it's for sure a lie.

To all our brothers and sisters who live in Islamic countries, they made you worry about your food, your safety, and your children, so no one has the time to question them; it's time to listen to your heart and read the Quran and go back to the Holly book. Change your way of thinking and try to learn for yourself, don't ever say that is what we found our fathers doing.

For many years I grew up in such countries, and I never read the Quran to understand it, I just read to recite it, but I was for sure one of the greatest defenders of Hadith, and I used to count on the Hadith in almost everything. For the past 10 years, I used to travel driving a lot, for longer hours, and I used to play the Quran in my car. The first year I heard the Quran, I didn't notice anything, and then some of the Ayat started to get stuck in my head; by the seventh year, the image started clear. And the journey of questioning started, and now I can remember many Ayat and start connecting the dots. And I started to understand the Ayah that says,

أَوْ زِدْ عَلَيْهِ وَرَتِّلِ ٱلْقُرْءَانَ تَرْتِيلًا ٤

"Or a little more—and recite the Quran ˹properly˺ in a measured way."

Al-Muzzammil4

Reciting the Quran will give you the ability to connect the dots, not just in Ramadan, like how we used to do, and quickly because we need to finish reading it before the end of Ramadan! We need to start reading it with love and passion, I swear every time I say I am in love with this Surah, I found another Surah I fall in love with, I can't say which Surah I am so deeply in love with because it's Magical and every Surah has a beauty like no other.

You are not a Sheep! It's your responsibility to find the truth and faith in yourself. In the end, you are the one who will be responsible for your actions. I shed some light on a portion of the lies that I grew up with millions of people thinking it's right, and there is more. That's why we need to think and question in an open mind and logical and scientific way.

قُلْ سِيرُوا فِى ٱلْأَرْضِ ثُمَّ ٱنظُرُوا كَيْفَ كَانَ عَـٰقِبَةُ ٱلْمُكَذِّبِينَ ١١

"Ask ˹them, O Prophet˺, "To whom belongs everything in the heavens and the earth?" Say, "To Allah!" He has taken upon Himself to be Merciful. He will certainly gather ˹all of˺ you together for the Day of Judgment—about which there is no doubt. But those who have ruined themselves will never believe."

Al-Anam11

قُلْ سِيرُوا۟ فِى ٱلْأَرْضِ فَٱنظُرُوا۟ كَيْفَ كَانَ عَٰقِبَةُ ٱلْمُجْرِمِينَ ٦٩

Say, ˹O Prophet, ˺ "Travel throughout the land and see the fate of the wicked."

An-naml69

۞ قُلْ سِيرُوا۟ فِى ٱلْأَرْضِ فَٱنظُرُوا۟ كَيْفَ بَدَأَ ٱلْخَلْقَ ۚ ثُمَّ ٱللَّهُ يُنشِئُ ٱلنَّشْأَةَ ٱلْءَاخِرَةَ إِنَّ ٱللَّهَ عَلَىٰ كُلِّ شَىْءٍ قَدِيرٌ ٢٠

Say, ˹O Prophet, ˺ "Travel throughout the land and see how He originated the creation, then Allah will bring it into being one more time. Surely Allah is Most Capable of everything."

Al-ankaboot20

قُلْ سِيرُوا۟ فِى ٱلْأَرْضِ فَٱنظُرُوا۟ كَيْفَ كَانَ عَٰقِبَةُ ٱلَّذِينَ مِن قَبْلُ ۚ كَانَ أَكْثَرُهُم مُّشْرِكِينَ ٤٢

Say, ˹O Prophet,˺ "Travel throughout the land and see what was the end of those ˹destroyed˺ before ˹you˺—most of them were polytheists."

Ar-room42

The most important question is, for many years and till now, people believe all that was written in Hadith, although there are horrific ones and damaging for Islam; so where is the men of clothes?

Most wrongdoing don't think they're wrongdoing. Islam leaders think they are right and insist on their path even if it's wrong; same as the devil did when GOD ask him to bow to Adam PBUH, self-delusional instead they all come together and discuss what is best for the nation under the roof of Quran, and agree that Islam is the religion of peace and love and humanity, not to kill each other's and kills others in the name of God. It's all hope and wishes; after all, if there is one thing many of them share, it is an incredible capacity for self-delusion.

فَمَن يُرِدِ ٱللَّهُ أَن يَهْدِيَهُ يَشْرَحْ صَدْرَهُ لِلْإِسْلَٰمِ ۖ وَمَن يُرِدْ أَن يُضِلَّهُ يَجْعَلْ صَدْرَهُ ضَيِّقًا حَرَجًا كَأَنَّمَا يَصَّعَّدُ فِى ٱلسَّمَآءِ ۚ كَذَٰلِكَ يَجْعَلُ ٱللَّهُ ٱلرِّجْسَ عَلَى ٱلَّذِينَ لَا يُؤْمِنُونَ ١٢٥

"Whoever Allah wills to guide, He opens their heart to Islam.[1] But whoever He wills to leave astray, He makes their chest tight and constricted as if they were climbing up into the sky. This is how Allah dooms those who disbelieve."

Al-An'am125

174

How Mohamad PBUH found out about going up in the sky, you can't breathe, did he fly or even climb a mountain?

FINALLY

In order to Islam, go back on the right path, burn all the books and go back to the Quran. Don't let the devil persuade you in the opposite direction. I know it's not easy if you grew up on some belief, and then you trying to change. It's very hard, I don't ask you to change; I want you to think for yourself and search for truth.

I ask the guidance from GOD for everything in my life and guidance for all human beings, and I pray for GOD to guide us and direct us to what is best for all.

مَن جَاءَ بِٱلْحَسَنَةِ فَلَهُ خَيْرٌ مِنْهَا وَهُم مِّن فَزَعٍ يَوْمَئِذٍ ءَامِنُونَ ٨٩

"Whoever comes with a good deed will be rewarded with what is better, and they will be secure from the horror on that Day."

An-Naml89

وَمَن جَاءَ بِٱلسَّيِّئَةِ فَكُبَّتْ وُجُوهُهُمْ فِى ٱلنَّارِ هَلْ تُجْزَوْنَ إِلَّا مَا كُنتُمْ تَعْمَلُونَ ٩٠

"And whoever comes with an evil deed will be hurled face-first into the Fire. Are you rewarded except for what you used to do?"

An-Naml90

إِنَّمَآ أُمِرْتُ أَنْ أَعْبُدَ رَبَّ هَٰذِهِ ٱلْبَلْدَةِ ٱلَّذِى حَرَّمَهَا وَلَهُ كُلُّ شَىْءٍ ۖ وَأُمِرْتُ أَنْ أَكُونَ مِنَ ٱلْمُسْلِمِينَ ٩١

"Say, ˹O Prophet, ˺ "I have only been commanded to worship the Lord of this city ˹of Mecca˺, Who has made it sacred, and to Him belongs everything. And I am commanded to be one of those who ˹fully˺ submit ˹to Him. ˺""

An-Naml91

وَأَنْ أَتْلُوَا ٱلْقُرْءَانَ ۖ فَمَنِ ٱهْتَدَىٰ فَإِنَّمَا يَهْتَدِى لِنَفْسِهِ ۖ وَمَن ضَلَّ فَقُلْ إِنَّمَآ أَنَا۠ مِنَ ٱلْمُنذِرِينَ ٩٢

And to recite the Quran." Then whoever chooses to be guided, it is only for their own good. But whoever chooses to stray, say, ˹O Prophet, ˺ "I am only a warner."

An-Naml92

وَقُلِ ٱلْحَمْدُ لِلَّهِ سَيُرِيكُمْ ءَايَٰتِهِ فَتَعْرِفُونَهَا ۚ وَمَا رَبُّكَ بِغَٰفِلٍ عَمَّا تَعْمَلُونَ ٩٣

And say, "All praise is for Allah! He will show you His signs, and you will recognize them. And your Lord is never unaware of what you do."

An-Naml93

REFERENCES

https://quran.com/

Youtube.com

Wikepedia.com

https://sunnahonline.com/library/fiqh-and-sunnah/278-rulings-regarding-the-wiping-over-the-socks-for-purification

https://www.thelastdialogue.org/article/the-topic-forbidden-mentioned-in-quran/

https://education.nationalgeographic.org/resource/equinox

فصول

وَأَنْ أَتْلُوَا۟ ٱلْقُرْءَانَ ۖ فَمَنِ ٱهْتَدَىٰ فَإِنَّمَا يَهْتَدِى لِنَفْسِهِ وَمَن ضَلَّ فَقُلْ إِنَّمَآ أَنَا۠ مِنَ ٱلْمُنذِرِينَ

٩٢ النمل

وَقُلِ ٱلْحَمْدُ لِلَّهِ سَيُرِيكُمْ ءَايَٰتِهِ فَتَعْرِفُونَهَا ۚ وَمَا رَبُّكَ بِغَٰفِلٍ عَمَّا تَعْمَلُونَ

٩٣ النمل

180

من أجل السلامة، عليك العودة إلى الطريق الصحيح وإلغاء جميع الكتب والعودة إلى القرآن. ولا تدع شياطين الجن والإنس تقنعك بشيء معاكس.

أطلب الإرشاد من الله في كل شيء في حياتي وأن يهديني وإياكم الصراط المستقيم، وأن يصلحنا ويرشدنا لما هو خير لنا.

مَن جَآءَ بِٱلْحَسَنَةِ فَلَهُۥ خَيْرٌ مِّنْهَا وَهُم مِّن فَزَعٍ يَوْمَئِذٍ ءَامِنُونَ

٨٩ النمل

وَمَن جَآءَ بِٱلسَّيِّئَةِ فَكُبَّتْ وُجُوهُهُمْ فِى ٱلنَّارِ هَلْ تُجْزَوْنَ إِلَّا مَا كُنتُمْ تَعْمَلُونَ

٩٠ النمل

إِنَّمَآ أُمِرْتُ أَنْ أَعْبُدَ رَبَّ هَٰذِهِ ٱلْبَلْدَةِ ٱلَّذِى حَرَّمَهَا وَلَهُۥ كُلُّ شَىْءٍ ۖ وَأُمِرْتُ أَنْ أَكُونَ مِنَ ٱلْمُسْلِمِينَ

٩١ النمل

وَأَنْ أَتْلُوَا۟ ٱلْقُرْءَانَ ۖ فَمَنِ ٱهْتَدَىٰ فَإِنَّمَا يَهْتَدِى لِنَفْسِهِۦ وَمَن ضَلَّ فَقُلْ إِنَّمَآ أَنَا۠ مِنَ ٱلْمُنذِرِينَ

معظم من يتصرفون خطأ لا يعتقدون أنهم يتصرفون خطأ، وهذا أيضا حال رجال الدين وقادة الأمم الإسلامية، فإنهم يعتقدون أنهم على حق بل ويصرون على أحقيتهم ويختلفون فيما بينهم. والكل يفعل تماما كما فعل الشيطان حين أمره الله بالسجود وقال أنا أفضل منه، وكل شخص يعتقد بأنه أفضل من الآخر، وأصبحوا يقتلون بعضهم باسم الله. فالقاسم المشترك الوحيد بينهم هو قدرتهم الخارقة على خداع ذاتهم.

فَمَن يُرِدِ ٱللَّهُ أَن يَهْدِيَهُ يَشْرَحْ صَدْرَهُ لِلْإِسْلَٰمِ ۖ وَمَن يُرِدْ أَن يُضِلَّهُ يَجْعَلْ صَدْرَهُ ضَيِّقًا حَرَجًا كَأَنَّمَا يَصَّعَّدُ فِى ٱلسَّمَآءِ ۚ كَذَٰلِكَ يَجْعَلُ ٱللَّهُ ٱلرِّجْسَ عَلَى ٱلَّذِينَ لَا يُؤْمِنُونَ

وهذه إحدى الآيات التي تدل على عظمة القرآن. ومن اللافت أيضا، كيف علم محمد عليه الصلاة والسلام بأنه عند الصعود في السماء، لا يمكنك التنفس؟ لأن هذه المعلومة لم تعرف إلا بعد اكتشاف الطيران! والجواب هو: لقد علمه إياه الخالق عز وجل.

أي سورة أحبها أكثر، لأن كل سورة لها سحرها وجمال
لا مثيل له.

أنت لست كالأنعام! أنت من أمر الله الملائكة أن تسجد
له! عليك مسؤولية العثور على الحقيقة وأن تجد السبيل
ولا تضله، لا تزر وازرة وزر أخرى، فالمسؤولية عليك
وحدك.

قُل سِيرُواْ فِى ٱلْأَرْضِ ثُمَّ ٱنظُرُواْ كَيْفَ كَانَ عَـٰقِبَةُ
ٱلْمُكَذِّبِينَ

١١١ الانعام

قُل سِيرُواْ فِى ٱلْأَرْضِ فَٱنظُرُواْ كَيْفَ كَانَ عَـٰقِبَةُ
ٱلْمُجْرِمِينَ

٦٩ النمل

قُلْ سِيرُواْ فِى ٱلْأَرْضِ فَٱنظُرُواْ كَيْفَ بَدَأَ ٱلْخَلْقَ ثُمَّ
ٱللَّهُ يُنشِئُ ٱلنَّشْأَةَ ٱلْـَٔاخِرَةَ ۚ إِنَّ ٱللَّهَ عَلَىٰ كُلِّ شَىْءٍ قَدِيرٌ

٢٠ العنكبوت

قُلْ سِيرُواْ فِى ٱلْأَرْضِ فَٱنظُرُواْ كَيْفَ كَانَ عَـٰقِبَةُ
ٱلَّذِينَ مِن قَبْلُ ۚ كَانَ أَكْثَرُهُم مُّشْرِكِينَ

إلى جميع الإخوة والأهل في البلدان الإسلامية، لقد جعلوكم تقلقون على طعامكم وسلامتكم لكي لا يكون لديكم الوقت لاستجوابهم. لقد حان الوقت أن تنفضوا غبارهم عنكم وتعودوا إلى كتاب الله ولا تقولوا كما قال السابقون هذا ما وجدنا آباءنا عليه. لقد نشأت في هذه البلدان لسنوات عديدة ولم أقرأ القرآن أبدا لفهمه والتمعن فيه، لكنني كنت من أكثر المدافعين عن رجال الدين والأحاديث بحيث كنت أتعرف على ديني من الأحاديث وليس من القرآن. منذ عشر سنوات، بدأت أسافر كثيرا بسبب عملي وأقود لمسافات طويلة، فبدأت الاستماع للقرآن الكريم خلال قيادتي. وبعد مضي خمس سنوات، بدأت رحلة الاستجواب، حيث علقت بعض الآيات في ذهني وبدأت بربط النقاط وفهم الآية التي تقول:

أَوْ زِدْ عَلَيْهِ وَرَتِّلِ ٱلْقُرْءَانَ تَرْتِيلًا
المزمل4
سيمنحك القرآن القدرة على ربط النقاط ببعضها،
وليس قراءة القرآن فقط في رمضان كما اعتدنا، وأن نختمه قبل نهاية الشهر سواء فهمناه أم لا. نحتاج أن نسمعه ونقرأه بحب وشغف. أقسم بالله أنني كلما استمعت إلى سورة أحببتها، وظننت أنها المفضلة لدي حتى أسمع أخرى، فأصبحت لا أستطيع أن أقول

يراك ويعرف ما في نفسك. الاحتيال على الدين عكس ذلك.

يَسْتَخْفُونَ مِنَ ٱلنَّاسِ وَلَا يَسْتَخْفُونَ مِنَ ٱللَّهِ وَهُوَ مَعَهُمْ إِذْ يُبَيِّتُونَ مَا لَا يَرْضَىٰ مِنَ ٱلْقَوْلِ ۚ وَكَانَ ٱللَّهُ بِمَا يَعْمَلُونَ مُحِيطًا

١٠٨ النساء

هَٰأَنتُمْ هَٰؤُلَاءِ جَٰدَلْتُمْ عَنْهُمْ فِى ٱلْحَيَوٰةِ ٱلدُّنْيَا فَمَن يُجَٰدِلُ ٱللَّهَ عَنْهُمْ يَوْمَ ٱلْقِيَٰمَةِ أَم مَّن يَكُونُ عَلَيْهِمْ وَكِيلًا

١٠٩ النساء

أدعو الجميع لقراءة القرآن أو الاستماع إليه عدة مرات، حيث تتعرف إلى الدين الحقيقي وتتعلق بحب الخالق أكثر، ولن تترك أصحاب العمائم أو غيرهم يتلاعبون بعقلك.

أدعوك لتبدأ التفكير بنفسك، فأنت لست جاهلا كما أرادوا أن يفهموك. إن أصحاب العمائم ليسوا بأذكى منك. أسهل الأمور أن تستمع للقرآن عدة مرات ولا تكتفي بواحدة فقط. وعندها، وإن لم تحفظه فبهداية من الله، سوف تستطيع التمييز بين الخطأ والصواب في الأحاديث.

الذين كتبوا حول مواضيع مشابهة. السؤال هنا هو: لماذا لا يجتمع أهل العلم وأهل الفتوى لمناقشة الأمر ولتصحيح المسار الذي اتخذته الأمة؟ الأمة مؤمنة بالله وبالقرآن. فلماذا اللغو وتغيير مسارهم؟

لَّا إِكْرَاهَ فِى ٱلدِّينِ ۖ قَد تَّبَيَّنَ ٱلرُّشْدُ مِنَ ٱلْغَىِّ ۚ فَمَن يَكْفُرْ بِٱلطَّٰغُوتِ وَيُؤْمِنۢ بِٱللَّهِ فَقَدِ ٱسْتَمْسَكَ بِٱلْعُرْوَةِ ٱلْوُثْقَىٰ لَا ٱنفِصَامَ لَهَا ۗ وَٱللَّهُ سَمِيعٌ عَلِيمٌ ٢٥٦ البقرة

حُرِّمَتْ عَلَيْكُمُ ٱلْمَيْتَةُ وَٱلدَّمُ وَلَحْمُ ٱلْخِنزِيرِ وَمَآ أُهِلَّ لِغَيْرِ ٱللَّهِ بِهِ وَٱلْمُنْخَنِقَةُ وَٱلْمَوْقُوذَةُ وَٱلْمُتَرَدِّيَةُ وَٱلنَّطِيحَةُ وَمَآ أَكَلَ ٱلسَّبُعُ إِلَّا مَا ذَكَّيْتُمْ وَمَا ذُبِحَ عَلَى ٱلنُّصُبِ وَأَن تَسْتَقْسِمُوا۟ بِٱلْأَزْلَٰمِ ۚ ذَٰلِكُمْ فِسْقٌ ۗ ٱلْيَوْمَ يَئِسَ ٱلَّذِينَ كَفَرُوا۟ مِن دِينِكُمْ فَلَا تَخْشَوْهُمْ وَٱخْشَوْنِ ۚ ٱلْيَوْمَ أَكْمَلْتُ لَكُمْ دِينَكُمْ وَأَتْمَمْتُ عَلَيْكُمْ نِعْمَتِى وَرَضِيتُ لَكُمُ ٱلْإِسْلَٰمَ دِينًا ۚ فَمَنِ ٱضْطُرَّ فِى مَخْمَصَةٍ غَيْرَ مُتَجَانِفٍ لِّإِثْمٍ ۙ فَإِنَّ ٱللَّهَ غَفُورٌ رَّحِيمٌ ٣ المائدة

الرسالة كاملة والأمر متروك لكل شخص سواء كان يؤمن أم لا. فالإسلام إيمان وعندما يدخل الإيمان إلى قلبك، فأنت لست بحاجة إلى فتوى من هذا أو ذاك، لأنك رقيب نفسك وتحاسب نفسك وتخاف الله في جميع أعمالك. هذا هو الإسلام، أن تؤمن بأن الله

خاتمة وأفكار

القصد من هذا الكتاب هو تسليط الضوء على موضوع مهم، وهو أنه قد تم الابتعاد عن الإسلام منذ زمن بعيد. أنا أعلم بأنه ليس الكتاب الوحيد الذي تطرق لهذا الموضوع، بل هنالك العديد من الرواد

أَفَلَا يَتَدَبَّرُونَ ٱلْقُرْءَانَ ۚ وَلَوْ كَانَ مِنْ عِندِ غَيْرِ ٱللَّهِ لَوَجَدُوا۟ فِيهِ ٱخْتِلَٰفًا كَثِيرًا (النساء ٨٢)

والشرائع والحكم لله وحده. على الرسول الكريم تبليغ الرسالة وعلينا طاعة الله والرسول، ولكنه لا يستطيع أن يسُنّ أو يُشَرع أو يحكم بأي موضوع خارج عما شرع الله. إذن، إن الحكم لله وحده وإنها سنة الله، ولن تجد لسنة الله تحويلا لذلك، فعلى كل من يعتقد بأن للرسول سنة، الرجوع إلى كتاب الله، لأن في ذلك شرك بالله. لقد أدى الرسول الكريم الأمانة وبلغها للأمة وجاهد فيها خير جهاد، فلا تنسبوا له السنن والأحكام لأنها خاصة بالله وحدد، وعلينا طاعة الرسول بالرسالة التي بلغها، ألا وهي القرآن الكريم. هذا عمل مدسوس، ظاهره جيد وباطنه الكفر والمعصية.

وَجَعَلُوا۟ لَهُۥ مِنْ عِبَادِهِۦ جُزْءًا ۚ إِنَّ ٱلْإِنسَٰنَ لَكَفُورٌ مُّبِينٌ (الزخرف) ١٥

لا أحد يشارك الله في الحكم والتنزيل وسن الشرائع، ولا يمكن أن يوجد، مهما علا شأنه. لذلك، فإنه علينا الانتباه جيدا لهذا الموضوع. إن محمد، سيد الخلق، قد نظم التشريع، ولكنه لم يُشرع، ولم يسن السنن وإنما دلنا عليها، وهدانا إلى عبادة الله الحق

أَفَلَا يَتَدَبَّرُونَ ٱلْقُرْءَانَ أَمْ عَلَىٰ قُلُوبٍ أَقْفَالُهَآ (محمد) ٢٤

وَمَا ٱخْتَلَفْتُمْ فِيهِ مِن شَيْءٍ فَحُكْمُهُ إِلَى ٱللَّهِ ۚ ذَٰلِكُمُ ٱللَّهُ رَبِّى عَلَيْهِ تَوَكَّلْتُ وَإِلَيْهِ أُنِيبُ (الشورى) ١٠

فحكمه الى الله.

فَلِذَٰلِكَ فَٱدْعُ ۖ وَٱسْتَقِمْ كَمَا أُمِرْتَ ۖ وَلَا تَتَّبِعْ أَهْوَآءَهُمْ ۖ وَقُلْ ءَامَنتُ بِمَا أَنزَلَ ٱللَّهُ مِن كِتَٰبٍ ۖ وَأُمِرْتُ لِأَعْدِلَ بَيْنَكُمُ ۖ ٱللَّهُ رَبُّنَا وَرَبُّكُمْ ۖ لَنَا أَعْمَٰلُنَا وَلَكُمْ أَعْمَٰلُكُمْ ۖ لَا حُجَّةَ بَيْنَنَا وَبَيْنَكُمُ ۖ ٱللَّهُ يَجْمَعُ بَيْنَنَا ۖ وَإِلَيْهِ ٱلْمَصِيرُ (الشورى) ١٥

فادعوا وقل امنت بما أنزل الله من كتاب وأمرت أن تحكم بالعدل.

ٱللَّهُ ٱلَّذِى أَنزَلَ ٱلْكِتَٰبَ بِٱلْحَقِّ وَٱلْمِيزَانَ ۗ وَمَا يُدْرِيكَ لَعَلَّ ٱلسَّاعَةَ قَرِيبٌ (الشورى) ١٧

لقد أمرنا الله في آيات كثيرة بطاعته وطاعة الرسول بالأمر الإلهي الذي أنزله، ألا وهو الرسالة. ونرى كيف ميز الله الطاعة والوعد وأن يقضي أمرا، وبالأنفال والقتال، وهذا أمر بديهي. فكيف نعرف أمر الله أو وعده إذا لم يعلمنا الرسول بهما؟ ولكن، علينا التمييز بأن الأمر صادر عن الله وليس عن الرسول، لأن الله قال في كتابه بطاعة الله ورسوله، ولكنه لم يجمع فيما أنزل أو فيما يحكم. إذن، إن التنزيل

ذُنُوبِهِمْ ۗ وَإِنَّ كَثِيرًا مِّنَ ٱلنَّاسِ لَفَٰسِقُونَ (المائدة) ٤٩

أحكم بما أنزل الله.

لَّٰكِنِ ٱلرَّٰسِخُونَ فِى ٱلْعِلْمِ مِنْهُمْ وَٱلْمُؤْمِنُونَ يُؤْمِنُونَ بِمَآ
أُنزِلَ إِلَيْكَ وَمَآ أُنزِلَ مِن قَبْلِكَ ۚ وَٱلْمُقِيمِينَ ٱلصَّلَوٰةَ ۚ
وَٱلْمُؤْتُونَ ٱلزَّكَوٰةَ وَٱلْمُؤْمِنُونَ بِٱللَّهِ وَٱلْيَوْمِ ٱلْءَاخِرِ أُو۟لَٰئِكَ
سَنُؤْتِيهِمْ أَجْرًا عَظِيمًا (النساء) ١٦٢

سُنَّةَ ٱللَّهِ ٱلَّتِى قَدْ خَلَتْ مِن قَبْلُ ۖ وَلَن تَجِدَ لِسُنَّةِ ٱللَّهِ
تَبْدِيلًا (الفتح) ٢٣

ولن تجد لسنة الله تبديلا.

سُنَّةَ مَن قَدْ أَرْسَلْنَا قَبْلَكَ مِن رُّسُلِنَا ۖ وَلَا تَجِدُ لِسُنَّتِنَا
تَحْوِيلًا (الاسراء) ٧٧

ولن تجد لسنة الله تحويلا.

مَّا كَانَ عَلَى ٱلنَّبِىِّ مِنْ حَرَجٍ فِيمَا فَرَضَ ٱللَّهُ لَهُ ۖ سُنَّةَ ٱللَّهِ
فِى ٱلَّذِينَ خَلَوْا۟ مِن قَبْلُ ۚ وَكَانَ أَمْرُ ٱللَّهِ قَدَرًا مَّقْدُورًا
(الأحزاب) ٣٨

إِنَّ ٱلَّذِينَ لَا يُؤْمِنُونَ بِـَٔايَٰتِ ٱللَّهِ لَا يَهْدِيهِمُ ٱللَّهُ وَلَهُمْ
عَذَابٌ أَلِيمٌ (النحل) ١٠٤

وَلَمَّا رَءَا ٱلْمُؤْمِنُونَ ٱلْأَحْزَابَ قَالُوا۟ هَٰذَا مَا وَعَدَنَا ٱللَّهُ وَرَسُولُهُۥ وَصَدَقَ ٱللَّهُ وَرَسُولُهُۥ ۚ وَمَا زَادَهُمْ إِلَّا إِيمَٰنًا وَتَسْلِيمًا (الأحزاب) ٢٢

وَأَطِيعُوا۟ ٱللَّهَ وَأَطِيعُوا۟ ٱلرَّسُولَ ۚ فَإِن تَوَلَّيْتُمْ فَإِنَّمَا عَلَىٰ رَسُولِنَا ٱلْبَلَٰغُ ٱلْمُبِينُ (التغابن) ١٢

فما على الرسول الا البلاغ.

۞ يَٰٓأَيُّهَا ٱلرَّسُولُ بَلِّغْ مَآ أُنزِلَ إِلَيْكَ مِن رَّبِّكَ ۖ وَإِن لَّمْ تَفْعَلْ فَمَا بَلَّغْتَ رِسَالَتَهُۥ ۚ وَٱللَّهُ يَعْصِمُكَ مِنَ ٱلنَّاسِ ۗ إِنَّ ٱللَّهَ لَا يَهْدِى ٱلْقَوْمَ ٱلْكَٰفِرِينَ (المائدة) ٦٧

يا أيها الرسول يلغ ما أنزل اليك من ربك.

وَٱلَّذِينَ يُؤْمِنُونَ بِمَآ أُنزِلَ إِلَيْكَ وَمَآ أُنزِلَ مِن قَبْلِكَ وَبِٱلْءَاخِرَةِ هُمْ يُوقِنُونَ (البقرة) ٤

ما أنزل أليك.

وَأَنِ ٱحْكُم بَيْنَهُم بِمَآ أَنزَلَ ٱللَّهُ وَلَا تَتَّبِعْ أَهْوَآءَهُمْ وَٱحْذَرْهُمْ أَن يَفْتِنُوكَ عَن بَعْضِ مَآ أَنزَلَ ٱللَّهُ إِلَيْكَ ۖ فَإِن تَوَلَّوْا۟ فَٱعْلَمْ أَنَّمَا يُرِيدُ ٱللَّهُ أَن يُصِيبَهُم بِبَعْضِ

وَإِذْ تَقُولُ لِلَّذِى أَنْعَمَ ٱللَّهُ عَلَيْهِ وَأَنْعَمْتَ عَلَيْهِ أَمْسِكْ عَلَيْكَ زَوْجَكَ وَٱتَّقِ ٱللَّهَ وَتُخْفِى فِى نَفْسِكَ مَا ٱللَّهُ مُبْدِيهِ وَتَخْشَى ٱلنَّاسَ وَٱللَّهُ أَحَقُّ أَن تَخْشَىٰهُ فَلَمَّا قَضَىٰ زَيْدٌ مِّنْهَا وَطَرًا زَوَّجْنَٰكَهَا لِكَىْ لَا يَكُونَ عَلَى ٱلْمُؤْمِنِينَ حَرَجٌ فِى أَزْوَٰجِ أَدْعِيَائِهِمْ إِذَا قَضَوْا مِنْهُنَّ وَطَرًا وَكَانَ أَمْرُ ٱللَّهِ مَفْعُولًا (الأحزاب) ٣٧

هنا فرق الله بما أنعم الله عليه وبما أنعم الرسول عليه. حيث أن الرسول رباه. ولكن الله أحق أن يخشى. الله مبديه.

مَّا كَانَ عَلَى ٱلنَّبِىِّ مِنْ حَرَجٍ فِيمَا فَرَضَ ٱللَّهُ لَهُ سُنَّةَ ٱللَّهِ فِى ٱلَّذِينَ خَلَوْا مِن قَبْلُ وَكَانَ أَمْرُ ٱللَّهِ قَدَرًا مَّقْدُورًا (الأحزاب) ٣٨

سنة الله. أمر الله.

وَأَذَٰنٌ مِّنَ ٱللَّهِ وَرَسُولِهِ إِلَى ٱلنَّاسِ يَوْمَ ٱلْحَجِّ ٱلْأَكْبَرِ أَنَّ ٱللَّهَ بَرِىءٌ مِّنَ ٱلْمُشْرِكِينَ وَرَسُولُهُ فَإِن تُبْتُمْ فَهُوَ خَيْرٌ لَّكُمْ وَإِن تَوَلَّيْتُمْ فَٱعْلَمُوا أَنَّكُمْ غَيْرُ مُعْجِزِى ٱللَّهِ وَبَشِّرِ ٱلَّذِينَ كَفَرُوا بِعَذَابٍ أَلِيمٍ (التوبة) ٣

غير معجزي الله. وآذان للناس الى الحج من خلال الرسول.

والله خبير بما تعملون. أطيعوا الله في الصدقات من خلال الرسول.

ذَٰلِكَ بِأَنَّهُمْ شَاقُّوا۟ ٱللَّهَ وَرَسُولَهُۥ ۚ وَمَن يُشَاقِقِ ٱللَّهَ وَرَسُولَهُۥ فَإِنَّ ٱللَّهَ شَدِيدُ ٱلْعِقَابِ (الانفال)١٣

فان الله شديد العقاب. من يشاقق امر الله من خلال مشاقة الرسول.

وَلَوْ أَنَّهُمْ رَضُوا۟ مَآ ءَاتَىٰهُمُ ٱللَّهُ وَرَسُولُهُۥ وَقَالُوا۟ حَسْبُنَا ٱللَّهُ سَيُؤْتِينَا ٱللَّهُ مِن فَضْلِهِ وَرَسُولُهُۥٓ إِنَّآ إِلَى ٱللَّهِ رَٰغِبُونَ ٥٩ (التوبة)

وقالو حسبنا الله ورسوله وسيؤتينا الله من فضله. لو انهم رضوا ما أتاهم الله من خلال الرسول.

قُل يَٰٓأَيُّهَا ٱلنَّاسُ إِنِّى رَسُولُ ٱللَّهِ إِلَيْكُمْ جَمِيعًا ٱلَّذِى لَهُۥ مُلْكُ ٱلسَّمَٰوَٰتِ وَٱلْأَرْضِ ۖ لَآ إِلَٰهَ إِلَّا هُوَ يُحْىِۦ وَيُمِيتُ ۖ فَـَٔامِنُوا۟ بِٱللَّهِ وَرَسُولِهِ ٱلنَّبِىِّ ٱلْأُمِّىِّ ٱلَّذِى يُؤْمِنُ بِٱللَّهِ وَكَلِمَٰتِهِۦ وَٱتَّبِعُوهُ لَعَلَّكُمْ تَهْتَدُونَ (الأعراف)١٥٨

وَمَا كَانَ لِمُؤْمِنٍ وَلَا مُؤْمِنَةٍ إِذَا قَضَى ٱللَّهُ وَرَسُولُهُۥٓ أَمْرًا أَن يَكُونَ لَهُمُ ٱلْخِيَرَةُ مِنْ أَمْرِهِمْ ۗ وَمَن يَعْصِ ٱللَّهَ وَرَسُولَهُۥ فَقَدْ ضَلَّ ضَلَٰلًا مُّبِينًا (الأحزاب)٣٦

قضى الله أمرا من خلال رسوله.

Is it Sunnah's God or Sunnah's messenger?

هل هي سنة الله أمْ سنة الرسول؟

وَأَطِيعُواْ ٱللَّهَ وَرَسُولَهُ وَلَا تَنَٰزَعُواْ فَتَفْشَلُواْ وَتَذْهَبَ رِيحُكُمْ ۖ وَٱصْبِرُوٓاْ ۚ إِنَّ ٱللَّهَ مَعَ ٱلصَّٰبِرِينَ (الانفال) ٤٦

ان الله مع الصابرين. وأطيعوا أمر الله من خلال الرسول.

يَسْـَٔلُونَكَ عَنِ ٱلْأَنفَالِ ۖ قُلِ ٱلْأَنفَالُ لِلَّهِ وَٱلرَّسُولِ ۖ فَٱتَّقُواْ ٱللَّهَ وَأَصْلِحُواْ ذَاتَ بَيْنِكُمْ ۖ وَأَطِيعُواْ ٱللَّهَ وَرَسُولَهُ إِن كُنتُم مُّؤْمِنِينَ (الانفال) ١

فاتقوا الله. وأطيعوا الله من خلال الرسول في الانفال.

ءَأَشْفَقْتُمْ أَن تُقَدِّمُواْ بَيْنَ يَدَىْ نَجْوَىٰكُمْ صَدَقَٰتٍ ۚ فَإِذْ لَمْ تَفْعَلُواْ وَتَابَ ٱللَّهُ عَلَيْكُمْ فَأَقِيمُواْ ٱلصَّلَوٰةَ وَءَاتُواْ ٱلزَّكَوٰةَ وَأَطِيعُواْ ٱللَّهَ وَرَسُولَهُ ۚ وَٱللَّهُ خَبِيرٌۢ بِمَا تَعْمَلُونَ (المجادلة) ١٣

هل ما زلت تشك؟ هل تعتقد بوجود أي كائن لديه المعرفة وعلم الغيب. أي قول يتعارض مع قول الله هو مختلق ولا يجوز حتى الاستماع له لأن الكفة ما بين الخالق والمخلوق غير مرجحة.

وَمَا خَلَقْنَا ٱلسَّمَٰوَٰتِ وَٱلْأَرْضَ وَمَا بَيْنَهُمَآ إِلَّا بِٱلْحَقِّ وَإِنَّ ٱلسَّاعَةَ لَءَاتِيَةٌ فَٱصْفَحِ ٱلصَّفْحَ ٱلْجَمِيلَ.

٨٥ الحجر

وَلِلَّهِ غَيْبُ ٱلسَّمَٰوَٰتِ وَٱلْأَرْضِ وَمَآ أَمْرُ ٱلسَّاعَةِ إِلَّا كَلَمْحِ ٱلْبَصَرِ أَوْ هُوَ أَقْرَبُ إِنَّ ٱللَّهَ عَلَىٰ كُلِّ شَىْءٍ قَدِيرٌ

٧٧ النحل

لا يستغرق الأمر سوى غمضة عين.

إِنَّ ٱللَّهَ عِندَهُ عِلْمُ ٱلسَّاعَةِ وَيُنَزِّلُ ٱلْغَيْثَ وَيَعْلَمُ مَا فِى ٱلْأَرْحَامِ وَمَا تَدْرِى نَفْسٌ مَّاذَا تَكْسِبُ غَدًا وَمَا تَدْرِى نَفْسٌ بِأَيِّ أَرْضٍ تَمُوتُ إِنَّ ٱللَّهَ عَلِيمٌ خَبِيرٌ

٣٤ لقمان

ٱلْيَوْمَ تُجْزَوْنَ عَذَابَ ٱلْهُونِ بِمَا كُنتُمْ تَقُولُونَ عَلَى
ٱللَّهِ غَيْرَ ٱلْحَقِّ وَكُنتُمْ عَنْ ءَايَتِهِ تَسْتَكْبِرُونَ

الانعام ٩٣

شائعات

في النهاية، نعلم أن كل القصص التي تدور في مجتمعنا الإسلامي عن يوم الساعة وعن العلامات التي رويت في صحيح البخاري ومسلم هي غير منطقية وغير علمية وتتعارض مع كتاب الله.

يَسْـَٔلُونَكَ عَنِ ٱلسَّاعَةِ أَيَّانَ مُرْسَىٰهَا قُلْ إِنَّمَا عِلْمُهَا عِندَ رَبِّي لَا يُجَلِّيهَا لِوَقْتِهَا إِلَّا هُوَ ثَقُلَتْ فِى ٱلسَّمَٰوَٰتِ وَٱلْأَرْضِ لَا تَأْتِيكُمْ إِلَّا بَغْتَةً يَسْـَٔلُونَكَ كَأَنَّكَ حَفِيٌّ عَنْهَا قُلْ إِنَّمَا عِلْمُهَا عِندَ ٱللَّهِ وَلَٰكِنَّ أَكْثَرَ ٱلنَّاسِ لَا يَعْلَمُونَ

١٨٧ الاعراف

تلك المعرفة عند الله فقط

عِندِ ٱللَّهِ وَمَا هُوَ مِنْ عِندِ ٱللَّهِ وَيَقُولُونَ عَلَى ٱللَّهِ ٱلْكَذِبَ وَهُمْ يَعْلَمُونَ

٧٨ آل عمران

وَمَا قَدَرُوا۟ ٱللَّهَ حَقَّ قَدْرِهِ إِذْ قَالُوا۟ مَا أَنزَلَ ٱللَّهُ عَلَىٰ بَشَرٍ مِّن شَىْءٍ قُلْ مَنْ أَنزَلَ ٱلْكِتَٰبَ ٱلَّذِى جَاءَ بِهِ مُوسَىٰ نُورًا وَهُدًى لِّلنَّاسِ تَجْعَلُونَهُ قَرَاطِيسَ تُبْدُونَهَا وَتُخْفُونَ كَثِيرًا وَعُلِّمْتُم مَّا لَمْ تَعْلَمُوٓا۟ أَنتُمْ وَلَآ ءَابَآؤُكُمْ قُلِ ٱللَّهُ ثُمَّ ذَرْهُمْ فِى خَوْضِهِمْ يَلْعَبُونَ

٩١ الانعام

وَهَٰذَا كِتَٰبٌ أَنزَلْنَٰهُ مُبَارَكٌ مُّصَدِّقُ ٱلَّذِى بَيْنَ يَدَيْهِ وَلِتُنذِرَ أُمَّ ٱلْقُرَىٰ وَمَنْ حَوْلَهَا وَٱلَّذِينَ يُؤْمِنُونَ بِٱلْءَاخِرَةِ يُؤْمِنُونَ بِهِ وَهُمْ عَلَىٰ صَلَاتِهِمْ يُحَافِظُونَ

الانعام ٩٢

وَمَنْ أَظْلَمُ مِمَّنِ ٱفْتَرَىٰ عَلَى ٱللَّهِ كَذِبًا أَوْ قَالَ أُوحِىَ إِلَىَّ وَلَمْ يُوحَ إِلَيْهِ شَىْءٌ وَمَن قَالَ سَأُنزِلُ مِثْلَ مَآ أَنزَلَ ٱللَّهُ وَلَوْ تَرَىٰٓ إِذِ ٱلظَّٰلِمُونَ فِى غَمَرَٰتِ ٱلْمَوْتِ وَٱلْمَلَٰئِكَةُ بَاسِطُوٓا۟ أَيْدِيهِمْ أَخْرِجُوٓا۟ أَنفُسَكُمُ

علامات الساعة (القيامة)

كذبة أخرى نشأنا معها وهي علامات الساعة. هناك قصص كثيرة متداولة بين المسلمين تُنِم عن الجهل، إلا أن أصحاب العمائم لم يمحصوها، بل يساهمون في نشرها لجهلهم بما جاء في كتاب الله. ومنهم من يعرف الحق ويخاف قوله أو أن يخسر وظيفته، لأنه هذا ما آل إليه ديننا، أصبح مجرد وظيفة.

وَإِنَّ مِنْهُمْ لَفَرِيقًا يَلْوُنَ أَلْسِنَتَهُم بِالْكِتَبِ لِتَحْسَبُوهُ مِنَ الْكِتَبِ وَمَا هُوَ مِنَ الْكِتَبِ وَيَقُولُونَ هُوَ مِنْ

وَأَيُّوبَ إِذْ نَادَىٰ رَبَّهُ أَنِّى مَسَّنِىَ ٱلضُّرُّ وَأَنتَ أَرْحَمُ ٱلرَّٰحِمِينَ ۞

وَذَا ٱلنُّونِ إِذ ذَّهَبَ مُغَٰضِبًا فَظَنَّ أَن لَّن نَّقْدِرَ عَلَيْهِ فَنَادَىٰ فِى ٱلظُّلُمَٰتِ أَن لَّآ إِلَٰهَ إِلَّآ أَنتَ سُبْحَٰنَكَ إِنِّى كُنتُ مِنَ ٱلظَّٰلِمِينَ

ممن يطلب الأنبياء والرسل العون والدعاء؟

إذا كان الرسل والأنبياء يرجون العون من الله، فلماذا ترجوه أنت من غيره؟

إنها لعنة الحديث! لقد أضل الحديث كثيرا من الخلق عن سبيل الله ودعاهم لتجاهل القرآن وأعادونا إلى عصور الظلام. ألسنا نعبد الله؟ أنا متأكد أنه يمكنك في عديد من الدول أن تسب الله ولا أحد سيكترث لك، ولكن إذا سببت زعيما روحيا من هنا أو من هناك، فسينزل عليك غضب الحد وتقتل. هذا من فعل أصحاب العمائم. يا له من بؤس وسخرية! عندما رسم الغرب سيدنا محمد عليه الصلاة والسلام، ثرنا وهجنا لنصرة رسول الله، ولكن لو قرأنا البخاري ومسلم، فسنجد أنهم رسموا ما في هذا الكتاب. نحن من أسأنا إلى رسول الله باحتواء كتب كهذه، بل بجعلها المصدر الرئيسي لعلومنا وحياتنا.

هُنَالِكَ دَعَا زَكَرِيَّا رَبَّهُ ۖ قَالَ رَبِّ هَبْ لِى مِن لَّدُنْكَ ذُرِّيَّةً طَيِّبَةً ۖ إِنَّكَ سَمِيعُ ٱلدُّعَآءِ

٣٨ آل عمران

وَنُوحًا إِذْ نَادَىٰ مِن قَبْلُ فَٱسْتَجَبْنَا لَهُ فَنَجَّيْنَٰهُ وَأَهْلَهُ مِنَ ٱلْكَرْبِ ٱلْعَظِيمِ

قُلْ إِنَّمَا أَنَا بَشَرٌ مِّثْلُكُمْ يُوحَىٰ إِلَيَّ أَنَّمَا إِلَٰهُكُمْ إِلَٰهٌ وَٰحِدٌ ۖ فَمَن كَانَ يَرْجُوا لِقَاءَ رَبِّهِ فَلْيَعْمَلْ عَمَلًا صَٰلِحًا وَلَا يُشْرِكْ بِعِبَادَةِ رَبِّهِ أَحَدًا

١١٠ الكهف

قُلْ إِنَّمَا أَنَا بَشَرٌ مِّثْلُكُمْ يُوحَىٰ إِلَيَّ أَنَّمَا إِلَٰهُكُمْ إِلَٰهٌ وَٰحِدٌ فَٱسْتَقِيمُوا إِلَيْهِ وَٱسْتَغْفِرُوهُ ۗ وَوَيْلٌ لِّلْمُشْرِكِينَ

٦ فصلت

وَمَا مُحَمَّدٌ إِلَّا رَسُولٌ قَدْ خَلَتْ مِن قَبْلِهِ ٱلرُّسُلُ ۚ أَفَإِن مَّاتَ أَوْ قُتِلَ ٱنقَلَبْتُمْ عَلَىٰ أَعْقَابِكُمْ ۚ وَمَن يَنقَلِبْ عَلَىٰ عَقِبَيْهِ فَلَن يَضُرَّ ٱللَّهَ شَيْئًا ۗ وَسَيَجْزِى ٱللَّهُ ٱلشَّاكِرِينَ

١٤٤ آل عمران

لَهُ دَعْوَةُ ٱلْحَقِّ ۖ وَٱلَّذِينَ يَدْعُونَ مِن دُونِهِ لَا يَسْتَجِيبُونَ لَهُم بِشَىْءٍ إِلَّا كَبَٰسِطِ كَفَّيْهِ إِلَى ٱلْمَاءِ لِيَبْلُغَ فَاهُ وَمَا هُوَ بِبَٰلِغِهِ ۚ وَمَا دُعَاءُ ٱلْكَٰفِرِينَ إِلَّا فِى ضَلَٰلٍ

١٤ الرعد

وَقَالَ رَبُّكُمُ ٱدْعُونِيَ أَسْتَجِبْ لَكُمْ إِنَّ ٱلَّذِينَ يَسْتَكْبِرُونَ عَنْ عِبَادَتِى سَيَدْخُلُونَ جَهَنَّمَ دَاخِرِينَ

٦٠ غافر

وَإِذَا سَأَلَكَ عِبَادِى عَنِّى فَإِنِّى قَرِيبٌ أُجِيبُ دَعْوَةَ ٱلدَّاعِ إِذَا دَعَانِ فَلْيَسْتَجِيبُواْ لِى وَلْيُؤْمِنُواْ بِى لَعَلَّهُمْ يَرْشُدُونَ

١٨٦ البقرة

مع كل ما ورد في القرآن من أدلة على قرب الله عز وجل منا، ولكن للأسف لسنا بمؤمنين ولا زلنا نطلب أشياء ومباركة ممن يرقدون تحت التراب أو ممن لا يضرون ولا ينفعون. عندما نؤمن بوحدانية الله، يصبح الله هو الملجأ الوحيد لنا. وأنا هنا لا أستثني أحدا (حتى ضريح رسول الله)

لَهُمْ أَوْ لَا تَسْتَغْفِرْ لَهُمْ إِن تَسْتَغْفِرْ لَهُمْ سَبْعِينَ مَرَّةً فَلَن يَغْفِرَ ٱللَّهُ لَهُمْ ذَلِكَ بِأَنَّهُمْ كَفَرُواْ بِٱللَّهِ وَرَسُولِهِ وَٱللَّهُ لَا يَهْدِى ٱلْقَوْمَ ٱلْفَاسِقِينَ

٨٠التوبة

يَدْعُواْ مِن دُونِ ٱللَّهِ مَا لَا يَضُرُّهُ وَمَا لَا يَنفَعُهُۥ ذَٰلِكَ هُوَ ٱلضَّلَٰلُ ٱلْبَعِيدُ

١٢ الحج

يَدْعُواْ لَمَن ضَرُّهُۥ أَقْرَبُ مِن نَّفْعِهِۦ لَبِئْسَ ٱلْمَوْلَىٰ وَلَبِئْسَ ٱلْعَشِيرُ

١٣ الحج

يَٰٓأَيُّهَا ٱلنَّاسُ ضُرِبَ مَثَلٌ فَٱسْتَمِعُواْ لَهُۥ إِنَّ ٱلَّذِينَ تَدْعُونَ مِن دُونِ ٱللَّهِ لَن يَخْلُقُواْ ذُبَابًا وَلَوِ ٱجْتَمَعُواْ لَهُۥ وَإِن يَسْلُبْهُمُ ٱلذُّبَابُ شَيْئًا لَّا يَسْتَنقِذُوهُ مِنْهُ ضَعُفَ ٱلطَّالِبُ وَٱلْمَطْلُوبُ

٧٣ الحج

وَمِنَ ٱلنَّاسِ مَن يَتَّخِذُ مِن دُونِ ٱللَّهِ أَندَادًا يُحِبُّونَهُمْ كَحُبِّ ٱللَّهِ وَٱلَّذِينَ ءَامَنُواْ أَشَدُّ حُبًّا لِّلَّهِ وَلَوْ يَرَى ٱلَّذِينَ ظَلَمُواْ إِذْ يَرَوْنَ ٱلْعَذَابَ أَنَّ ٱلْقُوَّةَ لِلَّهِ جَمِيعًا وَأَنَّ ٱللَّهَ شَدِيدُ ٱلْعَذَابِ

١٦٥ البقرة

٣ الزمر

أَمِ ٱتَّخَذُوا۟ مِن دُونِ ٱللَّهِ شُفَعَآءَ ۚ قُلْ أَوَلَوْ كَانُوا۟ لَا يَمْلِكُونَ شَيْـًٔا وَلَا يَعْقِلُونَ
٤٣ الزمر
قُل لِّلَّهِ ٱلشَّفَـٰعَةُ جَمِيعًا ۖ لَّهُۥ مُلْكُ ٱلسَّمَـٰوَٰتِ وَٱلْأَرْضِ ثُمَّ إِلَيْهِ تُرْجَعُونَ
٤٤ الزمر

إنه لأمر مدهش، أن تلجأ للخلق بدلا من الخالق، وعندما تسألهم، يجيبونك هذا ما وجدنا آباءنا عليه. إن من أصعب الأشياء في الحياة على الإطلاق هو تغيير شخص ما أو أن يغير هذا الشخص ما في عقله. حين يولد الإنسان، يعطى الاسم والدين والقومية والجنسية لسنوات، حتى يكبر ويصبح من أشد المدافعين عن فكر ليس فكره، واعتقاد ليس اعتقاده.

وَلَا يَمْلِكُ ٱلَّذِينَ يَدْعُونَ مِن دُونِهِ ٱلشَّفَـٰعَةَ إِلَّا مَن شَهِدَ بِٱلْحَقِّ وَهُمْ يَعْلَمُونَ
٨٦ الزخرف
وَلَئِن سَأَلْتَهُم مَّنْ خَلَقَهُمْ لَيَقُولُنَّ ٱللَّهُ ۖ فَأَنَّىٰ يُؤْفَكُونَ
٨٧ الزخرف

وماذا عن التضرع والدعاء لغير الله؟

وَمَن يَدْعُ مَعَ ٱللَّهِ إِلَٰهًا ءَاخَرَ لَا بُرْهَٰنَ لَهُۥ بِهِۦ فَإِنَّمَا حِسَابُهُۥ عِندَ رَبِّهِۦٓ إِنَّهُۥ لَا يُفْلِحُ ٱلْكَٰفِرُونَ ۝

سورة المؤمنون

إنه لأمر مدهش أننا نعيش في القرن الحادي والعشرين، ومع ذلك ترى هنالك أشخاصا يتضرعون بالقبور ويطلبون الدعاء من الموتى بدلا من طلبه من الله. إن مجرد التفكير بأن شخصا ما أو شيئا ما يمكن أن يمنحهم مبتغاهم، هو في حد ذاته اشراك بالله. تَنزِيلُ ٱلْكِتَٰبِ مِنَ ٱللَّهِ ٱلْعَزِيزِ ٱلْحَكِيمِ ١ إِنَّآ أَنزَلْنَآ إِلَيْكَ ٱلْكِتَٰبَ بِٱلْحَقِّ فَٱعْبُدِ ٱللَّهَ مُخْلِصًا لَّهُ ٱلدِّينَ ٢ أَلَا لِلَّهِ ٱلدِّينُ ٱلْخَالِصُ ۚ وَٱلَّذِينَ ٱتَّخَذُوا۟ مِن دُونِهِ أَوْلِيَآءَ مَا نَعْبُدُهُمْ إِلَّا لِيُقَرِّبُونَآ إِلَى ٱللَّهِ زُلْفَىٰٓ إِنَّ ٱللَّهَ يَحْكُمُ بَيْنَهُمْ فِى مَا هُمْ فِيهِ يَخْتَلِفُونَ ۗ إِنَّ ٱللَّهَ لَا يَهْدِى مَنْ هُوَ كَٰذِبٌ كَفَّارٌ

تَنزِيلُ ٱلْكِتَٰبِ لَا رَيْبَ فِيهِ مِن رَّبِّ ٱلْعَٰلَمِينَ

٢ السجدة

يمكنني الاستمرار في تقديم أمثلة من آيات الكتاب التي تظهر عظمة كلام الله، ولكن ما يدهشني، هو منذ متى أصبحنا نأخذ بأقاويل البشر ونفضلها على القرآن؟ لماذا نأخذ بالحديث ونستثني القرآن؟

لكي تأخذ آية وتفسرها كيفما تشاء لتقتل وتكفر هذا ليس بالإسلام ولا ايمان بالرسالة المحمدية. لقد صاحب الرسول العديد من الخلق من النصارى واليهود والمنافقين والكفار والرسول لم يهدر دم أحد حيث دأب على تأدية الرسالة. فاما المبتدعون على رسالة أهدى من رسالة محمد أو هم أصحاب ضلالة.

الٓر ۚ تِلْكَ ءَايَٰتُ ٱلْكِتَٰبِ وَقُرْءَانٍ مُّبِينٍ

١ الحجر

ٱلْحَمْدُ لِلَّهِ ٱلَّذِىٓ أَنزَلَ عَلَىٰ عَبْدِهِ ٱلْكِتَٰبَ وَلَمْ يَجْعَل لَّهُۥ عِوَجَاۜ

١ الكهف

مَآ أَنزَلْنَا عَلَيْكَ ٱلْقُرْءَانَ لِتَشْقَىٰ

٢ طه

تَبَارَكَ ٱلَّذِى نَزَّلَ ٱلْفُرْقَانَ عَلَىٰ عَبْدِهِۦ لِيَكُونَ لِلْعَٰلَمِينَ نَذِيرًا

١ الفرقان

تِلْكَ ءَايَٰتُ ٱلْكِتَٰبِ ٱلْمُبِينِ

٢ الشورى

طسٓ ۚ تِلْكَ ءَايَٰتُ ٱلْقُرْءَانِ وَكِتَابٍ مُّبِينٍ

١ النمل

كِتَـٰبٌ أُنزِلَ إِلَيْكَ فَلَا يَكُن فِى صَدْرِكَ حَرَجٌ مِّنْهُ لِتُنذِرَ بِهِۦ وَذِكْرَىٰ لِلْمُؤْمِنِينَ

٢ الانعام

الٓر ۚ كِتَـٰبٌ أُحْكِمَتْ ءَايَـٰتُهُۥ ثُمَّ فُصِّلَتْ مِن لَّدُنْ حَكِيمٍ خَبِيرٍ

الانفال 1

الٓر ۚ تِلْكَ ءَايَـٰتُ ٱلْكِتَـٰبِ ٱلْمُبِينِ

١ يوسف

إِنَّآ أَنزَلْنَـٰهُ قُرْءَٰنًا عَرَبِيًّا لَّعَلَّكُمْ تَعْقِلُونَ

٢ يوسف

الٓمٓر ۚ تِلْكَ ءَايَـٰتُ ٱلْكِتَـٰبِ ۗ وَٱلَّذِىٓ أُنزِلَ إِلَيْكَ مِن رَّبِّكَ ٱلْحَقُّ وَلَـٰكِنَّ أَكْثَرَ ٱلنَّاسِ لَا يُؤْمِنُونَ

١ الرعد

الٓر ۚ كِتَـٰبٌ أَنزَلْنَـٰهُ إِلَيْكَ لِتُخْرِجَ ٱلنَّاسَ مِنَ ٱلظُّلُمَـٰتِ إِلَى ٱلنُّورِ بِإِذْنِ رَبِّهِمْ إِلَىٰ صِرَٰطِ ٱلْعَزِيزِ ٱلْحَمِيدِ

١ ابراهيم

كما يعتمد الكثير من التاريخ لإسلامي المبكر المتاح اليوم أيضًا على الحديث، على الرغم من أنه قد تم الطعن فيه بسب بعد موجود أساس في المادة المصدرية الأولية والتناقضات الداخلية للمواد الثانوية المتاحة (بحاجة لمصدر).

أَفَلَا يَتَدَبَّرُونَ ٱلْقُرْءَانَ ۚ وَلَوْ كَانَ مِنْ عِندِ غَيْرِ ٱللَّهِ لَوَجَدُوا۟ فِيهِ ٱخْتِلَـٰفًا كَثِيرًا
النساء ٨٢

أَفَلَا يَتَدَبَّرُونَ ٱلْقُرْءَانَ أَمْ عَلَىٰ قُلُوبٍ أَقْفَالُهَآ
محمد ٢٤

يكاد يوجد في مقدمة كل سورة تذكير من الله بعظمة هذا الكتاب (القرآن). ومع ذلك، فقد ارتأى المسلمون ألا يقرؤوه! ولا يريدون تكرار قراءته. فحتى أصحاب العمائم، لا يقرؤون القرآن الكريم ويستشهدون بالأحاديث بدلا عن القرآن. لذا، فلا بد لنا أن ننفض غبار الجهل عن أدمغتنا.

ذَٰلِكَ ٱلْكِتَـٰبُ لَا رَيْبَ ۛ فِيهِ ۛ هُدًى لِّلْمُتَّقِينَ

البقرة

Born	21 July 810 C.E.
	13th Shawwal 194 A.H.
	Bukhara, Abbasid Caliphate
Died	1 September 870 (aged 60) C.E.
	1 Shawwal 256 A.H.
	Khartank, Samarkand, Abbasid Caliphate
Resting place	Khartank (Samarkand, Uzbekistan)
Religion	Islam
Era	Islamic Golden Age (Abbasid era)

كان للحديث تأثير عميق ومثير للجدل على التفسير . يُنسب التفسير الأول للقرآن، المعروف باسم تفسير ابن عباس، أحيانًا إلى الصحابي ابن عباس. لقد تم استخدام الحديث في تكوين أساس الشريعة (نظام القانون الديني الذي يشكل جزءًا من التقاليد الإسلامية)، والفقه (الفقه الإسلامي). والحديث هو أصل سبب عدم وجود نظام فقهي واحد، بل مجموعة من الأنظمة الموازية في الإسلام.

يتبعون نفس الدين. لقد جنوا فغيروا رسالة الحب إلى غرام وانتقام وجهل وكراهية.
انقسم المسلمون حول العالم إلى أحزاب وشيع وكل فرح بما لديه، أو لم يكن الأجدى أن يلتفوا حول كتاب الله كدستور للمسلمين بدل الالتفاف حول سنة مصطنعة؟

إن الجزء الواضح هو أن كل الأحاديث انتشرت في زمن العباسيين الذين أمعنوا في قتل المسلمين وخصوصا قتل الفاطميين إلى حد الإبادة. ولكن السؤال المطروح هو: لِمَ أغفل المسلمون كتاب الله واعتنقوا الأحاديث؟ مع العلم أن البخاري جمع الأحاديث في ذلك الوقت، والآن أصبح أهم من رسول الله لدى المسلمين؛ حيث أن أحاديثه تخالف القرآن ولا أحد يجرؤ عل دحضها؟ أصبح الحديث في أمتنا من أخطر الأمور على الدين الإسلامي.

Title   Imam al-Bukhari

Amir al-Mu'minin fi al-Hadith

Personal

إِنَّ ٱلَّذِينَ ءَامَنُوا۟ وَٱلَّذِينَ هَادُوا۟ وَٱلنَّصَٰرَىٰ وَٱلصَّٰبِـِٔينَ مَنْ ءَامَنَ بِٱللَّهِ وَٱلْيَوْمِ ٱلْءَاخِرِ وَعَمِلَ صَٰلِحًا فَلَهُمْ أَجْرُهُمْ عِندَ رَبِّهِمْ وَلَا خَوْفٌ عَلَيْهِمْ وَلَا هُمْ يَحْزَنُونَ
٦٢ البقرة

إِنَّ ٱلَّذِينَ ءَامَنُوا۟ وَٱلَّذِينَ هَادُوا۟ وَٱلصَّٰبِـُٔونَ وَٱلنَّصَٰرَىٰ مَنْ ءَامَنَ بِٱللَّهِ وَٱلْيَوْمِ ٱلْءَاخِرِ وَعَمِلَ صَٰلِحًا فَلَا خَوْفٌ عَلَيْهِمْ وَلَا هُمْ يَحْزَنُونَ
٦٩ المائدة

إِنَّ ٱلَّذِينَ ءَامَنُوا۟ وَٱلَّذِينَ هَادُوا۟ وَٱلصَّٰبِـِٔينَ وَٱلنَّصَٰرَىٰ وَٱلْمَجُوسَ وَٱلَّذِينَ أَشْرَكُوٓا۟ إِنَّ ٱللَّهَ يَفْصِلُ بَيْنَهُمْ يَوْمَ ٱلْقِيَٰمَةِ إِنَّ ٱللَّهَ عَلَىٰ كُلِّ شَىْءٍ شَهِيدٌ
١٧ الحج

من الواضح أن هذا الأمر يعود لله وحده، هو القاضي بين الناس. الرسالة اكتملت والخيار واضح للجميع، لا إكراه في الدين، تبين الرشد من الغي. لسوء الحظ، في يومنا هذا، الكل نصبوا أنفسهم ألهه، يكفر هذا ويكفر ذاك ويهدر دم هذا أو دم ذاك، لدرجة أن أصحاب العمائم منشقون على أنفسهم رغم أنهم

ٱللَّهَ يَفْصِلُ بَيْنَهُمْ يَوْمَ ٱلْقِيَامَةِ ۗ إِنَّ ٱللَّهَ عَلَىٰ كُلِّ شَىْءٍ شَهِيدٌ

١٧ الحج

وَأَنزَلْنَا إِلَيْكَ ٱلْكِتَابَ بِٱلْحَقِّ مُصَدِّقًا لِّمَا بَيْنَ يَدَيْهِ مِنَ ٱلْكِتَابِ وَمُهَيْمِنًا عَلَيْهِ ۖ فَٱحْكُم بَيْنَهُم بِمَآ أَنزَلَ ٱللَّهُ ۖ وَلَا تَتَّبِعْ أَهْوَآءَهُمْ عَمَّا جَآءَكَ مِنَ ٱلْحَقِّ ۚ لِكُلٍّ جَعَلْنَا مِنكُمْ شِرْعَةً وَمِنْهَاجًا ۚ وَلَوْ شَآءَ ٱللَّهُ لَجَعَلَكُمْ أُمَّةً وَاحِدَةً وَلَٰكِن لِّيَبْلُوَكُمْ فِي مَآ ءَاتَاكُمْ ۖ فَٱسْتَبِقُوا ٱلْخَيْرَاتِ ۚ إِلَى ٱللَّهِ مَرْجِعُكُمْ جَمِيعًا فَيُنَبِّئُكُم بِمَا كُنتُمْ فِيهِ تَخْتَلِفُونَ

٤٨ المائدة

يَٰٓأَيُّهَا ٱلَّذِينَ ءَامَنُوا عَلَيْكُمْ أَنفُسَكُمْ ۖ لَا يَضُرُّكُم مَّن ضَلَّ إِذَا ٱهْتَدَيْتُمْ ۚ إِلَى ٱللَّهِ مَرْجِعُكُمْ جَمِيعًا فَيُنَبِّئُكُم بِمَا كُنتُمْ تَعْمَلُونَ

١٠٥ المائدة

إِلَيْهِ مَرْجِعُكُمْ جَمِيعًا ۖ وَعْدَ ٱللَّهِ حَقًّا ۚ إِنَّهُ يَبْدَؤُا ٱلْخَلْقَ ثُمَّ يُعِيدُهُ لِيَجْزِيَ ٱلَّذِينَ ءَامَنُوا وَعَمِلُوا ٱلصَّالِحَاتِ بِٱلْقِسْطِ ۚ وَٱلَّذِينَ كَفَرُوا لَهُمْ شَرَابٌ مِّنْ حَمِيمٍ وَعَذَابٌ أَلِيمٌ بِمَا كَانُوا يَكْفُرُونَ

٤ يونس

من سيدخل الجنة ومن سيدخل النار؟

© Can Stock Photo - csp29794027

قُلِ ٱللَّهُمَّ فَاطِرَ ٱلسَّمَٰوَٰتِ وَٱلْأَرْضِ عَٰلِمَ ٱلْغَيْبِ ق وَٱلشَّهَٰدَةِ أَنتَ تَحْكُمُ بَيْنَ عِبَادِكَ فِى مَا كَانُواْ فِيهِ يَخْتَلِفُونَ
٤٦ الزمر

إِنَّ ٱلَّذِينَ ءَامَنُواْ وَٱلَّذِينَ هَادُواْ وَٱلصَّٰبِئِينَ وَٱلنَّصَٰرَىٰ وَٱلْمَجُوسَ وَٱلَّذِينَ أَشْرَكُوٓاْ إِنَّ

إن الخمر لا يعتبر من المحرمات، فلا تستطيع أن تقارنه بأكل الخنزير أو بنكاح الرجل لأمه!

وَعَلَى الَّذِينَ هَادُوا حَرَّمْنَا مَا قَصَصْنَا عَلَيْكَ مِنْ قَبْلُ وَمَا ظَلَمْنَاهُمْ وَلَكِنْ كَانُوا أَنْفُسَهُمْ يَظْلِمُونَ

النحل 118

وَلَا تَقْتُلُوا النَّفْسَ الَّتِي حَرَّمَ اللَّهُ إِلَّا بِالْحَقِّ وَمَنْ قُتِلَ مَظْلُومًا فَقَدْ جَعَلْنَا لِوَلِيِّهِ سُلْطَانًا فَلَا يُسْرِفْ فِي الْقَتْلِ إِنَّهُ كَانَ مَنْصُورًا

الاسراء 33

الزَّانِي لَا يَنْكِحُ إِلَّا زَانِيَةً أَوْ مُشْرِكَةً وَالزَّانِيَةُ لَا يَنْكِحُهَا إِلَّا زَانٍ أَوْ مُشْرِكٌ وَحُرِّمَ ذَلِكَ عَلَى الْمُؤْمِنِينَ

النور 3

وَالَّذِينَ لَا يَدْعُونَ مَعَ اللَّهِ إِلَهًا آخَرَ وَلَا يَقْتُلُونَ النَّفْسَ الَّتِي حَرَّمَ اللَّهُ إِلَّا بِالْحَقِّ وَلَا يَزْنُونَ وَمَنْ يَفْعَلْ ذَلِكَ يَلْقَ أَثَامًا

الفرقان 68

يَا أَيُّهَا النَّبِيُّ لِمَ تُحَرِّمُ مَا أَحَلَّ اللَّهُ لَكَ تَبْتَغِي مَرْضَاتَ أَزْوَاجِكَ وَاللَّهُ غَفُورٌ رَحِيمٌ

قُلْ أَرَأَيْتُمْ مَا أَنْزَلَ اللَّهُ لَكُمْ مِنْ رِزْقٍ فَجَعَلْتُمْ مِنْهُ
حَرَامًا وَحَلَالًا قُلْ آللَّهُ أَذِنَ لَكُمْ ۖ أَمْ عَلَى اللَّهِ تَفْتَرُونَ

يونس 59

وَقَالَ الَّذِينَ أَشْرَكُوا لَوْ شَاءَ اللَّهُ مَا عَبَدْنَا مِنْ دُونِهِ
مِنْ شَيْءٍ نَحْنُ وَلَا آبَاؤُنَا وَلَا حَرَّمْنَا مِنْ دُونِهِ
مِنْ شَيْءٍ ۚ كَذَٰلِكَ فَعَلَ الَّذِينَ مِنْ قَبْلِهِمْ ۚ فَهَلْ عَلَى
الرُّسُلِ إِلَّا الْبَلَاغُ الْمُبِينُ

النحل 115

إِنَّمَا حَرَّمَ عَلَيْكُمُ الْمَيْتَةَ وَالدَّمَ وَلَحْمَ الْخِنْزِيرِ وَمَا
أُهِلَّ لِغَيْرِ اللَّهِ بِهِ ۖ فَمَنِ اضْطُرَّ غَيْرَ بَاغٍ وَلَا عَادٍ فَإِنَّ
اللَّهَ غَفُورٌ رَحِيمٌ

النحل 115

وَلَا تَقُولُوا لِمَا تَصِفُ أَلْسِنَتُكُمُ الْكَذِبَ هَٰذَا حَلَالٌ
وَهَٰذَا حَرَامٌ لِتَفْتَرُوا عَلَى اللَّهِ الْكَذِبَ ۚ إِنَّ الَّذِينَ
يَفْتَرُونَ عَلَى اللَّهِ الْكَذِبَ لَا يُفْلِحُونَ

النحل 116

قُلْ إِنَّمَا حَرَّمَ رَبِّيَ الْفَوَاحِشَ مَا ظَهَرَ مِنْهَا وَمَا بَطَنَ
وَالْإِثْمَ وَالْبَغْيَ بِغَيْرِ الْحَقِّ وَأَنْ تُشْرِكُوا بِاللَّهِ مَا لَمْ يُنَزِّلْ
بِهِ سُلْطَانًا وَأَنْ تَقُولُوا عَلَى اللَّهِ مَا لَا تَعْلَمُونَ

الأعراف 33

الَّذِينَ يَتَّبِعُونَ الرَّسُولَ النَّبِيَّ الْأُمِّيَّ الَّذِي يَجِدُونَهُ
مَكْتُوبًا عِنْدَهُمْ فِي التَّوْرَاةِ وَالْإِنْجِيلِ يَأْمُرُهُمْ
بِالْمَعْرُوفِ وَيَنْهَاهُمْ عَنِ الْمُنْكَرِ وَيُحِلُّ لَهُمُ الطَّيِّبَاتِ
وَيُحَرِّمُ عَلَيْهِمُ الْخَبَائِثَ وَيَضَعُ عَنْهُمْ إِصْرَهُمْ
وَالْأَغْلَالَ الَّتِي كَانَتْ عَلَيْهِمْ ۚ فَالَّذِينَ آمَنُوا بِهِ
وَعَزَّرُوهُ وَنَصَرُوهُ وَاتَّبَعُوا النُّورَ الَّذِي أُنْزِلَ مَعَهُ
أُولَئِكَ هُمُ الْمُفْلِحُونَ

الأعراف 157

إِنَّمَا النَّسِيءُ زِيَادَةٌ فِي الْكُفْرِ ۖ يُضَلُّ بِهِ الَّذِينَ
كَفَرُوا يُحِلُّونَهُ عَامًا وَيُحَرِّمُونَهُ عَامًا لِيُوَاطِئُوا
عِدَّةَ مَا حَرَّمَ اللَّهُ فَيُحِلُّوا مَا حَرَّمَ اللَّهُ ۚ زُيِّنَ لَهُمْ سُوءُ
أَعْمَالِهِمْ ۗ وَاللَّهُ لَا يَهْدِي الْقَوْمَ الْكَافِرِينَ

التوبة 37

الانعام 148

قُلْ هَلُمَّ شُهَدَاءَكُمُ الَّذِينَ يَشْهَدُونَ أَنَّ اللَّهَ حَرَّمَ هَٰذَا فَإِنْ شَهِدُوا فَلَا تَشْهَدْ مَعَهُمْ وَلَا تَتَّبِعْ أَهْوَاءَ الَّذِينَ كَذَّبُوا بِآيَاتِنَا وَالَّذِينَ لَا يُؤْمِنُونَ بِالْآخِرَةِ وَهُم بِرَبِّهِمْ يَعْدِلُونَ

الانعام 150

قُلْ تَعَالَوْا أَتْلُ مَا حَرَّمَ رَبُّكُمْ عَلَيْكُمْ أَلَّا تُشْرِكُوا بِهِ شَيْئًا وَبِالْوَالِدَيْنِ إِحْسَانًا وَلَا تَقْتُلُوا أَوْلَادَكُم مِّنْ إِمْلَاقٍ نَّحْنُ نَرْزُقُكُمْ وَإِيَّاهُمْ وَلَا تَقْرَبُوا الْفَوَاحِشَ مَا ظَهَرَ مِنْهَا وَمَا بَطَنَ وَلَا تَقْتُلُوا النَّفْسَ الَّتِي حَرَّمَ اللَّهُ إِلَّا بِالْحَقِّ ذَٰلِكُمْ وَصَّاكُم بِهِ لَعَلَّكُمْ تَعْقِلُونَ

الانعام 151

قُلْ مَنْ حَرَّمَ زِينَةَ اللَّهِ الَّتِي أَخْرَجَ لِعِبَادِهِ وَالطَّيِّبَاتِ مِنَ الرِّزْقِ قُلْ هِيَ لِلَّذِينَ آمَنُوا فِي الْحَيَاةِ الدُّنْيَا خَالِصَةً يَوْمَ الْقِيَامَةِ كَذَٰلِكَ نُفَصِّلُ الْآيَاتِ لِقَوْمٍ يَعْلَمُونَ

الأعراف 32

وَمِنَ الْإِبِلِ اثْنَيْنِ وَمِنَ الْبَقَرِ اثْنَيْنِ ۗ قُلْ آلذَّكَرَيْنِ حَرَّمَ أَمِ الْأُنْثَيَيْنِ أَمَّا اشْتَمَلَتْ عَلَيْهِ أَرْحَامُ الْأُنْثَيَيْنِ ۖ أَمْ كُنْتُمْ شُهَدَاءَ إِذْ وَصَّاكُمُ اللَّهُ بِهَٰذَا ۚ فَمَنْ أَظْلَمُ مِمَّنِ افْتَرَىٰ عَلَى اللَّهِ كَذِبًا لِيُضِلَّ النَّاسَ بِغَيْرِ عِلْمٍ ۗ إِنَّ اللَّهَ لَا يَهْدِي الْقَوْمَ الظَّالِمِينَ

الانعام 144

قُلْ لَا أَجِدُ فِي مَا أُوحِيَ إِلَيَّ مُحَرَّمًا عَلَىٰ طَاعِمٍ يَطْعَمُهُ إِلَّا أَنْ يَكُونَ مَيْتَةً أَوْ دَمًا مَسْفُوحًا أَوْ لَحْمَ خِنْزِيرٍ فَإِنَّهُ رِجْسٌ أَوْ فِسْقًا أُهِلَّ لِغَيْرِ اللَّهِ بِهِ ۚ فَمَنِ اضْطُرَّ غَيْرَ بَاغٍ وَلَا عَادٍ فَإِنَّ رَبَّكَ غَفُورٌ رَحِيمٌ

الانعام 145

وَعَلَى الَّذِينَ هَادُوا حَرَّمْنَا كُلَّ ذِي ظُفُرٍ ۖ وَمِنَ الْبَقَرِ وَالْغَنَمِ حَرَّمْنَا عَلَيْهِمْ شُحُومَهُمَا إِلَّا مَا حَمَلَتْ ظُهُورُهُمَا أَوِ الْحَوَايَا أَوْ مَا اخْتَلَطَ بِعَظْمٍ ۚ ذَٰلِكَ جَزَيْنَاهُمْ بِبَغْيِهِمْ ۖ وَإِنَّا لَصَادِقُونَ

الانعام 146

سَيَقُولُ الَّذِينَ أَشْرَكُوا لَوْ شَاءَ اللَّهُ مَا أَشْرَكْنَا وَلَا آبَاؤُنَا وَلَا حَرَّمْنَا مِنْ شَيْءٍ ۚ كَذَٰلِكَ كَذَّبَ الَّذِينَ مِنْ قَبْلِهِمْ حَتَّىٰ ذَاقُوا بَأْسَنَا ۗ قُلْ هَلْ عِنْدَكُمْ مِنْ عِلْمٍ فَتُخْرِجُوهُ لَنَا ۖ إِنْ تَتَّبِعُونَ إِلَّا الظَّنَّ وَإِنْ أَنْتُمْ إِلَّا تَخْرُصُونَ

وَقَالُوا هَٰذِهِ أَنْعَامٌ وَحَرْثٌ حِجْرٌ لَا يَطْعَمُهَا إِلَّا مَن نَشَاءُ بِزَعْمِهِمْ وَأَنْعَامٌ حُرِّمَتْ ظُهُورُهَا وَأَنْعَامٌ لَا يَذْكُرُونَ اسْمَ اللَّهِ عَلَيْهَا افْتِرَاءً عَلَيْهِ ۚ سَيَجْزِيهِم بِمَا كَانُوا يَفْتَرُونَ

الانعام 138

وَقَالُوا مَا فِي بُطُونِ هَٰذِهِ الْأَنْعَامِ خَالِصَةٌ لِذُكُورِنَا وَمُحَرَّمٌ عَلَىٰ أَزْوَاجِنَا ۖ وَإِن يَكُن مَّيْتَةً فَهُمْ فِيهِ شُرَكَاءُ ۚ سَيَجْزِيهِمْ وَصْفَهُمْ ۚ إِنَّهُ حَكِيمٌ عَلِيمٌ

الانعام 139

قَدْ خَسِرَ الَّذِينَ قَتَلُوا أَوْلَادَهُمْ سَفَهًا بِغَيْرِ عِلْمٍ وَحَرَّمُوا مَا رَزَقَهُمُ اللَّهُ افْتِرَاءً عَلَى اللَّهِ ۚ قَدْ ضَلُّوا وَمَا كَانُوا مُهْتَدِينَ

الانعام 140

ثَمَانِيَةَ أَزْوَاجٍ ۖ مِنَ الضَّأْنِ اثْنَيْنِ وَمِنَ الْمَعْزِ اثْنَيْنِ ۗ قُلْ آلذَّكَرَيْنِ حَرَّمَ أَمِ الْأُنثَيَيْنِ أَمَّا اشْتَمَلَتْ عَلَيْهِ أَرْحَامُ الْأُنثَيَيْنِ ۖ نَبِّئُونِي بِعِلْمٍ إِن كُنتُمْ صَادِقِينَ

الانعام 143

223

المائدة 3

قَالَ فَإِنَّهَا مُحَرَّمَةٌ عَلَيْهِمْ ۚ أَرْبَعِينَ سَنَةً ۚ يَتِيهُونَ فِي الْأَرْضِ ۚ فَلَا تَأْسَ عَلَى الْقَوْمِ الْفَاسِقِينَ

المائدة26

يَا أَيُّهَا الَّذِينَ آمَنُوا لَا تُحَرِّمُوا طَيِّبَاتِ مَا أَحَلَّ اللَّهُ لَكُمْ وَلَا تَعْتَدُوا ۚ إِنَّ اللَّهَ لَا يُحِبُّ الْمُعْتَدِينَ

المائدة 87

أُحِلَّ لَكُمْ صَيْدُ الْبَحْرِ وَطَعَامُهُ مَتَاعًا لَكُمْ وَلِلسَّيَّارَةِ ۖ وَحُرِّمَ عَلَيْكُمْ صَيْدُ الْبَرِّ مَا دُمْتُمْ حُرُمًا ۗ وَاتَّقُوا اللَّهَ الَّذِي إِلَيْهِ تُحْشَرُونَ

المائدة 96

وَمَا لَكُمْ أَلَّا تَأْكُلُوا مِمَّا ذُكِرَ اسْمُ اللَّهِ عَلَيْهِ وَقَدْ فَصَّلَ لَكُمْ مَا حَرَّمَ عَلَيْكُمْ إِلَّا مَا اضْطُرِرْتُمْ إِلَيْهِ ۗ وَإِنَّ كَثِيرًا لَيُضِلُّونَ بِأَهْوَائِهِمْ بِغَيْرِ عِلْمٍ ۗ إِنَّ رَبَّكَ هُوَ أَعْلَمُ بِالْمُعْتَدِينَ

الانعام 119

الْأُخْتِ وَأُمَّهَاتُكُمُ اللَّاتِي أَرْضَعْنَكُمْ وَأَخَوَاتُكُم مِّنَ الرَّضَاعَةِ وَأُمَّهَاتُ نِسَائِكُمْ وَرَبَائِبُكُمُ اللَّاتِي فِي حُجُورِكُم مِّن نِّسَائِكُمُ اللَّاتِي دَخَلْتُم بِهِنَّ فَإِن لَّمْ تَكُونُوا دَخَلْتُم بِهِنَّ فَلَا جُنَاحَ عَلَيْكُمْ وَحَلَائِلُ أَبْنَائِكُمُ الَّذِينَ مِنْ أَصْلَابِكُمْ وَأَن تَجْمَعُوا بَيْنَ الْأُخْتَيْنِ إِلَّا مَا قَدْ سَلَفَ ۗ إِنَّ اللَّهَ كَانَ غَفُورًا رَّحِيمًا

النساء 23

فَبِظُلْمٍ مِّنَ الَّذِينَ هَادُوا حَرَّمْنَا عَلَيْهِمْ طَيِّبَاتٍ أُحِلَّتْ لَهُمْ وَبِصَدِّهِمْ عَن سَبِيلِ اللَّهِ كَثِيرًا

النساء 160

حُرِّمَتْ عَلَيْكُمُ الْمَيْتَةُ وَالدَّمُ وَلَحْمُ الْخِنْزِيرِ وَمَا أُهِلَّ لِغَيْرِ اللَّهِ بِهِ وَالْمُنْخَنِقَةُ وَالْمَوْقُوذَةُ وَالْمُتَرَدِّيَةُ وَالنَّطِيحَةُ وَمَا أَكَلَ السَّبُعُ إِلَّا مَا ذَكَّيْتُمْ وَمَا ذُبِحَ عَلَى النُّصُبِ وَأَن تَسْتَقْسِمُوا بِالْأَزْلَامِ ۚ ذَٰلِكُمْ فِسْقٌ ۗ الْيَوْمَ يَئِسَ الَّذِينَ كَفَرُوا مِن دِينِكُمْ فَلَا تَخْشَوْهُمْ وَاخْشَوْنِ ۚ الْيَوْمَ أَكْمَلْتُ لَكُمْ دِينَكُمْ وَأَتْمَمْتُ عَلَيْكُمْ نِعْمَتِي وَرَضِيتُ لَكُمُ الْإِسْلَامَ دِينًا ۚ فَمَنِ اضْطُرَّ فِي مَخْمَصَةٍ غَيْرَ مُتَجَانِفٍ لِّإِثْمٍ ۙ فَإِنَّ اللَّهَ غَفُورٌ رَّحِيمٌ

البقرة 173

الَّذِينَ يَأْكُلُونَ الرِّبَا لَا يَقُومُونَ إِلَّا كَمَا يَقُومُ الَّذِي يَتَخَبَّطُهُ الشَّيْطَانُ مِنَ الْمَسِّ ۚ ذَٰلِكَ بِأَنَّهُمْ قَالُوا إِنَّمَا الْبَيْعُ مِثْلُ الرِّبَا ۗ وَأَحَلَّ اللَّهُ الْبَيْعَ وَحَرَّمَ الرِّبَا ۚ فَمَنْ جَاءَهُ مَوْعِظَةٌ مِنْ رَبِّهِ فَانْتَهَىٰ فَلَهُ مَا سَلَفَ وَأَمْرُهُ إِلَى اللَّهِ ۖ وَمَنْ عَادَ فَأُولَٰئِكَ أَصْحَابُ النَّارِ ۖ هُمْ فِيهَا خَالِدُونَ

البقرة 275

وَمُصَدِّقًا لِمَا بَيْنَ يَدَيَّ مِنَ التَّوْرَاةِ وَلِأُحِلَّ لَكُمْ بَعْضَ الَّذِي حُرِّمَ عَلَيْكُمْ ۚ وَجِئْتُكُمْ بِآيَةٍ مِنْ رَبِّكُمْ فَاتَّقُوا اللَّهَ وَأَطِيعُونِ

آل عمران 50

كُلُّ الطَّعَامِ كَانَ حِلًّا لِبَنِي إِسْرَائِيلَ إِلَّا مَا حَرَّمَ إِسْرَائِيلُ عَلَىٰ نَفْسِهِ مِنْ قَبْلِ أَنْ تُنَزَّلَ التَّوْرَاةُ ۗ قُلْ فَأْتُوا بِالتَّوْرَاةِ فَاتْلُوهَا إِنْ كُنْتُمْ صَادِقِينَ

آل عمران 93

وَيَسْأَلُونَكَ مَاذَا يُنْفِقُونَ قُلِ الْعَفْوَ ۗ كَذَٰلِكَ يُبَيِّنُ اللَّهُ لَكُمُ الْآيَاتِ لَعَلَّكُمْ تَتَفَكَّرُونَ
البقرة ٢١٩

خلال مناقشة ما، لا تستطيع أن تجادل شخصا يقول قال الله بنقاش قال فلان ولا بعلو الصوت ولا بالتهديد والوعيد. لقد أرسل الله رسالة إلى كل البشر. فعلى كل مؤمن أن يقرأها وسيفهمها، لأن الله لن يرسل رسالة فقط لأصحاب العمائم، ومن الأولى تعليم الناس اللغة العربية بدلا من تعليمهم الأحاديث المضللة.

القرآن حدد ما محرم من خلال الآيات التالية
ثُمَّ أَنْتُمْ هَٰؤُلَاءِ تَقْتُلُونَ أَنْفُسَكُمْ وَتُخْرِجُونَ فَرِيقًا مِنْكُمْ مِنْ دِيَارِهِمْ تَظَاهَرُونَ عَلَيْهِمْ بِالْإِثْمِ وَالْعُدْوَانِ وَإِنْ يَأْتُوكُمْ أُسَارَىٰ تُفَادُوهُمْ وَهُوَ مُحَرَّمٌ عَلَيْكُمْ إِخْرَاجُهُمْ ۚ أَفَتُؤْمِنُونَ بِبَعْضِ الْكِتَابِ وَتَكْفُرُونَ بِبَعْضٍ ۚ فَمَا جَزَاءُ مَنْ يَفْعَلُ ذَٰلِكَ مِنْكُمْ إِلَّا خِزْيٌ فِي الْحَيَاةِ الدُّنْيَا ۖ وَيَوْمَ الْقِيَامَةِ يُرَدُّونَ إِلَىٰ أَشَدِّ الْعَذَابِ ۗ وَمَا اللَّهُ بِغَافِلٍ عَمَّا تَعْمَلُونَ
البقرة 85
إِنَّمَا حَرَّمَ عَلَيْكُمُ الْمَيْتَةَ وَالدَّمَ وَلَحْمَ الْخِنْزِيرِ وَمَا أُهِلَّ بِهِ لِغَيْرِ اللَّهِ ۖ فَمَنِ اضْطُرَّ غَيْرَ بَاغٍ وَلَا عَادٍ فَلَا إِثْمَ عَلَيْهِ ۚ إِنَّ اللَّهَ غَفُورٌ رَحِيمٌ

منهم من يقول بأن الله حرم الخمر على مراحل! تعالى الله أن يكون خائفا من البشر ليحرمه على مراحل. إن الله عندما وضع المحرمات وضعها بكل صراحة ووضوح وجزم وإن لم تؤمنوا فيستبدلكم بقوم آخرين. لم يحرم الله شيئا يمكن أن يكون فيه منفعة للبشرية. يدخل الكحول في أمور عديدة من حياتنا، من تطهير الجروح واستخدامها في العمليات الجراحية، حبذا لو يتبع أصحاب العمائم ما يعلموا وألا يدخلوا المستشفيات لأنها تعج بالكحول.

سلط الباحث الدكتور محمد شحرور الضوء على هذا الموضوع وشرح تفاصيله من القرآن، وانتقده بعض الدعاة أرجو من الجميع أن يستعمل ما قاله الاثنان ويحكم بينهم. شخصيا، وجدت أن الدكتور شحرور اعتمد في حجته على القرآن وقول الله، بينما اعتمد الآخر على ابن مسعود وعلى الأحاديث الضعيفة.

https://www.youtube.com/watch?v=EV
ENWrWQ3cE

إن استخدام الأحاديث التي تناقض قول الله وافتراء الكذب على الله بزعمهم هذا حلال وهذا حرام، يستعمل لتوجيه الشباب وغسل أدمغتهم، وذلك لتنفيذ أجندتهم الخاصة

النساء ٤٣ .

۞ يَسْـَٔلُونَكَ عَنِ ٱلْخَمْرِ وَٱلْمَيْسِرِ ۖ قُلْ فِيهِمَآ إِثْمٌ كَبِيرٌ وَمَنَٰفِعُ لِلنَّاسِ وَإِثْمُهُمَآ أَكْبَرُ مِن نَّفْعِهِمَا ۗ وَيَسْـَٔلُونَكَ مَاذَا يُنفِقُونَ قُلِ ٱلْعَفْوَ ۗ كَذَٰلِكَ يُبَيِّنُ ٱللَّهُ لَكُمُ ٱلْـَٔايَٰتِ لَعَلَّكُمْ تَتَفَكَّرُونَ
البقرة ٢١٩

يَٰٓأَيُّهَا ٱلَّذِينَ ءَامَنُوٓا۟ إِنَّمَا ٱلْخَمْرُ وَٱلْمَيْسِرُ وَٱلْأَنصَابُ وَٱلْأَزْلَٰمُ رِجْسٌ مِّنْ عَمَلِ ٱلشَّيْطَٰنِ فَٱجْتَنِبُوهُ لَعَلَّكُمْ تُفْلِحُونَ
المائدة ٩٠

إِنَّمَا يُرِيدُ ٱلشَّيْطَٰنُ أَن يُوقِعَ بَيْنَكُمُ ٱلْعَدَٰوَةَ وَٱلْبَغْضَآءَ فِى ٱلْخَمْرِ وَٱلْمَيْسِرِ وَيَصُدَّكُمْ عَن ذِكْرِ ٱللَّهِ وَعَنِ ٱلصَّلَوٰةِ ۖ فَهَلْ أَنتُم مُّنتَهُونَ
المائدة ٩١

وَإِنَّ لَكُمْ فِى ٱلْأَنْعَٰمِ لَعِبْرَةً ۖ نُّسْقِيكُم مِّمَّا فِى بُطُونِهِۦ مِنۢ بَيْنِ فَرْثٍ وَدَمٍ لَّبَنًا خَالِصًا سَآئِغًا لِّلشَّٰرِبِينَ
النحل ٦٦

إِنَّ فِى ذَٰلِكَ لَـَٔايَةً لِّقَوْمٍ يَعْقِلُونَ
النحل ٦٧

مجددا، لا نرى آية تحرم الخمر، بل هناك آية تدعو إلى تجنب الرجس الناتج عنه، ألا وهو السكر. ما أراه هو أنه تحديد للاستهلاك أكثر منه تحريما. حيث وضع الحد الأعلى وهو السكر. مثل موضوع النساء، حيث حدد الله ولم يحرم، ووعد المؤمنين النساء والخمر!

للإنسان، ولكنها ليست محرمة. لذلك، فإنه لا يحق لأي تحريم شيء، حتى لو كان رسول الله عليه الصلاة والسلام، إنه شيء موكول لله وهو الوحيد الذي يملك ذلك الحق. فإذا قرأت حديثا يقول سمعت فلان عن رسول الله قال إن هذه حرام أو هذه حلال، فاعلم أنه حديث مفبرك.

بل حتى في الأمور التي حرمها الله، فستجد عظمة الخالق في كونه سيغفر لك إذا حدث أن ارتكبتها مضطرا!

يَٰٓأَيُّهَا ٱلنَّبِىُّ لِمَ تُحَرِّمُ مَآ أَحَلَّ ٱللَّهُ لَكَ ۖ تَبۡتَغِى مَرۡضَاتَ أَزۡوَٰجِكَ ۚ وَٱللَّهُ غَفُورٌ رَّحِيمٌ .
التحريم ١

إِنَّمَا حَرَّمَ عَلَيۡكُمُ ٱلۡمَيۡتَةَ وَٱلدَّمَ وَلَحۡمَ ٱلۡخِنزِيرِ وَمَآ أُهِلَّ بِهِۦ لِغَيۡرِ ٱللَّهِ ۖ فَمَنِ ٱضۡطُرَّ غَيۡرَ بَاغٍ وَلَا عَادٍ فَلَآ إِثۡمَ عَلَيۡهِ ۚ إِنَّ ٱللَّهَ غَفُورٌ رَّحِيمٌ
البقرة ١٧٣

الخمر في القرآن
يَٰٓأَيُّهَا ٱلَّذِينَ ءَامَنُواْ لَا تَقۡرَبُواْ ٱلصَّلَوٰةَ وَأَنتُمۡ سُكَٰرَىٰ حَتَّىٰ تَعۡلَمُواْ مَا تَقُولُونَ وَلَا جُنُبًا إِلَّا عَابِرِى سَبِيلٍ حَتَّىٰ تَغۡتَسِلُواْ ۚ وَإِن كُنتُم مَّرۡضَىٰٓ أَوۡ عَلَىٰ سَفَرٍ أَوۡ جَآءَ أَحَدٌ مِّنكُم مِّنَ ٱلۡغَآئِطِ أَوۡ لَٰمَسۡتُمُ ٱلنِّسَآءَ فَلَمۡ تَجِدُواْ مَآءً فَتَيَمَّمُواْ صَعِيدًا طَيِّبًا فَٱمۡسَحُواْ بِوُجُوهِكُمۡ وَأَيۡدِيكُمۡ ۗ إِنَّ ٱللَّهَ كَانَ عَفُوًّا غَفُورًا

هل الخمر حرام؟؟

تم ذكر الخمر بشكل مباشر في ثلاثة مواضع في القرآن، وإن كنا نسلط الضوء على الموضوع، فليس من باب التشجيع على شرب الكحول، بل للفصل ما بين ما حرمه الله أو ما لم يحرمه. فالتحريم أمر خاص بالله وحده عز وجل. وهناك أمور ضارة

سيرينا الله مدى حكمته في أنفسنا وفي الآفاق وفي مخلوقات الله وفي كل شيء، حتى ندرك أن القرآن هو العلم والحق من ربنا. والله يريدنا أن نسعى ونسأل ونتعلم ونحاور ونناقش ونكتشف.

قُلْ سِيرُوا۟ فِى ٱلْأَرْضِ ثُمَّ ٱنظُرُوا۟ كَيْفَ كَانَ عَٰقِبَةُ ٱلْمُكَذِّبِينَ

الانعام
١١

سَنُرِيهِمْ ءَايَٰتِنَا فِى ٱلْءَافَاقِ وَفِىٓ أَنفُسِهِمْ حَتَّىٰ يَتَبَيَّنَ لَهُمْ أَنَّهُ ٱلْحَقُّ ۗ أَوَلَمْ يَكْفِ بِرَبِّكَ أَنَّهُ عَلَىٰ كُلِّ شَىْءٍ شَهِيدٌ

٥٣ فصلت

يَـٰٓأَيُّهَا ٱلَّذِينَ ءَامَنُوٓاْ إِذَا قُمْتُمْ إِلَى ٱلصَّلَوٰةِ فَٱغْسِلُواْ وُجُوهَكُمْ وَأَيْدِيَكُمْ إِلَى ٱلْمَرَافِقِ وَٱمْسَحُواْ بِرُءُوسِكُمْ وَأَرْجُلَكُمْ إِلَى ٱلْكَعْبَيْنِ ۚ وَإِن كُنتُمْ جُنُبًا فَٱطَّهَّرُواْ ۚ وَإِن كُنتُم مَّرْضَىٰٓ أَوْ عَلَىٰ سَفَرٍ أَوْ جَآءَ أَحَدٌ مِّنكُم مِّنَ ٱلْغَآئِطِ أَوْ لَـٰمَسْتُمُ ٱلنِّسَآءَ فَلَمْ تَجِدُواْ مَآءً فَتَيَمَّمُواْ صَعِيدًا طَيِّبًا فَٱمْسَحُواْ بِوُجُوهِكُمْ وَأَيْدِيكُم مِّنْهُ ۚ مَا يُرِيدُ ٱللَّهُ لِيَجْعَلَ عَلَيْكُم مِّنْ حَرَجٍ وَلَـٰكِن يُرِيدُ لِيُطَهِّرَكُمْ وَلِيُتِمَّ نِعْمَتَهُۥ عَلَيْكُمْ لَعَلَّكُمْ تَشْكُرُونَ
٦ المائدة

بما أن الله أمر بالوضوء وحدد شروطه، فلا أحد على الإطلاق سيستطيع تغيير هذه الشروط وإلا فسيكون ذلك افتراءً على الله بالكذب. بدأ أمر الله بأن نغسل وجوهنا وأيدينا إلى المرافق. وبما أننا في الجزء العلوي من الجسد، فقد أرادنا الله أن نمسح رؤوسنا قبل غسل أرجلنا. فمن أين أتى المسح على الخف؟ ولماذا لا تغسل قدماك؟ حدد الله غسل الأرجل إلى الكعبين، على ألا يوجد عازل بينهم كالخف! أمر واضح وبسيط فلِمَ تغيير حدود الله؟ الدين علم ومنطق. لماذا التذاكي على الله واضاعة معجزات الله.

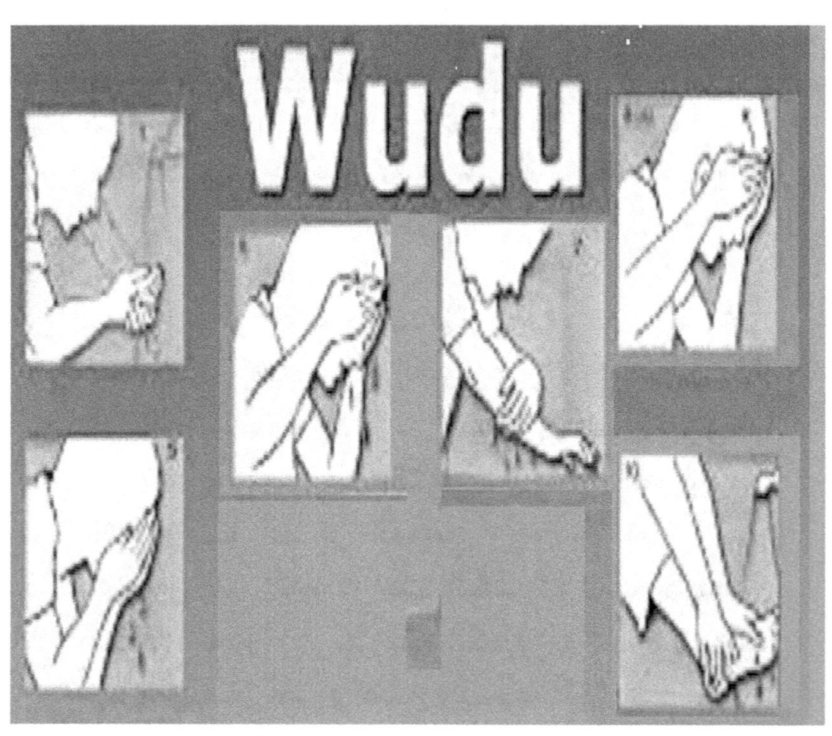

Wudu

أو لم تكتب فيحق لك أن تكتب الثلث فقط!) ماذا لو قام الشخص ببيع كل شيء قبل الوفاة أو إعطائها لمن يريد، أليس ذلك حقه؟ وكيف تستطيع منع ذلك؟ تخالف الله لتجعلها مشقة للناس، والدين سهل. هكذا أمر الله الخَلق، ولكن طمع الحكام في السيطرة على الأموال الموصي بها والأملاك، دفعهم إلى نشر هكذا قانون من خلال علماء السلاطين.

قرأت أحكاما لا تمت للإسلام بصلة وليست صحيحة، وهذا المقطع نسخة من أحد المواقع الالكترونية:
نرى الناس يمسحون على الخفين العلوي والسفلي. فما حكم هذا المسح وما حكم صلاتهم؟
صلاتهم ووضوؤهم صحيحان، ولكن يجب على الجميع أن يعلم أن مسح أسفل الخفين ليس من السنة. ففي السنة حديث علي بن أبي طالب رضي الله عنه، قال: لو كان الدين على القول، فمسح جانب الخفين، لكني رأيت رسول الله صلى الله عليه وسلم مسح سلام على الجزء العلوي من الخفين ". وهذا يدل على أن الجزء العلوي فقط من الخفين يشرع في المسح، للتنقية.

مرة أخرى، بما أنهم لم يتمكنوا من تغيير القرآن، فإنهم يريدون الاستخفاف بعقول المسلمين.
لماذا يعتبر رجال الدين أن الوصية في الثلث فقط مما يملك الشخص؟

ما الدليل على ذلك؟

لماذا يؤكد الله في كتابه الكريم على توزيع التركة بعد وصية أو دين؟

على سبيل المثال، أنا شخص يملك 1000 دولار، بينما علي دين 1000 دولار، فلن يبقى إذا أي شيء للورثة! إن الله قد ساوى ما بين الوصية والدين. فلذلك، لا يمكن أن تحكم الوصية في ثلث التركة فقط، بل تطالها بأكملها، ما عدا ما لم يتم ذكره أو جمعه بعد كتابة الوصية وغفل عن إضافته للوصية. فهنا يجري التقسيم الشرعي. في حالة ما لم تكتب الوصية، يجري أيضا التقسيم الشرعي. ومن خلال هذا التقسيم الإلهي الذي يعتبر إرشادا لنا حول كيف يجب أن نوزع التركة بالعدل من خلال الوصية، فعلى رجال الدين أن يشجعوا المسلمين على كتابة الوصية وليس إحباطهم (من خلال إحلال قانون، سواء كتبت

يَـٰٓأَيُّهَا ٱلَّذِينَ ءَامَنُوا۟ شَهَـٰدَةُ بَيْنِكُمْ إِذَا حَضَرَ أَحَدَكُمُ ٱلْمَوْتُ حِينَ ٱلْوَصِيَّةِ ٱثْنَانِ ذَوَا عَدْلٍ مِّنكُمْ أَوْ ءَاخَرَانِ مِنْ غَيْرِكُمْ إِنْ أَنتُمْ ضَرَبْتُمْ فِى ٱلْأَرْضِ فَأَصَـٰبَتْكُم مُّصِيبَةُ ٱلْمَوْتِ ۚ تَحْبِسُونَهُمَا مِنۢ بَعْدِ ٱلصَّلَوٰةِ فَيُقْسِمَانِ بِٱللَّهِ إِنِ ٱرْتَبْتُمْ لَا نَشْتَرِى بِهِۦ ثَمَنًا وَلَوْ كَانَ ذَا قُرْبَىٰ ۙ وَلَا نَكْتُمُ شَهَـٰدَةَ ٱللَّهِ إِنَّآ إِذًا لَّمِنَ ٱلْـَٔاثِمِينَ ١٠٦ المائدة

236

يُوصِيكُمُ ٱللَّهُ فِىٓ أَوْلَٰدِكُمْ ۖ لِلذَّكَرِ مِثْلُ حَظِّ ٱلْأُنثَيَيْنِ ۚ فَإِن كُنَّ نِسَآءً فَوْقَ ٱثْنَتَيْنِ فَلَهُنَّ ثُلُثَا مَا تَرَكَ ۖ وَإِن كَانَتْ وَٰحِدَةً فَلَهَا ٱلنِّصْفُ ۚ وَلِأَبَوَيْهِ لِكُلِّ وَٰحِدٍ مِّنْهُمَا ٱلسُّدُسُ مِمَّا تَرَكَ إِن كَانَ لَهُۥ وَلَدٌ ۚ فَإِن لَّمْ يَكُن لَّهُۥ وَلَدٌ وَوَرِثَهُۥٓ أَبَوَاهُ فَلِأُمِّهِ ٱلثُّلُثُ ۚ فَإِن كَانَ لَهُۥٓ إِخْوَةٌ فَلِأُمِّهِ ٱلسُّدُسُ ۚ مِنۢ بَعْدِ وَصِيَّةٍ يُوصِى بِهَآ أَوْ دَيْنٍ ۗ ءَابَآؤُكُمْ وَأَبْنَآؤُكُمْ لَا تَدْرُونَ أَيُّهُمْ أَقْرَبُ لَكُمْ نَفْعًا ۚ فَرِيضَةً مِّنَ ٱللَّهِ ۗ إِنَّ ٱللَّهَ كَانَ عَلِيمًا حَكِيمًا

١١ النساء

وَلَكُمْ نِصْفُ مَا تَرَكَ أَزْوَٰجُكُمْ إِن لَّمْ يَكُن لَّهُنَّ ۞ وَلَدٌ ۚ فَإِن كَانَ لَهُنَّ وَلَدٌ فَلَكُمُ ٱلرُّبُعُ مِمَّا تَرَكْنَ ۚ مِنۢ بَعْدِ وَصِيَّةٍ يُوصِينَ بِهَآ أَوْ دَيْنٍ ۚ وَلَهُنَّ ٱلرُّبُعُ مِمَّا تَرَكْتُمْ إِن لَّمْ يَكُن لَّكُمْ وَلَدٌ ۚ فَإِن كَانَ لَكُمْ وَلَدٌ فَلَهُنَّ ٱلثُّمُنُ مِمَّا تَرَكْتُم ۚ مِّنۢ بَعْدِ وَصِيَّةٍ تُوصُونَ بِهَآ أَوْ دَيْنٍ ۗ وَإِن كَانَ رَجُلٌ يُورَثُ كَلَٰلَةً أَوِ ٱمْرَأَةٌ وَلَهُۥٓ أَخٌ أَوْ أُخْتٌ فَلِكُلِّ وَٰحِدٍ مِّنْهُمَا ٱلسُّدُسُ ۚ فَإِن كَانُوٓا۟ أَكْثَرَ مِن ذَٰلِكَ فَهُمْ شُرَكَآءُ فِى ٱلثُّلُثِ ۚ مِنۢ بَعْدِ وَصِيَّةٍ يُوصَىٰ بِهَآ أَوْ دَيْنٍ غَيْرَ مُضَآرٍّ ۚ وَصِيَّةً مِّنَ ٱللَّهِ ۗ وَٱللَّهُ عَلِيمٌ حَلِيمٌ

١٢ النساء

كُتِبَ عَلَيْكُمْ إِذَا حَضَرَ أَحَدَكُمُ ٱلْمَوْتُ إِن تَرَكَ خَيْرًا ٱلْوَصِيَّةُ لِلْوَلِدَيْنِ وَٱلْأَقْرَبِينَ بِٱلْمَعْرُوفِ حَقًّا عَلَى ٱلْمُتَّقِينَ

١٨٠ البقرة

فَمَن بَدَّلَهُ بَعْدَ مَا سَمِعَهُ فَإِنَّمَآ إِثْمُهُ عَلَى ٱلَّذِينَ يُبَدِّلُونَهُ إِنَّ ٱللَّهَ سَمِيعٌ عَلِيمٌ

١٨١ البقرة

أمر الله بالوصية!

يكن سهلا أن يستطيعوا تغيير حرف في القرآن، فحاولوا من خلال الأحاديث. إن تصديق مثل هذه الأضاليل يعتبر في غاية الخطورة، فهو نسف للقرآن واتهام لمحمد عليه الصلاة والسلام بأنه لم يكمل الرسالة ولم يؤدِ الدعوة. كل هذا من إبعاد المسلمين عن الكتاب لإخفاء الإعجاز القرآني وليمسحوا الكتاب الكريم من عقول المسلمين وقلوبهم.

لَا إِكْرَاهَ فِي ٱلدِّينِ ۖ قَد تَّبَيَّنَ ٱلرُّشْدُ مِنَ ٱلْغَيِّ ۚ فَمَن يَكْفُرْ بِٱلطَّـٰغُوتِ وَيُؤْمِنۢ بِٱللَّهِ فَقَدِ ٱسْتَمْسَكَ بِٱلْعُرْوَةِ ٱلْوُثْقَىٰ لَا ٱنفِصَامَ لَهَا ۗ وَٱللَّهُ سَمِيعٌ عَلِيمٌ
٢٥٦ البقرة

سَأَصْرِفُ عَنْ ءَايَـٰتِيَ ٱلَّذِينَ يَتَكَبَّرُونَ فِي ٱلْأَرْضِ بِغَيْرِ ٱلْحَقِّ وَإِن يَرَوْا۟ كُلَّ ءَايَةٍ لَّا يُؤْمِنُوا۟ بِهَا وَإِن يَرَوْا۟ سَبِيلَ ٱلرُّشْدِ لَا يَتَّخِذُوهُ سَبِيلًا وَإِن يَرَوْا۟ سَبِيلَ ٱلْغَيِّ يَتَّخِذُوهُ سَبِيلًا ۚ ذَٰلِكَ بِأَنَّهُمْ كَذَّبُوا۟ بِـَٔايَـٰتِنَا وَكَانُوا۟ عَنْهَا غَـٰفِلِينَ
١٤٦ الأعراف

قُلْ أُوحِيَ إِلَيَّ أَنَّهُ ٱسْتَمَعَ نَفَرٌ مِّنَ ٱلْجِنِّ فَقَالُوٓا۟ إِنَّا سَمِعْنَا قُرْءَانًا عَجَبًا
١ الجن

يَهْدِىٓ إِلَى ٱلرُّشْدِ فَـَٔامَنَّا بِهِ ۖ وَلَن نُّشْرِكَ بِرَبِّنَآ أَحَدًا
٢ الجن

يهدي إلى الرشد، اللهم اهدنا رشدا.

لقد تمت الرسالة وقام الرسول بتأديتها حق تأدية، الإيحاء بظهور أي شخص آخر، فهو ليس إلا نسفا للقرآن، وإهانة لرسول الله بأنه لم يكمل رسالته، مع العلم أن الله أخبرنا في القرآن أن الرسالة قد تمت. فماذا سيغير ظهورهم؟ وهل سيأتون بدين أهدى من الدين الإسلامي؟

مَّا كَانَ مُحَمَّدٌ أَبَآ أَحَدٍ مِّن رِّجَالِكُمْ وَلَٰكِن رَّسُولَ ٱللَّهِ وَخَاتَمَ ٱلنَّبِيِّۧنَ ۗ وَكَانَ ٱللَّهُ بِكُلِّ شَىْءٍ عَلِيمًا
٤٠ الاحزاب

لماذا؟

تؤمن الديانة اليهودية بأن المسيح عليه السلام سوف يظهر لأنهم لم يؤمنوا بالسيد المسيح ابن العذراء مريم عليها السلام. وهم لا زالوا ينتظرون ظهوره. وبما أن الإسلام قد أكد ظهور المسيح عليه السلام واعترف بنبوءته ورسالته بالإنجيل إلى بني إسرائيل، فإنهم سوف يكونون في حالة عداء مع المسيحيين عموما. فلذلك نشروا مقولة ظهور المسيح عندما لم يوجد أي جسد في المغارة كان الأمر سهلا للغاية بالنسبة لهم، أما بالنسبة للمسلمين، فقد كان أسهل بكثير، لأن كل ما عليهم فعله هو أن يدسوا الأحاديث، وهذا ما فعلوه. لم

يَـٰيَحْيَىٰ خُذِ ٱلْكِتَـٰبَ بِقُوَّةٍ ۖ وَءَاتَيْنَـٰهُ ٱلْحُكْمَ صَبِيًّا ١٢

وَحَنَانًا مِّن لَّدُنَّا وَزَكَوٰةً ۖ وَكَانَ تَقِيًّا ١٣ وَبَرًّۢا بِوَٰلِدَيْهِ
وَلَمْ يَكُن جَبَّارًا عَصِيًّا ١٤ وَسَلَـٰمٌ عَلَيْهِ يَوْمَ وُلِدَ
وَيَوْمَ يَمُوتُ وَيَوْمَ يُبْعَثُ حَيًّا
١٥ مريم

إِذْ قَالَ ٱللَّهُ يَـٰعِيسَىٰٓ إِنِّى مُتَوَفِّيكَ وَرَافِعُكَ إِلَىَّ وَمُطَهِّرُكَ
مِنَ ٱلَّذِينَ كَفَرُوا۟ وَجَاعِلُ ٱلَّذِينَ ٱتَّبَعُوكَ فَوْقَ ٱلَّذِينَ
كَفَرُوٓا۟ إِلَىٰ يَوْمِ ٱلْقِيَـٰمَةِ ۖ ثُمَّ إِلَىَّ مَرْجِعُكُمْ فَأَحْكُمُ
بَيْنَكُمْ فِيمَا كُنتُمْ فِيهِ تَخْتَلِفُونَ
٥٥ آل عمران

١١٧ المائدة

حُرِّمَتْ عَلَيْكُمُ ٱلْمَيْتَةُ وَٱلدَّمُ وَلَحْمُ ٱلْخِنزِيرِ وَمَآ أُهِلَّ
لِغَيْرِ ٱللَّهِ بِهِۦ وَٱلْمُنْخَنِقَةُ وَٱلْمَوْقُوذَةُ وَٱلْمُتَرَدِّيَةُ
وَٱلنَّطِيحَةُ وَمَآ أَكَلَ ٱلسَّبُعُ إِلَّا مَا ذَكَّيْتُمْ وَمَا
ذُبِحَ عَلَى ٱلنُّصُبِ وَأَن تَسْتَقْسِمُوا۟ بِٱلْأَزْلَـٰمِ ۚ ذَٰلِكُمْ
فِسْقٌ ۗ ٱلْيَوْمَ يَئِسَ ٱلَّذِينَ كَفَرُوا۟ مِن دِينِكُمْ فَلَا
تَخْشَوْهُمْ وَٱخْشَوْنِ ۚ ٱلْيَوْمَ أَكْمَلْتُ لَكُمْ دِينَكُمْ
وَأَتْمَمْتُ عَلَيْكُمْ نِعْمَتِى وَرَضِيتُ لَكُمُ ٱلْإِسْلَـٰمَ دِينًا ۚ
فَمَنِ ٱضْطُرَّ فِى مَخْمَصَةٍ غَيْرَ مُتَجَانِفٍ لِّإِثْمٍ
فَإِنَّ ٱللَّهَ غَفُورٌ رَّحِيمٌ
٣ المائدة

ثمة اعتقاد آخر مستمر حتى الآن، وهو عودة السيد المسيح عليه السلام وظهور المسيح الدجال وكذلك المهدي، والسؤال هنا هو: لماذا؟ ولماذا نفاه القرآن؟

إِنَّ مَثَلَ عِيسَىٰ عِندَ ٱللَّهِ كَمَثَلِ ءَادَمَ ۖ خَلَقَهُۥ مِن تُرَابٍ ثُمَّ قَالَ لَهُۥ كُن فَيَكُونُ ٥٩ آل عمران

هل سيعود آدم عليه السلام؟؟
بِأُخْتَ هَٰرُونَ مَا كَانَ أَبُوكِ ٱمْرَأَ سَوْءٍ وَمَا كَانَتْ أُمُّكِ بَغِيًّا ٢٨ فَأَشَارَتْ إِلَيْهِ ۖ قَالُوا كَيْفَ نُكَلِّمُ مَن كَانَ فِى ٱلْمَهْدِ صَبِيًّا ٢٩ قَالَ إِنِّى عَبْدُ ٱللَّهِ ءَاتَىٰنِىَ ٱلْكِتَٰبَ وَجَعَلَنِى نَبِيًّا ٣٠ وَجَعَلَنِى مُبَارَكًا أَيْنَ مَا كُنتُ وَأَوْصَٰنِى بِٱلصَّلَوٰةِ وَٱلزَّكَوٰةِ مَا دُمْتُ حَيًّا ٣١ وَبَرًّا بِوَٰلِدَتِى وَلَمْ يَجْعَلْنِى جَبَّارًا شَقِيًّا ٣٢ وَٱلسَّلَٰمُ عَلَىَّ يَوْمَ وُلِدتُّ وَيَوْمَ أَمُوتُ وَيَوْمَ أُبْعَثُ حَيًّا ٣٣ ذَٰلِكَ عِيسَى ٱبْنُ مَرْيَمَ ۚ قَوْلَ ٱلْحَقِّ ٱلَّذِى فِيهِ يَمْتَرُونَ ٣٤

لقد ذكر القرآن أن السيد المسيح عليه السلام قال: السلام على يوم ولدت (وقد ولد) ويوم أموت (وقد مات) ويوم أبعث حيا (اليوم الذي يبعث حيا). والسؤال هو: هل حدد له يوم بعث غير يوم بعثنا جميعا؟ مع العلم أن الله قال في كتابه الكريم عن يحي عليه السلام نفس الشيء، فهل سيعود يحي عليه السلام أيضا؟

هل سيعود المسيح؟؟ ماذا عن المهدي؟؟؟

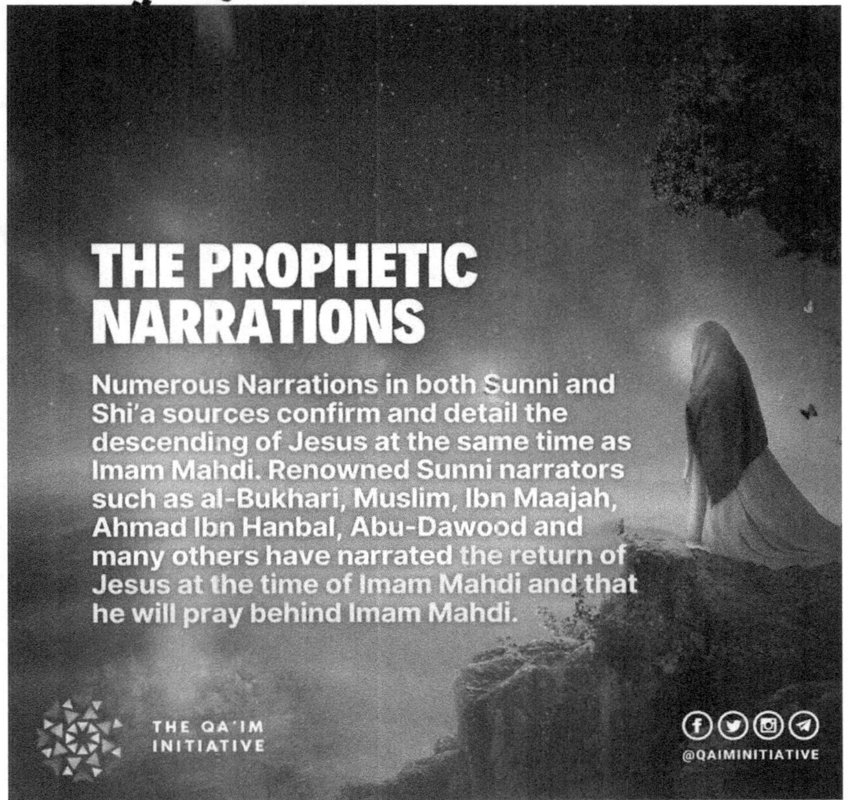

إذا مررت في حارة وسمعت القرآن بصوت عالٍ، فلأن هناك حالة وفاة! حولنا كتاب الحياة إلى علامة على الموت، أستغفر الله!

لِّيُنذِرَ مَن كَانَ حَيًّا وَيَحِقَّ ٱلْقَوْلُ عَلَى ٱلْكَٰفِرِينَ
يس ٧٠

بَوْرِقِكُمْ هَٰذِهِ إِلَى ٱلْمَدِينَةِ فَلْيَنظُرْ أَيُّهَا أَزْكَىٰ طَعَامًا فَلْيَأْتِكُم بِرِزْقٍ مِّنْهُ وَلْيَتَلَطَّفْ وَلَا يُشْعِرَنَّ بِكُمْ أَحَدًا
الكهف 18 19

أَوْ كَٱلَّذِى مَرَّ عَلَىٰ قَرْيَةٍ وَهِىَ خَاوِيَةٌ عَلَىٰ عُرُوشِهَا قَالَ أَنَّىٰ يُحْىِۦ هَٰذِهِ ٱللَّهُ بَعْدَ مَوْتِهَا ۖ فَأَمَاتَهُ ٱللَّهُ مِائَةَ عَامٍ ثُمَّ بَعَثَهُ ۖ قَالَ كَمْ لَبِثْتَ ۖ قَالَ لَبِثْتُ يَوْمًا أَوْ بَعْضَ يَوْمٍ ۖ قَالَ بَل لَّبِثْتَ مِائَةَ عَامٍ فَٱنظُرْ إِلَىٰ طَعَامِكَ وَشَرَابِكَ لَمْ يَتَسَنَّهْ ۖ وَٱنظُرْ إِلَىٰ حِمَارِكَ وَلِنَجْعَلَكَ ءَايَةً لِّلنَّاسِ ۖ وَٱنظُرْ إِلَى ٱلْعِظَامِ كَيْفَ نُنشِزُهَا ثُمَّ نَكْسُوهَا لَحْمًا ۚ فَلَمَّا تَبَيَّنَ لَهُ قَالَ أَعْلَمُ أَنَّ ٱللَّهَ عَلَىٰ كُلِّ شَىْءٍ قَدِيرٌ
البقرة ٢٥٩".

في كلتا الحالتين، نرى أن مفهوم الوقت قد توقف بالنسبة لهم.

مع كل الأدلة التي عرضناها عن عدم وجود عذاب القبر، فإنه علينا ألا نخاف من عذاب القبر، بل من الخلود في النار والذي هو أعظم.

إن الكذب هو مفتاح تدمير كل شيء، ولكشف الكذب، هنالك طريقة وحيدة، ألا وهي المقارنة بالقرآن.

لسوء الحظ، يعرف معظم المسلمين الحديث ولا يعرفون القرآن. وإذا قرؤوه، لا يفعلوه للفهم أو الإنصات أو الاستماع إليه. لقد أصبح القرآن في عديد من الدول الإسلامية علامة على الموت، بحيث

إِنَّكَ لَا تُسْمِعُ ٱلْمَوْتَىٰ وَلَا تُسْمِعُ ٱلصُّمَّ ٱلدُّعَآءَ إِذَا وَلَّوْاْ مُدْبِرِينَ

النمل ٨٠

سبحان الله جل جلاله بحكمته، إنك لا تسمع الموتى الدعاء ولا الصم إذا ولوا مدبرين. لأن الأصم يمكن أن يقرأ الشفاه أو تعابير الوجه، ولكن لا يمكنه ذلك إذا ولى مدبرا.

الوقت والنوم

إن النوم كالموت. حين ننام، يقرر الله من سيستيقظ أم لا، فالوقت ملك الله، وعندما يموت الإنسان يتوقف وقته إلى حين البعث، بالضبط كما هو حال النوم بالنسبة للاستيقاظ.

ٱللَّهُ يَتَوَفَّى ٱلْأَنفُسَ حِينَ مَوْتِهَا وَٱلَّتِى لَمْ تَمُتْ فِى مَنَامِهَا ۖ فَيُمْسِكُ ٱلَّتِى قَضَىٰ عَلَيْهَا ٱلْمَوْتَ وَيُرْسِلُ ٱلْأُخْرَىٰ إِلَىٰ أَجَلٍ مُّسَمًّى ۚ إِنَّ فِى ذَٰلِكَ لَآيَٰتٍ لِّقَوْمٍ يَتَفَكَّرُونَ

٤٢ الزمر

وَتَحْسَبُهُمْ أَيْقَاظًا وَهُمْ رُقُودٌ ۚ وَنُقَلِّبُهُمْ ذَاتَ ٱلْيَمِينِ وَذَاتَ ٱلشِّمَالِ ۖ وَكَلْبُهُم بَٰسِطٌ ذِرَاعَيْهِ بِٱلْوَصِيدِ ۚ لَوِ ٱطَّلَعْتَ عَلَيْهِمْ لَوَلَّيْتَ مِنْهُمْ فِرَارًا وَلَمُلِئْتَ مِنْهُمْ رُعْبًا ١٨ وَكَذَٰلِكَ بَعَثْنَٰهُمْ لِيَتَسَآءَلُواْ بَيْنَهُمْ ۚ قَالَ قَآئِلٌ مِّنْهُمْ كَمْ لَبِثْتُمْ ۖ قَالُواْ لَبِثْنَا يَوْمًا أَوْ بَعْضَ يَوْمٍ ۚ قَالُواْ رَبُّكُمْ أَعْلَمُ بِمَا لَبِثْتُمْ فَٱبْعَثُواْ أَحَدَكُم

لم يرد اسم عزرائيل نهائيا في القرآن لأنه ليس ملاكا واحدا مكلفا، بل ملائكة كرام.

قُلْ يَتَوَفَّىٰكُم مَّلَكُ ٱلْمَوْتِ ٱلَّذِى وُكِّلَ بِكُمْ ثُمَّ إِلَىٰ رَبِّكُمْ تُرْجَعُونَ ١١
(11) السجدة

إنما أسلط الضوء على بعض ما يشاع بين العامة من أقاويل وأحاديث، والتي كان الغرض منها هو التسلل إلى ديننا الحنيف.

وَقَالُوا لِجُلُودِهِمْ لِمَ شَهِدتُّمْ عَلَيْنَا قَالُوا أَنطَقَنَا ٱللَّهُ ٱلَّذِى أَنطَقَ كُلَّ شَىْءٍ وَهُوَ خَلَقَكُمْ أَوَّلَ مَرَّةٍ وَإِلَيْهِ تُرْجَعُونَ
21 فصلت
وَمَا كُنتُمْ تَسْتَتِرُونَ أَن يَشْهَدَ عَلَيْكُمْ سَمْعُكُمْ وَلَا أَبْصَٰرُكُمْ وَلَا جُلُودُكُمْ وَلَٰكِن ظَنَنتُمْ أَنَّ ٱللَّهَ لَا يَعْلَمُ كَثِيرًا مِّمَّا تَعْمَلُونَ ٢٢
22 فصلت

بعد كل هذا، ألا تزال تؤمن بعذاب القبر؟ ألم يحن الوقت للصحوة والعودة للقرآن؟

وعندما نتناقش في أحاديث عذاب القبر، يطل علينا أصحاب العمائم ليذكروا هذه الآية. وهذا يدل على جهلهم بالقرآن.

فَكَيْفَ إِذَا تَوَفَّتْهُمُ ٱلْمَلَٰئِكَةُ يَضْرِبُونَ وُجُوهَهُمْ وَأَدْبَٰرَهُمْ ٢٧

27محمد

وهذه الآية تحدثت عن موقعة قتالية حيث حاربت الملائكة إلى جانب المؤمنين، والضرب يحصل خلال عملية الوفاة وليست بعدها.

البعض فقط يعلم أنه حديث كاذب، ولكنهم يبررون ذلك بأنه على الناس أن يخافوا الله، أليس من الخير أن يخافوا الخلود في جهنم؟ أي تبرير لأي حديث هو فتح لباب التضليل، لأن عامة الناس لا يعرفون من القرآن سوى أنه قدسي، وقداسته ألا تمسه وتقرأه. إحدى الأضاليل المتداولة بين الناس اسم عزرائيل، وهو ملك الموت الذي يقبض أرواح الناس. ما شاء الله! لقد أعطوه اسما كما أعطوه لمنكر ونكير!

ٱلَّذِينَ تَتَوَفَّاهُمُ ٱلْمَلَٰئِكَةُ طَيِّبِينَ ۙ يَقُولُونَ سَلَٰمٌ عَلَيْكُمُ ٱدْخُلُوا۟ ٱلْجَنَّةَ بِمَا كُنتُمْ تَعْمَلُونَ ٣٢

32النحل

ٱلَّذِينَ تَتَوَفَّاهُمُ ٱلْمَلَٰئِكَةُ ظَالِمِي أَنفُسِهِمْ ۖ فَأَلْقَوُا۟ ٱلسَّلَمَ مَا كُنَّا نَعْمَلُ مِن سُوٓءٍ ۚ بَلَىٰٓ إِنَّ ٱللَّهَ عَلِيمٌۢ بِمَا كُنتُمْ تَعْمَلُونَ ٢٨

28النحل

الدفن إنه الآن يسأل! هذا إلى جانب الأسماء التي أتوا بها كمنكر ونكير وعدة أحاديث لا تنم إلا عن جهل بكتاب الله. أستغفر الله والعياذ بالله. توجد في القرآن كل الإجابات التي نحتاج إليها، ولكن رجال الدين أوهموا الناس بأنهم لن يفهموا القرآن وأنه لم يتحدث عن كيفية الصلاة وغيرها، وذلك من أجل إبعادهم عن الكتاب أو إذا قرؤوه فقط للقراءة. لقد أثروا على الناس نفسيا ونشروا بينهم فكرة أنهم بحاجة إلى أصحاب العمائم.

قبل أن أجيب عليهم، أود أن أفرق بين نوعين من الحديث: المرئي والمكتوب.

الحديث المرئي وهو ما رأت ملايين المسلمين الرسول يفعله وتناقلوه بينهم، وبالرغم من صعوبة تزويره، فقد تمكن المدسوسون من تغيير معظمه. الحديث المكتوب وهو ما نسب إلى رسول الله، مع العلم أن الخلفاء الأربعة ومن بعدهم لم يداولوا الحديث لأنه كان غير موجود في زمنهم، وإنما ابتدع لاحقا. فكيف لرسول الله أن يخبر شخصا بشيء ما دون بقية الأمة، وكأنه يهمس في أذنه، والعياذ بالله. لقد قضى الرسول كل أيامه يدرس المؤمنون القرآن ولا كلمة تعلو فوق كلام الله.

تثبت الدراسات أن أي حديث يتناقل بين أشخاص وعبر مسافة زمنية، يختلف اختلافا عميقا عن الحديث الأصل.

خطب الجمعة؟ وكيف لم تنقل أي واحدة منها؟ ولكنهم رأوا في الأحاديث ملجأ ووسيلة لضمان بقائهم في وظائفهم ولجمع الأموال.

إِنَّا نَحْنُ نَزَّلْنَا الذِّكْرَ وَإِنَّا لَهُ لَحَافِظُونَ9
9الحجر-

وَمَا أَرْسَلْنَا قَبْلَكَ إِلَّا رِجَالًا نُوحِي إِلَيْهِمْ ۖ فَاسْأَلُوا أَهْلَ الذِّكْرِ إِنْ 43كُنْتُمْ لَا تَعْلَمُونَ

43النحل-

وَهَٰذَا ذِكْرٌ مُّبَارَكٌ أَنزَلْنَاهُ ۚ أَفَأَنتُمْ لَهُ مُنكِرُونَ ٥٠
50الانبياء

إن الرسالة واضحة وضوح الشمس، يجب علينا أن نتبع الذكر، القرآن، وأي حديث مخالف للقرآن فهو حديث كاذب. ولكن، كيف يمكننا أن نعرف الحديث الصحيح إذا لم نقرأ ونحفظ القرآن؟ هل يجب أن نعتمد على رجال الدين؟ لو قرأ رجال الدين القرآن

ما وصلنا إلى ما وصلنا، ولما سمحوا للأحاديث الكاذبة أن تنتشر. ثم يمعنون في القول عند

لقد اكتشف يوم البعث ما ستكون عليه عقوبته، وهو يتمنى لو لم يكن يعلم لماذا؟ ألم يخبره الملكان بذلك في القبر؟

الْيَوْمَ نَخْتِمُ عَلَى أَفْوَاهِهِمْ وَتُكَلِّمُنَا أَيْدِيهِمْ وَتَشْهَدُ أَرْجُلُهُمْ بِمَا كَانُوا يَكْسِبُونَ
65يس

هل هذا يحدث في القبر؟

يوجد في كل سورة تقريبا دليل على عدم وجود عذاب القبر، أو حساب قبل يوم الحساب. ولا يوجد ملكان يطرحان أسئلة ويحاسبون الموتى. الله هو القاضي يوم القيامة. كل الأدلة التي نحتاجها توجد أمام أعيننا وما زلنا نرجح الحديث على كلام الله، بل ونكفر من ينكر هذا الحديث. أما إنكار آيات الله فهو أمر غير مهم. متى سنعود إلى القرآن العظيم لنتقرب من خلاله إلى الله؟

لقد واجه الدين الإسلامي هجمات شرسة هادفة إلى إبعاد المسلمين عن الكتاب، وذلك لتعمي أعينهم عن الصواب وإظهار المسلمين بأنهم جهلة ومتخلفين لأنهم فشلوا في تغيير كتاب الله، فلجأوا إلى نسب الأحاديث إلى الرسول. وللأسف، لم يطرح رجال الدين أي سؤال بهذا الخصوص. ماذا حل بجميع

يَوْمَ نَدْعُوا۟ كُلَّ أُنَاسٍ بِإِمَٰمِهِمْ ۖ فَمَنْ أُوتِىَ كِتَٰبَهُۥ بِيَمِينِهِۦ

فَأُو۟لَٰٓئِكَ يَقْرَءُونَ كِتَٰبَهُمْ وَلَا يُظْلَمُونَ فَتِيلًا ﴿٧١﴾
[الاسراء71]

ٱللَّهُ يَحْكُمُ بَيْنَكُمْ يَوْمَ ٱلْقِيَٰمَةِ فِيمَا كُنتُمْ فِيهِ

تَخْتَلِفُونَ ﴿٦٩﴾
الحج69

وَيَوْمَ يُعْرَضُ ٱلَّذِينَ كَفَرُوا۟ عَلَى ٱلنَّارِ أَلَيْسَ هَٰذَا بِٱلْحَقِّ ۖ قَالُوا۟ بَلَىٰ وَرَبِّنَا ۚ

قَالَ فَذُوقُوا۟ ٱلْعَذَابَ بِمَا كُنتُمْ تَكْفُرُونَ ﴿٣٤﴾
الاحقاف34

وَيَوْمَ تَقُومُ ٱلسَّاعَةُ يُقْسِمُ ٱلْمُجْرِمُونَ مَا لَبِثُوا۟ غَيْرَ

﴿٥٥﴾ سَاعَةٍ ۚ كَذَٰلِكَ كَانُوا۟ يُؤْفَكُونَ
الروم55

إذا أقسم المجرمون بأنهم لبثوا ساعات قليلة، فأين عذاب القبر وهم الأحق بأن يعذبوا؟؟

مَنْ أُوتِيَ كِتَابَهُ بِشِمَالِهِ فَيَقُولُ يَا لَيْتَنِي لَمْ أُوتَ كِتَابِيَهْ
الاحقاف25

نائمون عامل الوقت معدوم!

وَوُضِعَ ٱلْكِتَٰبُ فَتَرَى ٱلْمُجْرِمِينَ مُشْفِقِينَ مِمَّا فِيهِ وَيَقُولُونَ يَٰوَيْلَتَنَا مَالِ هَٰذَا ٱلْكِتَٰبِ لَا يُغَادِرُ صَغِيرَةً وَلَا كَبِيرَةً إِلَّا أَحْصَىٰهَا ۚ وَوَجَدُوا۟ مَا عَمِلُوا۟ حَاضِرًا ۗ وَلَا يَظْلِمُ رَبُّكَ أَحَدًا ۩ ﴿٤٩﴾ وَعُرِضُوا۟ عَلَىٰ رَبِّكَ صَفًّا لَّقَدْ جِئْتُمُونَا كَمَا خَلَقْنَٰكُمْ أَوَّلَ مَرَّةٍ ۚ بَلْ زَعَمْتُمْ أَلَّن نَّجْعَلَ لَكُم مَّوْعِدًا ﴿٤٨﴾

الكهف 48 49

فلنسأل أنفسنا هذا السؤال؟ هل سيحدث ذلك في القبر أم يوم القيامة؟؟

ٱقْرَأْ كِتَٰبَكَ كَفَىٰ بِنَفْسِكَ ٱلْيَوْمَ عَلَيْكَ حَسِيبًا ﴿١٤﴾

الاسراء 14

مرة أخرى، إذا كنت سأقرأ كتابي يوم القيامة، فلماذا سيسألني الملكان في القبر؟؟

هل هنالك عذاب القبر؟

يؤكد القرآن الكريم في جميع الآيات على أنه عند حدوث الموت، يتوقف الزمن أو الوقت بالنسبة للميت. ويوم البعث، حين سيبعث الناس، سوف يظنون أنهم ناموا لساعات فقط. وقد ذكرت هذه المعلومات في العديد من الآيات.

قَالُواْ يَٰوَيْلَنَا مَنۢ بَعَثَنَا مِن مَّرْقَدِنَا ۜ هَٰذَا مَا وَعَدَ ٱلرَّحْمَٰنُ وَصَدَقَ ٱلْمُرْسَلُونَ

٥٢ يس

هناك بعض الدول لا تغيب عنها الشمس لبضعة شهور، أربعة إلى خمسة أشهر! فكيف يصومون من طلوع الشمس إلى غروبها؟

خُلِقَ ٱلْإِنسَٰنُ مِنْ عَجَلٍ ۚ سَأُورِيكُمْ ءَايَٰتِى فَلَا تَسْتَعْجِلُونِ

١٣٧الانبياء

https://www.sunrise-and-sunset.com/en									
Jul-22						number of hours	Sep-22		number of hours
Longyearbyen						24 hours sun never set for four months april to aug	Longyearbyen		13 hrs it will shift by 10 days per year average from 2020 2021 2022
Oslo norway						18 hrs average	Oslo Norway		13 hrs average
Russia Moscow						16 hrs Average	Russia Moscow		12.5 hrs average
London, United Kingdom						16 hrs average	London, United Kingdom		12.5 hrs average
new york						15 hrs average	new york		12.5hrs average
shanghi, China						14 hrs Average	shanghi, China		12.5 hrs average
Mecca , Saudi Arabia						13.5 Hrs average	Mecca , Saudi Arabia		12.5 hrs average
Buenos Aires, Argentine						10 Hrs average	Buenos Aires, Argentine		12 hrs average
Australia melbourne						9.5 Hrs average	Australia melbourne		12 hrs average

الجواب

الجواب على العدل الإلهي، ما عليك سوى إلقاء نظرة على البيانات الخاصة بشهر أيلول(سبتمبر)في جميع أنحاء العالم.

١١٣ فَتَعَٰلَى ٱللَّهُ ٱلْمَلِكُ ٱلْحَقُّ ۗ وَلَا تَعْجَلْ بِٱلْقُرْءَانِ مِن قَبْلِ أَن يُقْضَىٰٓ إِلَيْكَ وَحْيُهُۥ ۖ وَقُل رَّبِّ زِدْنِى عِلْمًا

١١٤ طه

يمكننا الآن التعرف على السنة الهجرية التي بدأت 17 عاما بعد وفاة الرسول عليه السلام وأفسدت حساب السنين والأشهر، لأن من فعل ذلك، لم يفهم ما هي حكمة الله ومعجزة القرآن. ولذلك ففي أي شيء يغاير القرآن، توجد إمكانية هدر معجزة من معجزات الله.

الْحَجُّ أَشْهُرٌ مَعْلُومَاتٌ فَمَن فَرَضَ فِيهِنَّ الْحَجَّ فَلَا رَفَثَ وَلَا فُسُوقَ وَلَا جِدَالَ فِي الْحَجِّ وَمَا تَفْعَلُوا مِنْ خَيْرٍ يَعْلَمْهُ اللَّهُ وَتَزَوَّدُوا فَإِنَّ خَيْرَ الزَّادِ التَّقْوَىٰ وَاتَّقُونِ يَا أُولِي الْأَلْبَابِ ﴿١١٧﴾

لكي يتسنى لجميع المسلمين الحج الله جعله أشهر وليس يوم واحد وفقط جزء بسيط من عامة المسلمين.

شديدي الثراء، و20 % و20 % من الأثرياء من الوسط والبقية من الفقراء. لو افتدى هؤلاء 50% بإطعام الفقراء لمدة شهر، أليست هذه هي الإنسانية؟ كما أن الصيام مفيد لهم إذا ما قرروا الصيام ولكن لا أحد يريد أن يتحدث عن العطاء، وهذا قمة الأنانية وشيء مغاير للصيام، الصيام ذكر قليلا ولكن العطاء والصدقة والعمل الحسن تكررت مرات عديدة.

هل شهر رمضان (بصيغته الحالية) عادلا بين الشعوب في جميع أنحاء العالم (إذا لم يتم تصحيح السنة الهجرية)؟ ما علينا سوى إلقاء نظرة على البيانات الخاصة بشروق وغياب الشمس في كل بلد لندرك كم أجحفنا في حق رمضان وخالفنا القرآن.

الحج

كيف لموسم الحج أن يأتي في الصيف؟ وتزهق الأنفس كل سنة من شدة الحر؟ بينما لو لم يغيروا التقويم، لكان الحج في شهر كانون الأول(ديسمبر) وهو من أفضل الشهور في مكة وألطفها طقسا بخلاف باقي دول العالم! لو علموا !!

وَكَذَٰلِكَ أَنزَلْنَٰهُ قُرْءَانًا عَرَبِيًّا وَصَرَّفْنَا فِيهِ مِنَ ٱلْوَعِيدِ لَعَلَّهُمْ يَتَّقُونَ أَوْ يُحْدِثُ لَهُمْ ذِكْرًا

أَيَّامًا مَّعْدُودَٰتٍ ۚ فَمَن كَانَ مِنكُم مَّرِيضًا أَوْ عَلَىٰ سَفَرٍ فَعِدَّةٌ مِّنْ أَيَّامٍ أُخَرَ ۚ وَعَلَى ٱلَّذِينَ يُطِيقُونَهُ فِدْيَةٌ طَعَامُ مِسْكِينٍ ۖ فَمَن تَطَوَّعَ خَيْرًا فَهُوَ خَيْرٌ لَّهُ ۚ وَأَن تَصُومُوا خَيْرٌ لَّكُمْ ۖ إِن كُنتُمْ تَعْلَمُونَ

١٨٤ البقرة

لقد حددت في هذه الآيات شروط الصيام بوضوح، فعلى الذين يطيقونه فدية إطعام مسكين. أما إذا أطعمت مسكينا وتطوعت للصيام، فهو خير لك لتنال منفعة الصيام. والفدية معروفة بنفس المعنى الذي افتدى الله به سيدنا إبراهيم ابنه بكبش. أي أن الفدية تحل محل المطلوب.

إنها ليست مشقة

لديك إذن خيارات، لأن الإسلام هو دين يسر وليس عسر، لذلك لا داعي أن تتلاعب بالدين، أو تظن أنه هناك ثغرة في هذا الدين الحنيف، حيث تختلق الأعذار كي لا تصوم (كقيادة السيارة لمسافة معينة ليسقط عنك التكليف، وهذا هراء لأنه ليس بالسفر المقصود في القرآن). دعنا نفترض أن عدد المسلمين في العالم 1.7 مليار شخص و10% من

وإحرامه عاما آخر كي لا يقاتل الفاسقون جبنا وكفرا، لأنه لا قتال في الأشهر الحرم. والكفر هنا في التغيير والتلاعب بقواعد التقييم الذي استخدمه العرب لسنين طويلة تعود إلى ما قبل الإسلام، وحتى أن محمد عليه السلام لم يغيره برغم نزول الآية الكريمة وهذا ما يؤكد ما نقول.

في الواقع، إن إلغاء التقويم كالتلاعب به، إذ لهما نفس النتيجة وكلاهما ينسف مبدأ المعجزة الإلهية. تغيير الأشهر ومواقعها يخالف القرآن. ويمكن تعديل هذا الخطأ بعملية حسابية سهلة وبسيطة بإضافة شهر قمري كل عامين وثمانية أشهر. ويمكن أن نحتسب رمضان لعدة سنين قادمة وأن يكون لدينا تقويم سنوي (روزنامة) حيث يتم احتساب كل شيء وليس فقط اعتماد السنة الهجرية لمعرفة رمضان. لقد علمنا الله الحساب وعدة الشهور وما زال المسلمون يختلفون فيما بينهم على شهر رمضان. لهذا ينظر الغرب إلينا باستغراب ويتعجبون من غباءنا.

يَـٰٓأَيُّهَا ٱلَّذِينَ ءَامَنُوا۟ كُتِبَ عَلَيْكُمُ ٱلصِّيَامُ كَمَا كُتِبَ عَلَى ٱلَّذِينَ مِن قَبْلِكُمْ لَعَلَّكُمْ تَتَّقُونَ

البقرة ١٨٣

يكتمل نمو هذه الحيوانات. ولكن كيف نكون منصفين ونتبع أمر الله بعدم الصيد إذا كنا نداور الأشهر الحرم على مدى السنين؟ وكيف الربيع ليس ربيعا؟ وذو الحجة يتداول أيضا! على مدى السنين؟ وماذا حصل لثرواتنا الحيوانية؟ أهذا ما أمر الرحمن؟

عندما اعتمد المسلمون السنة الهجرية وألغوا التقويم العربي الذي كان سائدا في عهد الرسول، كان مخالفة لأمر الله برغم النية الحسنة، لأنهم يجهلون، ولم يؤتوا من العلم ما أوتي محمد عليه السلام. ولو كان لديهم ما لدينا من علوم، لما فعلوها! لذلك فإن اتباع أوامر الله، حسب النص القرآني أمر لا يجب الاستهانة به.

إِنَّمَا ٱلنَّسِيٓءُ زِيَادَةٌ فِى ٱلْكُفْرِ ۖ يُضَلُّ بِهِ ٱلَّذِينَ كَفَرُوا۟ يُحِلُّونَهُۥ عَامًا وَيُحَرِّمُونَهُۥ عَامًا لِّيُوَاطِـُٔوا۟ عِدَّةَ مَا حَرَّمَ ٱللَّهُ فَيُحِلُّوا۟ مَا حَرَّمَ ٱللَّهُ ۚ زُيِّنَ لَهُمْ سُوٓءُ أَعْمَـٰلِهِمْ ۗ وَٱللَّهُ لَا يَهْدِى ٱلْقَوْمَ ٱلْكَـٰفِرِينَ

التوبة ٣٧

بكل بساطة، لقد ذكر الله التلاعب بشهر النسيء وهو شهر التقويم، والكفر في إحلاله عاما

11. •ذو القعدة: يترجم هذا الشهر حرفياً إلى" يوم الجلوس / الهدنة "لأن القتال توقف خلال هذا الشهر.

12. •ذو الحجة: يسمى هذا الشهر" شهر الحج " لأنه الشهر الذي تؤدى فيه فريضة الحج.

•الأشهر المقدسة

•هناك أربعة أشهر في التقويم الهجري تُعرف باسم "الأشهر الحرم "أو" الأشهر المقدسة "وهي: محرم، ورجب، وذو القعدة، وذو الحجة. وقد سميت على هذا النحو لأن الله حرم القتال والصيد خلال هذه الأشهر بالذات، إلا في الحالات التي يهاجم فيها فرد أو جماعة أولاً ويحتاج إلى القتال دفاعًا عن النفس:

تخصيص الشهور

لكي نكون منصفين للبيئة والحيوانات، حرم الله الصيد في أربعة أشهر حرم، (ليس فقط القتال) حيث تحتاج الحيوانات هذه الأشهر للتكاثر وإن كان شهر رجب ليس متواليا مع الأشهر الحرم الثلاثة الأخرى، ولكنه من الأشهر المهمة حيث

جفاف الأرض، ولهذا يطلق عليه أحيانًا اسم "جمادى الآخرة"أو الآخر، أي نهاية موسم الجفاف.

7. •رجب :هذا الشهر مشتق من كلمة "رجابه" التي تعني" الاحترام". فكلما رأى النبي محمد هلال رجب، كان ينطق بهذا الدعاء:" يا الله ! اجعل شهري رجب وشعبان مباركين لنا، ودعنا نبلغ شهر رمضان."

8. •شعبان :هذا الشهر يعني" مبعثر "لأنه يشير إلى الوقت من العام الذي تتشتت فيه القبائل العربية للعثور على المياه والمراعي الجديدة.

9. •رمضان :مشتق من أصل كلمة"رماد"التي تعني" الحرق"، في إشارة إلى الحر الشديد الذي اتسم به هذا الشهر. وبمعنى آخر من الرمضاء أول نزول المطر.

10. •شوال :اسم هذا الشهر يعني الحمل أو الرفع لأن إناث الإبل تحمل في هذا الوقت جنيناً جديداً من الإبل، وبالتالي يقل إنتاجها من اللبن.

2. •صفر :معنى" فارغ"، سمي هذا الشهر بهذا الاسم لأن العرب قبل الإسلام كانوا يغادرون منازلهم بحثًا عن الطعام خلال هذا الشهر. وتقول بعض المصادر إن هذا الاسم مشتق فعليًا من قيام العرب قبل الإسلام بمداهمة المنازل خلال هذه الفترة وتركها"فارغة."

3. •ربيع الأول :كلمة ربيع تعني الربيع. الأول يعني "الأول "، هذا الشهر يعني" الربيع الأول."

4. ربيع الثاني :يعني" الربيع الثاني "،ويشار إليه أحيانًا باسم ربيع الآخر أو" الربيع الأخير "لأنه يشير إلى نهاية فصل الربيع.

5. •جمادى الأول :كلمة جمادى تعني "جاف/جاف ."في زمن العرب الجاهليين، كانت الأرض تميل إلى الجفاف الشديد خلال هذا الشهر، إما بسبب الحرارة الشديدة أو بسبب تجمد مصادر المياه بسبب درجات الحرارة الباردة.

6. •جمادى الثاني :كان الذي المعنى نفس له وهذا عليه الشهر السابق، ولكنه يشير إلى انتهاء

النبوة ورمضان

دعونا الآن نعود إلى رمضان، فكيف عرف رجل من الصحراء عليه السلام هذه المعلومة، لكي يصوم نفس الشهر لعدة أعوام، إلى حدود وفاته. ولماذا حدد القرآن رمضان شهر الصيام؟ إنه يستحيل ألا يكون الأمر إلهيا. علينا إصلاح السنة الهجرية، وبعدها ستستقيم الأشهر تلقائيا، وإلا فإننا نتجاهل هذه المعجزة الإلهية ونكون قد غيرنا أهم شيء في الرسالة المحمدية.
وهل من إجابة على عدم تطابق أسماء الأشهر مع الأشهر الفعلية؟ وماذا عن شهر الحج؟

1. ●محرم :هو الشهر الأول في التقويم الهجري ويعني "ممنوع". جاء هذا الشهر لمنع العرب من القتال.

خلال شهر أيلول، يتساوى الليل والنهار في العالم كله، بفرق ساعة أو أقل أو أكثر، وذلك لأن الأرض والشمس يواجهان بعضهما البعض في نفس الخط. هذه عدالة الله للإنسان في الصوم في شهر رمضان. وللتأكد من صحة المعلومات، يمكنك مراجعة الموقع الالكتروني وابحث عن أي بلد تريد وستجد حكمة الله في اختيار رمضان من باقي الشهور   وأن رمضان يتوافق وشهر أيلول إلى أن تم تعديل السنة الهجرية وستعلم أنه هناك دول لا تغرب عنها الشمس لعدة أشهر. فماذا يفعلون؟ فكيف يصومون، وكلنا نعرف حكم الصيام من شروق الشمس إلى المغيب؟

https://www.sunrise-and-sunset.com

هذه المعلومات أصبحت متاحة   بعد التقدم العلمي الحاصل حاليا. وهي معلومات يستحيل أن يعرفها شخص قبل ما يزيد من 1500 عام مضى.
إذن، متى يحل شهر رمضان؟
يجب أن يتصادف حلول شهر رمضان في عدة مواقِ مع السابع من أيلول (سبتمبر)، ثم في السابع عشر منه في السنة التالية، ومن ثم في اليوم السابع والعشرين منه في السنة التي تليها، على أن يعود إلى السابع من أيلول (سبتمبر) في السنة التي تليها بعد إضافة شهر التقويم، وهكذا دواليك.

شهرة هي روشهاشناه ويوم كيبور، ''الأيام المقدسة العليا'' في اليهودية. رأس السنة اليهودية هو العام اليهودي الجديد، الذي يصادف حلول الاعتدال في أيلول(سبتمبر) (يتم احتساب روشهاشناه على أنه 163 يومًا بعد اليوم الأول من عيد الفصح (والذي يتم حسابه في حد ذاته من خلال الاعتدال في مارس). رنين البوق، وهو قرن كبش يستخدم كبوق لآلاف السنين في الطقوس اليهودية، يرحب بروشهاشناه. يوم كيبور، أقدس يوم في التقويم اليهودي، يصادف حوالي 10 أيام بعد رأس السنة. يوم الغفران هو يوم عطلة رسمي يُعرف باسم ''يوم الكفارة''. يتم الاحتفال به تقليديا من خلال صيام يوم كامل مع صلاة الاستغفار. وترتبط معظم الأحداث الثقافية التي لها علاقة بالاعتدال الربيعي في سبتمبر، بمهرجان الحصاد الخريفي، تشوسوك، الذي يتم الاحتفال به على مدى ثلاثة أيام في الكوريتين، وهو أحد أكثر المهرجانات الشعبية شهرة. يُطلق على تشوسوك أحيانًا اسم''عيد الشكر الكوري''، وهو احتفال بالعائلة والتراث الزراعي الغني بكوريا

لقد كان نوروز ولأكثر من 3000 عام عيدا،

تشمل عطلة النوروز شخصيات أسطورية (مثل آمونوروز، الملقب أحيانًا بـ" سانتا كلوز الإيراني")، (والتجمعات العائلية التقليدية، وعناصر" الخطيئة . "هفت ـ سينهي سبعة أطعمة رمزية مرتبطة بالنيروز، وكلها تبدأ بالحرف العربي أو الفارسي الخطيئة :سابزي) براعم ترمز إلى الولادة (سامانو) بودنغ حلو، يرمز إلى الثروة (سنجد) فواكه مجففة، شبيهة بالتمر، ترمز إلى الحب (الرائي) الثوم، يرمز إلى الصحة (السيب) التفاح، يرمز إلى الجمال (السماق) فاكهة السماق الأحمر، ترمز إلى لون شروق الشمس (والسركه) الخل يرمز إلى العمر والحكمة (خارج احتفالات العام الجديد، يتم الاحتفال بالاعتدال الربيعي لشهر مارس في الأعياد في جميع أنحاء العالم . يوم الاعتدال الربيعي هو يوم عطلة رسمية في اليابان . يبدأ عيد الفصح اليهودي ليلة اكتمال القمر بعد اعتدال مارس. ويتم احتساب تاريخ عيد الفصح، وهو أحد أهم الأعياد في التقويم المسيحي، باستخدام الاعتدال لشهر مارس. الاعتدال الشتوي لشهر سبتمبر :أقل من الأحداث التي تشير إلى الاعتدال لشهر سبتمبر .ولعل أكثرها

رقيقة جدًا، بعرض كيلومتر واحد فقط. خلال اعتدال زحل، (الحلقات وخط استواء زحل تصطف بشكل مثالي مع الشمس) تكشف الصور المأخوذة من المنظور الشمسي عن الحلقات على أنها خطر للغاية. ثقافة الاعتدال هي مثل الانقلابات الشتوية، إذ تعتبر الاعتدال علامات تاريخية للتغير الموسمي. الاعتدال الربيعي، بشكل غير رسمي هو مناسبة فصل الربيع، يُنظر إليه تقليديًا على أنه وقت ولادة جديدة وتجديد. لهذا السبب، احتفلت العديد من الثقافات بالاعتدال الربيعي لشهر مارس باعتباره اليوم الأول من العام الجديد. بدأ التقويم البابلي القديم عند اكتمال القمر الأول بعد اعتدال مارس، واليوم، تستمر العديد من التقويمات الثقافية والدينية في الاحتفال بالعام الجديد في الربيع. ربما يكون عيد النوروز هو أكثر أيام الاعتدال انتشارًا وشهرة، وهو اليوم الأول من السنة في التقويم الفارسي. لقد كان نوروز ولأكثر من 3000 عام، عيدًا دينيًا في الزرادشتية، لكنه اليوم يتميز بالاحتفالات العلمانية في جميع أنحاء أوروبا الشرقية وآسيا الوسطى.

الشمس بعد الاعتدال الربيعي في مارس وقبل الاعتدال الربيعي في سبتمبر. أما أثناء الاعتدال، فتكون الشمس بمحاذاة مباشرة خلف الأقمار الصناعية في مدار ثابت بالنسبة للأرض عند خط الاستواء. تقع الأقمار الصناعية مباشرة فوق النقطة تحت الشمسية، وهي مغمورة بالإشعاع الشمسي المباشر، يمكن أن يتداخل هذا الإشعاع الشمسي مع الأقمار الصناعية وحتى يمنعها من إرسال الإشارات. تدور العديد من أقمار الاتصالات حول خط الاستواء، وقد يعاني المستهلكون من بطء اتصالات الإنترنت، أو الراديو الثابت، أو شاشات التلفزيون المجمدة أثناء فترات انقطاع الشمس الاعتدال. يتم تحديد توقيت الاعتدال من خلال الخصائص المدارية والميل المحوري للكوكب. عملاق الغاز زحل، على سبيل المثال، تكون الاعتدال مثيرة بشكل خاص. حوالي 15 عامًا تفصل بين الاعتدال على زحل، وتستمر حوالي أربعة أيام. ويدور نظام حلقات زحل المذهل في نفس مستوى خط استواء الكوكب، وعلى الرغم من أن الحلقات تمتد لآلاف الكيلومترات في الفضاء، إلا أنها في الواقع

النهار أطول بحوالي ثماني دقائق من الليل عند خط عرض30 درجة تقريبًا هذا ويكون الانكسار الجوي في المناطق القطبية أكثر إثارة في القطب الشمالي والقارة القطبية الجنوبية، حيث يمتد ضوء النهار حوالي 12ساعة و16 دقيقة. وبهذه الطريقة، فإن الاعتدال في المناطق القطبية تشير إلى التغيير البطيء من "شمس منتصف الليل" إلى "الليل القطبي. "يطلق اسم شمس منتصف الليل" على الظاهرة التي لا تنخفض فيها الشمس أبدًا تحت الأفق، مما يبقي المنطقة مغمورة في ضوء الشمس 24 ساعة في اليوم. كما تسمى الظاهرة المعاكسة بـ "الليلة قطبية" وهي فترة لا تشرق فيها الشمس أبدًا. مما يجعل المنطقة مظلمة لمدة 24 ساعة. الفترات: الاضطرابات الكهربية عرضة للاضطرابات في الأيام التي تسبق الاعتدال وبعده. "يوصف هذا الاضطراب "بانقطاع الشمس" في النصف الشمالي من الكرة الأرضية، تحدث انقطاعات لأشعة

على الرغم من أن الاعتدال قريب من هذه الظاهرة كما يحدث على الأرض، إلا أنه حتى أثناء الاعتدال، لا يتساوى النهار والليل تمامًا. يرجع هذا إلى حد كبير إلى الانكسار في الغلاف الجوي، حيث يصف الانكسار في الغلاف الجوي الطريقة التي يبدو أن الضوء ينحني بها أو ينحرف عن خط مستقيم أثناء مروره عبر الغلاف الجوي للأرض. وينتج الانكسار عن زيادة كثافة الهواء، مما يقلل من سرعة الضوء عبره وبسببه يمكننا رؤية الشمس قبل دقائق من شروقها وغروبها. المناطق الاستوائية: يتلقى خط الاستواء، عند خط عرض 0 درجة، أقصى كثافة لأشعة الشمس طوال العام. نتيجة لذلك، تتعرض المناطق القريبة من خط الاستواء للأرض لضوء شمس ثابت نسبيًا وتباين قليل في الاعتدال. عادةً ما يكون للاعتدال والمواسم السماوية تأثير أقل من الأنماط التي يحركها المناخ مثل هطول الأمطار (مواسم الأمطار والمواسم الجافة) ويزيد التباين الموسمي مع خطوط العرض كما يزيد الانكسار الجوي أيضًا من التباين في طول" الاعتدال "بين النهار والليل. ويكون

خط الاستواء. وقبل الاعتدال وبعده، تهاجر النقطة الفرعية شمالاً أو جنوباً. أما بعد الاعتدال، في مارس، فتهاجر النقطة الفرعية شمالًا، حيث يميل نصف الكرة الشمالي نحو الشمس. في حوالي 21 يونيو، تضرب النقطة الفرعية مدار السرطان (23.5 درجة شم (، وهذا هو الانقلاب الشمسي لشهر يونيو، وبعد ذلك تبدأ النقطة الفرعية في الهجرة جنوبًا.بعد الاعتدال الربيعي لشهر سبتمبر، تستمر النقطة الفرعية في التحرك جنوبًا، حيث يميل نصف الكرة الجنوبي نحو الشمس. في حوالي 21 ديسمبر، تضرب النقطة تحت الشمسية مدار الجدي (23.5درجة جنوبا. هذا هو الانقلاب الشمسي لشهر ديسمبر. كما يوحي اسمها، يشير الاعتدال إلى نصفي الكرة الأرضية المضيئين بشكل متساوٍ، حيث يقسم الفاصل الشمسي الأرض بالتساوي من الشمال إلى الجنوب) فاصل الطاقة الشمسية هو الخط المظلل الذي يشير إلى ضوء النهار وضوء الشمس على الكرة الأرضية. (يشير الاعتدال الحقيقي

إلى 12 ساعة من النهار والليل

الاعتدال هو حدث تمر فيه النقطة الفرعية للكوكب عبر خط الاستواء. والاعتدال هي الوقت الوحيد الذي يتساوى فيه طول النهار والليل في نصفي الكرة الأرضية الشمالي والجنوبي، هناك اعتدالان كل عام على الأرض: واحد في حوالي 21 مارس والآخر حوالي 22 سبتمبر. في بعض الأحيان، يُطلق عليه الاعتدال الربيعي"(الاعتدال الربيعي) و "(") الاعتدال الخريفي) على الرغم من اختلافهما. إن الاعتدال الربيعي في نصف الكرة الشمالي والاعتدال الخريفي في الجنوب. يصف الانحراف الشمس بخط عرض الأرض حيث تكون الشمس مباشرة في الظهيرة. (خط الاستواء، بالطبع، هو خط عرض 0 درجة.) لذا، فإن الاعتدال هي الأوقات الوحيدة في السنة عندما تكون النقطة الفرعية مباشرة على خط الاستواء. النقطة الفرعية هي منطقة تسطع فيها أشعة الشمس بشكل عامودي على سطح الأرض-وهي زاوية قائمة. غير أنه أثناء فترة الاعتدال، لا يميل محور الأرض البالغ 23.5 درجة نحو الشمس أو بعيدًا عنها: يكون المركز المدرك لقرص الشمس في نفس مستوى

السنة العربية مثل السنة الميلادية، حيث يتم إضافة يوم إلى شهر شباط في السنة الميلادية كل أربع سنوات وتدعى سنة كبيسة وكالسنة اليهودية وكالسنة الصينية أيضا تقوم. كما تتم إضافة شهر قمري في السنة العربية كل سنتين وثمانية أشهر، لكي تعود السنة للاستقامة؛ بحيث كان العرب يتبعون السنة القمرية. لماذا يأتي ربيع الأول وربيع الثاني في الشتاء القارس؟ إنه ليتناقض مع تسميته.

إكوينوكس

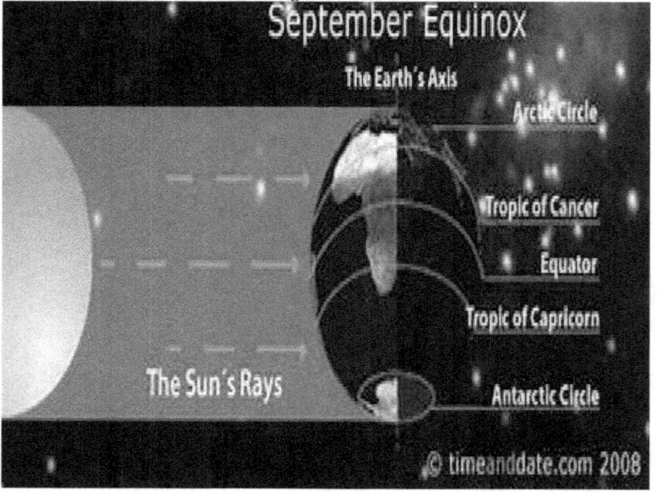

تحدث ظاهرة الاعتدال في 23 سبتمبر

بن ياسر (570 م) باسم "عام الفيل". كما سميت السنة الأولى للهجرة (622-23م) سميت بـ" إذن [4]السفر "في هذا التقويم[3] .

بعد 17سنة من الهجرة، [5] [3]أدت شكوى تقدم بها أبو موسى الأشعري دفعت بالخليفة عمر إلى إلغاء العمل بالسنوات المذكورة وتأسيس عصر تقويمي جديد . اختار عمر الهجرة، وهجرة محمد و 70مسلمًا من مكة إلى المدينة، كفترة للتقويم الإسلامي الجديد [6] . وينسب هذا التقليد لعثمان بالاقتراح الناجح.

ببساطة، تم ترتيب السنة باستمرار ترتيب الأشهر التي تم وضعها بالفعل، بدءًا من شهر محرم، ثم تم اعتماد هذا التقويم من قبل عمر.

كان النبي عليه الصلاة والسلام يصوم رمضان في نفس الشهر كل عام حسب التقويم العربي، وبقي حتى وفاته يصوم نفس الشهر. فمن غير السنة العربية؟ وألغى التقويم العربي؟ ولماذا غير بعد الرسول عليه السلام؟ هل يعد من قام بهذا التغيير أهدى من الرسول عليه السلام؟ أسئلة يجب أن نطرحها لأن تغيير شيء بسيط أضاع المعجزة التي نحن بصدد التكلم عنها!

السنة. وبالتالي، فإن يوم رأس السنة الجديدة يحدث قبل عشرة أيام من كل عام بالنسبة للتقويم الغريغوري. يتوافق عام 2022مع السنوات الإسلامية 1443- 1444 ويوافق عام 1443هـ الموافق 2022 - 2021 في العصر العام.[أ]

التعريف] عدل]

انظر أيضا التقويم القمري والتقويم الشمسي:

يُحسب العصر الهجري وفقًا للتقويم القمري الإسلامي، وعصره (السنة الأولى) هو عام هجرة محمد، ويبدأ في اليوم الأول من شهر محرم (ما يعادل تاريخ التقويم اليولياني في 19أبريل 622م[2]).

تاريخ الهجرة نفسه لم يشكل السنة الهجرية الجديدة. بدلاً من ذلك، يستمر النظام في الترتيب السابق للأشهر، مع حدوث الهجرة في اليوم الثامن من ربيع الأول، بعد 66 يومًا من السنة الأولى.

بحلول عصر محمد، كان هناك بالفعل تقويم قمري وبالمثل، استخدمت سنوات .عربي له أشهر محددة على سبيل [3] :التقويم أسماء تقليدية بدلاً من الأرقام المثال، عُرِفت سنة ميلاد محمد وعمار

السنة الهجريّة

السنة الهجريّة (العربية :سَنة هِجْريّة) أو العصر (التقويم الهجري في التقويم الهجري) هو العصر المستخدم في التقويم القمري الإسلامي. يبدأ إحصاءه من السنة الهجرية الجديدة التي هاجر فيها محمد وأتباعه من مكة إلى يثرب (المدينة المنورة الآن). هذا الحدث، المعروف باسم الهجرة، يتم الاحتفال به في الإسلام لدوره في تأسيس أو لمجتمع مسلم (الأمة).

في الغرب، يُشار إلى هذا العصر على أنه (AHباللاتينية / ˈænoʊ Anno Hegirae : / ˈhɛdʒɪriː، في عام الهجرة (بالتوازي مع العصر المسيحي (AD)، والعصر العام (CE)واليهودي (AM)ويمكن أيضًا وضعها قبل التاريخ أو بعده. في البلدان ذات الغالبية المسلمة، يتم أيضًا اختصارها بشكل شائع (H هـ Hijra)من اختصارها العربي. (السنوات السابقة للهجرة الأولى تُحسب باللغة الإنجليزية على أنها " (" BHقبل الهجرة ("، والتي يجب أن تتبع التاريخ[1] .

تتكون السنة في التقويم القمري الإسلامي من اثني عشر شهرًا قمريًا ولها فقط355 أو 354يوما في

Fasting times across the world

Tuesday, April 13, 2021

Country	Hours of Fasting	
Ushuaia, Argentina	12.23	
Santiago, Chile	12.41	
Rio de Janeiro, Brazil	12.51	
Lima, Peru	13.01	
Dar Es Salam, Tanzania	13.08	
Manilla, Philipines	13.39	
Sanaa, Yemen	13.47	
Hyderabad, India	13.48	
Miami, USA	13.49	
Kerala, India	13.56	
e Saudi Arabia	14.02	
Muscat, Oman	14.02	
Dubai, United Arab Emirates	14.05	
Cairo, Egypt	14.22	
Jersualem, Palestine	14.23	
Islamabad, Pakistan	14.29	
Delhi, India	14.33	
New York, USA	14.34	
Los Angeles, USA	14.36	
Baghdad, Iraq	14.36	
Beirut, Lebanon	14.38	
Tehran, Iran	14.38	
Athens, Greece	14.42	
Toronto, Canada	14.47	
Rome, Italy	14.58	
Paris, France	15.18	
London, England	15.21	
Edinburgh, Scottland	15.43	
Copenhagen, Denmark	16.02	
Moscow, Russia	16.11	
Berlin, Germany	16.15	
Lulea, Swden	16.52	
Anchorage, Alaska	16.57	
Oslo, Norway	17.18	
Helsinki, Finnland	17.19	
Fairbanks, Alaska	17.20	
Stockholm, Sweden	17.24	
Reykjavík, Iceland	17.39	
Svalbard, Iceland	17.51	
Murmansk, Russia	17.55	

هل توقيت المسلمين
للصيام صحيح؟؟
لماذا حدد الله رمضان
للصيام؟؟

قال الله عز وجل أن أمما أخرى لم تكن على الفلك، وأخيرا، فإن الرسالة الأهم هي أن الإسلام ليس دين عنف كما يرغبون في إظهاره، وقد يقدم البعض كحجة بأن القرآن شجع على القتال. دعونا نفحص ما أتى به القرآن، ألا وهو التشجيع على الدفاع عن النفس وعلى حرية المعتقد، ولكن ليس لقتل الناس بغير حق ولو كانوا على دين غير دينك. وللأسف شرّع المسلمون لأنفسهم قتل إخوانهم المسلمين وهو إجرام، وهم ليسوا بمسلمين. لقد أضرت أعمالهم بالصورة الحقيقية للإسلام. كما أن التاريخ شجع على إظهار المسلمين كأنهم همجيين، غير آبه بأنهم بعيدين كل البعد عن الإسلام.

وَقَٰتِلُواْ فِى سَبِيلِ ٱللَّهِ ٱلَّذِينَ يُقَٰتِلُونَكُمْ وَلَا تَعْتَدُوٓاْ ۚ إِنَّ ٱللَّهَ لَا يُحِبُّ ٱلْمُعْتَدِينَ

١٩٠ البقرة

ٱلشَّهْرُ ٱلْحَرَامُ بِٱلشَّهْرِ ٱلْحَرَامِ وَٱلْحُرُمَٰتُ قِصَاصٌ فَمَنِ ٱعْتَدَىٰ عَلَيْكُمْ فَٱعْتَدُواْ عَلَيْهِ بِمِثْلِ مَا ٱعْتَدَىٰ عَلَيْكُمْ ۚ وَٱتَّقُواْ ٱللَّهَ وَٱعْلَمُوٓاْ أَنَّ ٱللَّهَ مَعَ ٱلْمُتَّقِينَ

١٩٤ البقرة

العالمين، وقد كان الفلك الذي بناه نوح عليه السلام، مجرد ألواح خشبية متصلة ببعضها، وكافية لنقل نوح عليه السلام وأهله والمؤمنين وما آمن معه إلا قليل، وأن الحيوانات التي كان يحملها معه هي الحيوانات الأليفة فقط التي يحتاجها ليعيش منها ومن معه.

وَحَمَلْنَاهُ عَلَىٰ ذَاتِ أَلْوَاحٍ وَدُسُرٍ

١٣ القمر

حَتَّىٰ إِذَا جَآءَ أَمْرُنَا وَفَارَ ٱلتَّنُّورُ قُلْنَا ٱحْمِلْ فِيهَا مِن كُلٍّ زَوْجَيْنِ ٱثْنَيْنِ وَأَهْلَكَ إِلَّا مَن سَبَقَ عَلَيْهِ ٱلْقَوْلُ وَمَنْ ءَامَنَ ۚ وَمَآ ءَامَنَ مَعَهُۥٓ إِلَّا قَلِيلٌ

٤٠ هود

قِيلَ يَٰنُوحُ ٱهْبِطْ بِسَلَٰمٍ مِّنَّا وَبَرَكَٰتٍ عَلَيْكَ وَعَلَىٰٓ أُمَمٍ مِّمَّن مَّعَكَ ۚ وَأُمَمٌ سَنُمَتِّعُهُمْ ثُمَّ يَمَسُّهُم مِّنَّا عَذَابٌ أَلِيمٌ

٤٨ هود

۞ وَٱتْلُ عَلَيْهِمْ نَبَأَ نُوحٍ إِذْ قَالَ لِقَوْمِهِۦ يَٰقَوْمِ إِن كَانَ كَبُرَ عَلَيْكُم مَّقَامِى وَتَذْكِيرِى بِـَٔايَٰتِ ٱللَّهِ فَعَلَى ٱللَّهِ تَوَكَّلْتُ فَأَجْمِعُوٓا۟ أَمْرَكُمْ وَشُرَكَآءَكُمْ ثُمَّ لَا يَكُنْ أَمْرُكُمْ عَلَيْكُمْ غُمَّةً ثُمَّ ٱقْضُوٓا۟ إِلَىَّ وَلَا تُنظِرُونِ. يونس ٧١

يتطابق الحديث مع القرآن، ولكن إذا أتى الحديث بشيء مغاير لما قاله الله عز وجل، فإنه مجرد هراء وملفق ربما سيجادل البعض: لماذا ينتظر المسلمون الغرب حتى يكتشف شيئا وينسبوه للقرآن؟ الجواب بسيط: بأن المسلمين كادوا ليكتشفوه قبل الغرب لولا تغيير مسارهم وابتعادهم عن كتاب الله وتعلقهم بأحاديث علماء السلاطين. المشكلة ليست في الغرب، وإنما في أنفسنا. ورغم ذلك، فإن هذا لا يغير الحقيقة بأن القرآن كتاب معرفة وليس قصة خيالية.

أَمْ تَحْسَبُ أَنَّ أَكْثَرَهُمْ يَسْمَعُونَ أَوْ يَعْقِلُونَ ۚ إِنْ هُمْ إِلَّا كَالْأَنْعَامِ ۖ بَلْ هُمْ أَضَلُّ سَبِيلًا

٤٤ الفرقان

نوح عليه السلام

إحدى القصص التي ألقى القرآن الضوء عليها هي قصة نوح عليه السلام، حيث يعتقد الجميع بأن الكرة الأرضية قد غمرت كليا بالماء وأن سفينة نوح حملت من كل الحيوانات زوج، وهذا غير علمي وغير منطقي. وما حدث فعلا، هو أن الطوفان قد حصل في منطقة معينة وقد تكون بين جبال تركيا والعراق. حدث ذلك في منطقة فقط وليس في الكرة الأرضية كلها. حيث أن نوح أرسل إلى قومه فقط وليس إلى

هل هي صدفة، أنه في العصر العباسي قرر البخاري جمع الأحاديث، بعد 194 عاما على وفاة الرسول؟ لماذا؟ لم يفكر المسلمون طيلة هذه السنين في الأحاديث، بل عرفوا دينهم ونشطوا في كل شيء، وفجأة أصبح الدين غير مفهوم بدون البخاري ومسلم! لا أدري إذا كان البخاري قد تكلم اللغة العربية أصلا. ولماذا كل الأحاديث متناقلة عن فلان وعن فلان إلى أن ينتهي الأمر بأني سمعت رسول الله يقول! وكأن الرسول همس بأذن هذا الشخص دوننا عن الأمة. وأنا هنا لا أقصد التقليل من شأن أي أحد، ولكن حتى البخاري ومسلم يمكن أن تنسب لهما أحاديث. مع كل الاحترام للمسلمين الذين يهتمون بصدق حمل الرسالة، كل ما أقول لكم هو أنه لقد تفرق الإسلام إلى أحزاب وطوائف وأقوام، حيث كان من السهل نشر البدع ودس الضلال، حتى أن المسلمين قاتلوا المسلمين بحروب أشد ضراوة من مقاتلة الكفار أنفسهم (إلى درجة قتل حفيد رسول الله بأبشع الطرق والمسلمون مخدرون خائفين مذعنين للسلاطين). كما أن الغزاة قد غزوا البلاد الإسلامية وفرضوا أشياء لا تمت للدين بصلة. لذا، يجب أن

أكبر مدينة في العالم في ذلك الوقت، حيث كان العلماء المسلمون والمثقفون من مختلف أنحاء العالم مع خلفيات ثقافية مختلفة يعملون لجمع وترجمة كل المعارف الكلاسيكية المعروفة في العالم إلى الآرامية والعربية. [4]

يقال إن هذه الفترة انتهت بانهيار الخلافة العباسية بسبب الغزوات المغولية وحصار بغداد عام 1258 [5]. يؤرخ عدد قليل من العلماء نهاية العصر الذهبي حوالي عام 1350 بالارتباط مع عصر النهضة التيموري، [6] [7] في حين أن العديد من المؤرخين والعلماء المعاصرين يضعون نهاية العصر الذهبي الإسلامي في أواخر القرن الخامس عشر حتى القرن السادس عشر بالاجتماع مع إمبراطوريات البارود الإسلامية [1] [2] [3] (فترة الإسلام في العصور الوسطى متشابهة جدًا إن لم تكن متشابهة، حيث حددها مصدر واحد بأنها 1300-900 م.) [8]

كثر العلماء في جميع المجالات، حتى تدخل رجال الدين مستندين إلى أحاديث موضوعة وأصبحوا يتهمون العلماء بالزندقة والكفر وإحراق الكتب العلمية، فقط لخدمة سلاطينهم. وقد ساهموا في انهيار الإسلام ونشر الجهل في مجتمعات المسلمين، فأصبحوا أشر من الشياطين. قسمت الشعوب إلى دويلات وأحزاب وبدأ تأليف الأحاديث حسب المصالح الشخصية. كما تم تدمير كل ما وصل إليه رواد المسلمين من علم. للأسف، نجحوا في هذا، فقط لأننا ابتعدنا عن كتاب الله وأصبح القرآن جامع الغبار في كل منزل، وأصبحت الشعوب تتبع علماء السلاطين والمعممين الذين غرتهم الدنيا فلا يريدون الهداية.

العصر الذهبي الإسلامي

كان العصر الذهبي الإسلامي فترة ازدهار ثقافي واقتصادي وعلمي في تاريخ الإسلام، ويرجع تاريخه تقليديًا إلى القرن الثامن إلى القرن الرابع عشر [2] [1] من المفهوم تقليديًا أن هذه الفترة قد بدأت في عهد الخليفة العباسي هارون الرشيد[3] (786إلى809)مع افتتاح بيت الحكمة في بغداد ،

ʿAbdAllāh al-Lawātī al-Ṭanjī ibn
Baṭṭūṭah, /ˌɪbənbætˈtuːtɑː/; 24
February 1304 – 1368/1369) أ [المعروف،
باسم ابن بطوطة، كان بربريًا مغربيًا [3] [2] [1]
باحثًا ومستكشفًا سافر كثيرًا في أراضي الأفرو-
أوراسيا،إلى حد كبير في العالم الإسلامي، وسافر أكثر
من أي مستكشف آخر في تاريخ ما قبل الحديث، بلغ
إجمالي ما قطعه حوالي 117000
كم(73000ميل)،متجاوزًا تشنغ هي بحوالي 50000
كم(31000ميل)وماركو بولو بمقدار 24000 كم
(15000ميل). على مدى ثلاثين عامًا، زار ابن بطوطة
معظم جنوب أوراسيا، بما في ذلك آسيا الوسطى
وجنوب شرق آسيا وجنوب آسيا والصين وشبه
الجزيرة الأيبيرية .قرب نهاية حياته، أملى رواية
أسفاره بعنوان" هدية لمن يتأملون في عجائب المدن
وعجائب السفر"، ولكن يُعرف باسم الرحلة.

يُعتقد أنه كتبها، نجا منها حوالي240 ،بما في ذلك 150. في الفلسفة و 40 في الطب

حسن بن الهيثم، لاتيني باسم الحزن [10] (/ علي الحزن/ ؛ [11] الاسم الكامل أبو علي الحسن بن الحسن بن الهيثم أبو علي، الحسن بن الحسن بن الهيثم؛ حوالي 965 - ج. 1040)،عالم رياضيات وفلك وفيزيائي عربي من العصر الذهبي الإسلامي. [12] [13] [14] [15] [16] يُشار إليه بـ "أبو البصريات الحديثة" ، [17] [18] وقد قدم مساهمات كبيرة في مبادئ البصريات والإدراك البصري على وجه الخصوص. كان أكثر أعماله تأثيراً بعنوان "كتاب المناصير" (بالعربية: كتاب المناظر، "كتاب البصريات")، الذي كتب خلال الفترة 1011-1021، والذي نجا من طبعة لاتينية. [19] وهو متعدد المواهب، كما كتب في الفلسفة واللاهوت والطب

Abu Abdullah Muhammad ibn.

Battutah

أَبُو عَبْدُ اللهِ مُحَمَّدُ بْنُ عَبْدِ اللهِ اللَّوَاتِي :Arabic)
romanized: ,الطَّنْجِي بْنُ بَطُّوطَةَ

Abū ʿAbdAllāhMuḥammad ibn

الإسلام دين المعرفة، وعندما كانت أوروبا تغرق في العصور المظلمة، كان العالم الإسلامي يعيش عصورًا ذهبية، حيث حصلت كل الاختراعات وتطورت كل العلوم.

محمد بن موسى الخوارزمي] الحاشية [1بالفارسية: محمد بن موسى خوارزمى، بالحروف اللاتينية: محمد بن موسى خوارزمي، حوالي (850 - 780) ،أو الخوارزمي كان موسيقيًا فارسيًا من خوارزم، [6] 7] [8] [9] [10] [11] الذي أنتج أعمالًا ذات تأثير كبير في الرياضيات وعلم الفلك والجغرافيا. حوالي عام 820 م،تم تعيينه عالم فلك ورئيساً لمكتبة بيت الحكمة في بغداد. [12]: 14

ابن سينا (الفارسية: ابن سينا؛ 980 - يونيو 1037 م(،المعروف في الغرب باسم ابن سينا /) كان موسيقيًا فارسيًا [4]   (/ -ɪvːɑˌ ، enɜsˌ ɪvæˌ يُعتبر أحد أهم الأطباء وعلماء الفلك [6] [7] [8] [6] [7] [8] وصف سجاد رضوي ابن سينا بأنه" الفيلسوف الأكثر تأثيرًا في عصر ما قبل الحداثة". كان فيلسوفًا مسلمًا متجولًا متأثرًا بالفلسفة الأرسطية اليونانية. من بين 450عملاً

بمجرد أن تبني قاعدة على ما قاله الإنسان، والذي قد يكون مغايرا لما قاله الله أو تتجاهل قول الله، بإرساء قول الإنسان، يصبح خطف الدين أمرا سهلا. ويعتبر الحديث الذي هو مغاير لما قاله الله أهم الأمثلة على ما أقول. فهناك شريحة كبيرة من الناس يؤمنون بأحاديث ولو كانت مغايرة للقرآن وحتى لو أريتهم ما قال الله، لولوا وجوههم وحاربوك إلى درجة إهدار دمك. حجتهم في ذلك بأن أحاديث الرسول علمه إياها الله. وهو صحيح، فقد علم الله القرآن للرسول، ولكن الأحاديث المتضاربة عن القرآن شيء آخر. فكيف سيقول الله شيئا في القرآن ويقول الرسول عكسه في الأحاديث؟ ولكن من المستحيل تزوير القرآن ولكن من السهل أن تنسب الروايات للرسول، مع العلم أن التداول بالأحاديث تم بعد الرسول بـ 200 عام. لماذا؟ لكي يتم إدخال ما لم ينزل الله به من سلطان أو ليخدم حكام الدنيا من قبل علماء السلاطين. فمن الواجب إقفال هذا الباب والتحصين بقلعتنا القرآنية الغير قابلة للتدمير.

معرفة

هناك ترتيبًا للبشرية جمعاء. قال الله: انزلوا منها جميعًا، وعندما يأتي إليكم الهدى مني(الله) فمن اتبع هداي لن يكون هناك خوف عليهم ولن يحزنوا. هنا تشير الآية إلى الجنة حيث نزل آدم وزوجه من الجنة. قد يعني أن الجنة التي عاش فيها آدم وحواء قبل أن يرتكبان خطأهما كانت على الأرض، وتقع على ارتفاع فوق مستوى سطح البحر. يتناسب هذا بشكل جيد مع خصائص جبل سينين الذي يُطلق عليه الآن جبل الخنق في إثيوبيا وإفريقيا، ويصادف أيضًا أنه المكان الذي تطور فيه البشر لأول مرة. باختصار، يؤكد القرآن الكريم ببساطة الجذور الإفريقية لشجرة العائلة البشرية. قبل وقت طويل من استخدام داروين للتطور كآلية لشرح التنوع وتطور أنواع البشر، تناول القرآن الكريم نفسه ظهور التنوع وأصول الحياة على الأرض.

شرح هذا المقال جيدًا بواسطة كلير فوستر كلير فوستر تتحدث عن الإسلام

https://www.youtube.com/watch؟

في مصر، والذي اكتشفناه مؤخرًا بفضل خرائط الأقمار الصناعية؟ باختصار لم يكن يعرف. فأين هذا الجبل الغامض الذي اتضح أنه ذو أهمية كبيرة؟ يقع جبل سينين في مدينة أمهري لا يعرفها معظم الإثيوبيين، ويطلق عليه الآن جبل الخنق ويمكن العثور عليه في المرتفعات الإثيوبية الواقعة في ولاية أمهرة الوطنية الإقليمية، منطقة شرق جوجام شمال غرب مدينة ديبريماركوس. تنتمي المنطقة إدارياً إلى منطقتي فيريداسسنان ومشاكال حيث توجد سينين وتقع على بعد حوالي330 كم شمال العاصمة أديس أبابا عن طريق البر. كما تقع هذه المرتفعات على خط عرض 2،386 متر فوق مستوى سطح البحر. تنبع العديد من أنهار أعالي النيل من هذه السلسلة الجبلية البالغ مجموعها 59 نهراً والعديد من الينابيع التي تم تحديدها في مجمعات المياه العليا لجبل الاختناق. من المعروف أن مناخ منطقة جبل الخنق يتسم بالدفء بين شهري فبراير ومايو وقد يبلغ متوسط درجة الحرارة 17.80 درجة مئوية، بينما يصل متوسط درجة الحرارة الشهرية خلال أبرد الشهور بين يونيو وأغسطس إلى 15.60 درجة مئوية. يخبرنا الله في الفصل 2، الآية 38 من القرآن الكريم أن

إفريقيا حوالي 80 مليون سنة، وبالزيتون الذي عاش من شجرة أسلافها المشتركة قبل حوالي 1.5 مليون سنة وبجبل سينين الموجود في إثيوبيا ويسمى الآن جبل الخنق. وأخيراً، أقسم بمكة أرض الإسلام، أن الله خلق الإنسان في أفضل شكل(تقويم). كلمة تقويم في اللغة العربية تعني نصبها، برفعها ووضعها في وضع قائم أو رأسي. ويقول الله بعد ذلك نعود بالإنسان إلى أدنى مستوى. والآن، يبحث العلماء عن أسلافنا في صحراء إئيوبيا البعيدة وهو ما يحدث ليس مصادفة. لتكون أدنى نقطة في إثيوبيا هي الأدنى في إفريقيا وأدنى نقطة على هذا الكوكب. هكذا يلخص فصل موجز من ثمانية مقاطع مقابل ملايين السنين من التطور البشري في كتاب كشفه الله قبل 1400 عام. كيف يمكن للنبي محمد أن يعرف عن الصلة بين خلق الإنسان بشكل منتصب وملايين السنين من التطور الذي حدث بين ظهور التين والزيتون، وكيف يمكن أن يعلم عن الارتباط بين خلق الإنسان في جبل إفريقي أمهري منتصب في إئيوبيا؟ أو حتى عن موقع جبل سينين الذي تمت ترجمته بشكل خاطئ لسنوات على أنه جبل سيناء

هذا هو المثال الأكثر تطرفًا في البشر الذي يمكنك أن تجده. كما قال راسموس نيلسن، عالم الأحياء التطوري في جامعة كاليفورنيا في بيركلي، بتكيف البشر مع البيئات الجبلية تمامًا كما تنبأ تشارلز داروين. وكشفت مقالة بيبيسينيوز في مارس 2015 أن فريقا للبحث بقيادة البروفيسور برايان فيلمور من جامعة نيفادا في لاس فيغاس، قد اكتشف ما وصفوه بأنه أهم تحول في التطور البشري هذا.

هذا هو الانتقال من ساكن الشجرة إلى المشاة المنتصبة، حدث هذا الانتقال واكتشف في إثيوبيا منذ مليون سنة، مما أدى إلى ظهور الإنسان المنتصب أو الرجل المستقيم الذي كان أول مخلوق يقف منتصبًا تمامًا. فما علاقة النتائج التي ذكرت في كل هذه المقالات بهذا الفصل القصير من القرآن الذي ذكرناه ببساطة؟ يشير القرآن الكريم إلى إفريقيا، ويخبرنا أن تاريخ تطور الرجل المستقيم بدأ مع تطور الرئيسيات قبل 80 مليون سنة على الأقل، وأدى إلى رجل مستقيم قبل مليون ونصف المليون سنة على الأقل. كيف يفعل القرآن الكريم هذا، بأن الله أقسم بالتين الذي نما لأول مرة في

نظرية تشير إلى أن أيدينا تطورت كأدوات لمعالجة التين الناعم، وبالتالي الحلو والغني بالطاقة، بينما استفاد البشر الأوائل من بيولوجيا التين التي أتقنتها أحفادهم. وأين بالضبط تنمو شجرة التين العالمية في أو بالقرب من القرن FicusVastea المسماة الإفريقي؟ وهي مستوطنة في المقام الأول في إثيوبيا. والآن إلى الزيتون الذي سميت شجرته شجرة الحياة. وقد أوضح ذلك الدكتور بيسنارد من المركز الوطني الفرنسي للبحث العلمي، في مقال نشره على موقع هيئات الإذاعة الأسترالية في السابع من فبراير.2013 وقد خلص باحثو المركز المذكور إلى أن ثلاثة فروع رئيسية للزيتون البري قد انفصلت عن شجرة مشتركة لا تقل عن 1.5 مليون سنة. لنذهب الآن إلى الجبال (ففي نيويورك تايمز بقلم كارل زيمر أو في30 مايو(2013 ذكر زيمر أن الجبال تحتل مكانًا خاصًا في قلوب علماء الأحياء التطورية، فهي ليست جبالا فقط بعظمتها المادية، بل لديها أيضًا قوة لا مثيل لها لدفع التطور البشري لأسلافنا. حيث انتقل أسلافنا إلى ارتفاعات عالية لتقوي خبرتهم في الانتقاء الطبيعي الذي أعاد صياغة بيولوجيتهم، كتعديل مستويات الهيموغلوبين على سبيل المثال.

القارة الإفريقية. ويؤكد القرآن الكريم ذلك عندما يقول في سورة قصيرة للغاية تتكون من ثماني آيات فقط عن طريق التين والزيتون وطور سينين وهذا البلد الأمين. لقد خلقنا الإنسان في أحسن تقويم ثم رددناه أسفل سافلين، إلا الذين آمنوا وعملوا الصالحات، فلهم أجر غير ممنون فما الذي يكذبك بعد بالدين أليس الله بأحكم الحاكمين؟ دعنا نلقي نظرة على الكيفية التي يوضح بها هذا الفصل القصير عن الزيتون والتين وجبل سينين، أصول البشرية، لذلك دعونا نتحدث عن التين الذي يُعرف أنه من الفواكه الطرية الحلوة التي تأتي من زهرة مزهرة داخليًا. في 17 يناير BBC earth مقال نشر على موقع 2017، كتب مايك شاناهان أن أشجار التين لم تشهد التاريخ فحسب، بل شكّلت أشجار التين البري لأول مرة في إفريقيا منذ حوالي 80 مليون سنة. وقد كان البشر دائما يأكلون التين عبر التاريخ. ولم يقتصر الأمر على تناوله من طرف الحيوانات فحسب، وإنما أيضًا على مدار العام من وجود التين. كان من الممكن أن يساعد التين الناضج في الحفاظ على أسلافنا البشر الأوائل، وربما ساعدهم بما يحتوي عليه من سعرات على تطوير أدمغة أكبر. وهناك أيضًا

متتالية. يخبرنا القرآن الكريم أن الله خلقنا على مراحل متتالية عندما يقول ما بك أن أنت لا تأمل أن يكرمك الله عندما خلقك في مراحل متتالية. اعتقد تشارلز داروين أن البشر قد تطوروا في إفريقيا وأن جذور الشجرة البشرية كانت متأصلة بعمق هناك. وفي عام 1962، ظهر أن جذورنا في إفريقيا هي علماء الوراثة. قادر على تحديد تسلسلات أو علامات وراثية معينة في كل واحد منا. قام بالإشارة إليها من خلال عدد من قواعد البيانات الدولية المتزايدة باستمرار حيث يوجد تطابق من المحتم أن يكون هنا كسلف مشترك ومن الناحية الجينية تشير جميع العلامات إلى إفريقيا من خلال تعيين الجينوم البشري في عام 2003 جنبًا إلى جنب مع الآلاف من الأشخاص حول العالم الذين قدموا الحمض النووي الخاص بهم للاختبار. هنا دليل مادي واضح على أننا بدأنا جميعًا في إفريقيا قبل الهجرة إلى جميع أنحاء العالم. علاوة على ذلك، فإن اختبار الحمض النووي المتقدم جنبًا إلى جنب مع الاكتشافات التي وقعت مؤخرًا يعزز الاعتقاد بأنه إذا نظرت إلى الوراء بعيدًا بما فيه الكفاية، ستجد أن جميع البشر الأحياء هم من نسل مجموعة صغيرة مبتكرة وطموحة من الناس في

وسوف تتقارب إلى نقطة واحدة عن أصل بداية الحياة. كان تشارلز داروين مترددًا في نشر آرائه حول أصول الحياة. فقط كتب حول هذا الموضوع وعرفه من رسالة خاصة إلى صديقه وزميله جوزيف هوكر، حيث تحدث عن الجزئية الأولى لتكوين الخلق، وكيف يمكن أن تكون جزيئات الحياة قد تكونت. يخبرنا القرآن الكريم المكتوب منذ أكثر من 1400 عام أن كل أشكال الحياة على الأرض مرتبطة ببعضها البعض عندما يقول أنا خلقنا (أي الله) من الماء كل الكائنات الحية. ثانيًا، هذا التنوع في الحياة هو نتاج تعديلات على السكان عن طريق الانتقاء الطبيعي، حيث تم تفضيل بعض الصفات في بيئة على غيرها. ويخبرنا القرآن الكريم أن تاريخ الخلق هو تاريخ كل من الخلق والاختيار عندما يقول إن الله يخلق ما يشاء ويختار. كما يخبرنا أن النبي آدم كان جلب إلى النبوة عن طريق الاختيار عندما يقول حقًا أن الله اختار آدم ونوح وأسرة إبراهيم وعائلة عمران على العالمين. فإن الناس طبقا لنظرية داروين للتطور هو النسخ والاختلافات التي تخلقها، بمعنى أنها هو نسخ النتائج في عدة مراحل تطورية

٢ وَطُورِ سِينِينَ

٣ وَهَٰذَا ٱلْبَلَدِ ٱلْأَمِينِ

٤ لَقَدْ خَلَقْنَا ٱلْإِنسَٰنَ فِى أَحْسَنِ تَقْوِيمٍ

٥ ثُمَّ رَدَدْنَٰهُ أَسْفَلَ سَٰفِلِينَ

يشتهر تشارلز داروين بالطبع بنظريته في التطور، من خلال الانتقاء الطبيعي، وقدتم الإعلان عن عمل داروين لأول مرة في عام 1859، وقام بصدم المؤسسة الدينية البريطانية، وبينما يتم قبولها اليوم من قبل جميع العلماء تقريبًا، لا تزال نظرية التطور مرفوضة من طرف العديد من الأمريكيين في كثير من الأحيان لأنها تتعارض مع معتقداتهم الدينية حول الخلق الإلهي. ولكن قد تميل إلى التفكير بأن نظرية التطور لداروين مناهضة

للدين وقد تتفاجا عندما تعلم أن نظرية داروين

والقرآن الكريم يشتركان في بعض القواسم. لنبدأ بإلقاء نظرة فاحصة على النظرية التي تحتوي على نقطتين رئيسيتين. أولاً، كل الحياة على الأرض مرتبطة. ومرتبطة بتتبع كل منها للخطوط المنفصلة عن كل الكائنات الحية التي عاشت على الإطلاق

وَإِذْ قَالَ رَبُّكَ لِلْمَلَٰئِكَةِ إِنِّى جَاعِلٌ فِى ٱلْأَرْضِ خَلِيفَةً قَالُوٓا۟ أَتَجْعَلُ فِيهَا مَن يُفْسِدُ فِيهَا وَيَسْفِكُ ٱلدِّمَآءَ وَنَحْنُ نُسَبِّحُ بِحَمْدِكَ وَنُقَدِّسُ لَكَ ۖ قَالَ إِنِّىٓ أَعْلَمُ مَا لَا تَعْلَمُونَ

٣٠ البقرة

من الواضح من هذه الآية وجود مخلوقات شبيهة بآدم موجودة في الأرض وكانوا يتقاتلون ويتصرفون بطريقة حيوانية من غير روح، هؤلاء الخلق قومهم الله من قبل خلق آدم عليه السلام. وتزاوج أولاده منهم حيث تطور الإنسان بعد ذلك عبر الأجيال المتعاقبة. لأن الله علم آدم عليه السلام ونفخ فيه من روحه، وكان الملائكة يعرفون ويرون ما يجري على الأرض، لكنهم لا يعلمون ما علم الله آدم، ولا ما هو أمر الله جل جلاله، لأنهم لا يعلمون الغيب. ليس كما يقولون بأن أولاد آدم تزوجوا أخواتهم. أستغفر لله من هذا الكلام.

البرهان

التين

وَٱلتِّينِ وَٱلزَّيْتُونِ

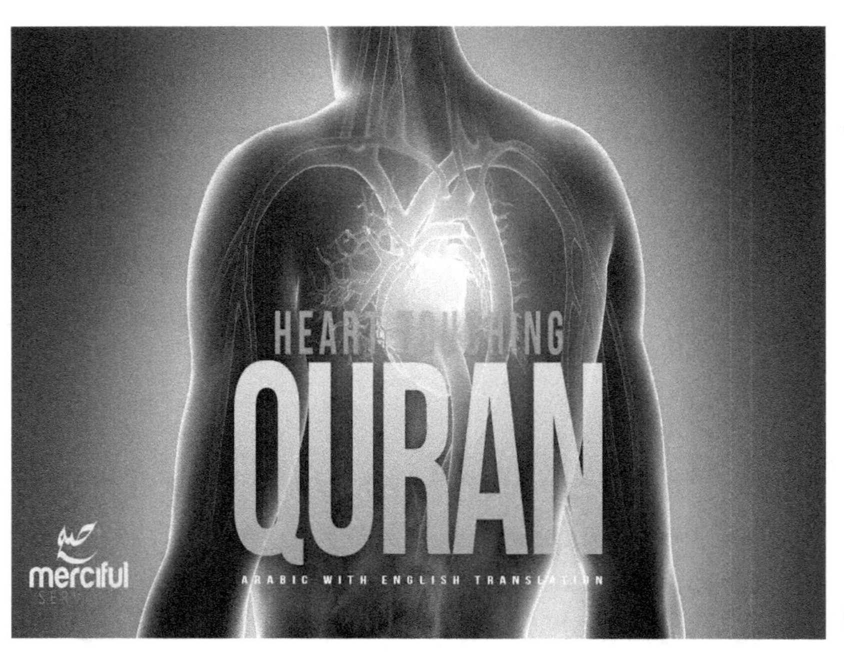

HEART TOUCHING
QURAN
ARABIC WITH ENGLISH TRANSLATION
merciful

المعنى

دعونا نرجع للإسلام لنفهم المعنى، وهو أن تسلم لله رب العالمين إله واحد، وهو نفسه في كل الرسالات. كل الرسل والأنبياء أسلموا لله، هو مولاهم الحق. فلِم لا نفعل نفس الشيء؟

إِنِّى وَجَّهْتُ وَجْهِىَ لِلَّذِى فَطَرَ ٱلسَّمَٰوَٰتِ وَٱلْأَرْضَ حَنِيفًا وَمَآ أَنَا۠ مِنَ ٱلْمُشْرِكِينَ

الانعام ١٧٩

الداروينية

إحدى النظريات التي لا نزال نسمع عنها هي نظرية التطور الداروينية. أشارت الداروينية لاحقًا إلى المفاهيم المحددة للانتقاء الطبيعي، أو حاجز وايزمان، أو العقيدة المركزية للبيولوجيا الجزيئية. على الرغم من أن المصطلح يشير بشكل صارم إلى التطور البيولوجي، فقد خصصه للإشارة إلى أصل الحياة أو إلى التطور الكوني، والتي تختلف عن التطور البيولوجي.

يتفق الإسلام مع نظرية التطور هذه

موسى عليه السلام، ونسوا الخالق وكذلك فعل المسيحيون عندما وقعوا في حب عيسى عليه السلام ونسوا خالقهم. كما فعل المسلمون نفس الشيء عندما وقعوا في حب محمد عليه السلام ونسوا الخالق. لقد ترك أتباع الرسالات الكتب المقدسة الإلهية، واتبعوا كتب العباد التي هي بعيدة كل البعد عما أنزل الله، ليس لشيء، فقط لأنها نسبت إلى الرسل. فتفرقوا إلى طوائف وأحزاب، كل فرح بما لديه. الدين واحد، وهو الإسلام، ولكن الرسالات متعددة.

سألني الرجل بعد ذلك عن الفرق بين السنة والشيعة، فقلت: نفس الشيء، فقط أن البعض أحب الرسول والبعض الآخر أحب ابن عمه. الهدف من إخباركم هذه القصة هو للتأكيد بأن الله هو من نعبد، ونؤمن به ونجله ونعظمه، والباقي مخلوقات سواء كانوا أنبياء أو رسل، لهم ما كسبوا ولنا ما كسبنا. لذلك فرغم محبتنا واحترامنا للرسل والأنبياء، علينا أن نتذكر أنهم مخلوقات مثلنا ومرجعنا إلى الخالق.

ءَامَنَ ٱلرَّسُولُ بِمَا أُنزِلَ إِلَيْهِ مِن رَّبِّهِ وَٱلْمُؤْمِنُونَ كُلٌّ ءَامَنَ بِٱللَّهِ وَمَلَٰئِكَتِهِ وَكُتُبِهِ وَرُسُلِهِ لَا نُفَرِّقُ بَيْنَ أَحَدٍ مِّن رُّسُلِهِ وَقَالُوا سَمِعْنَا وَأَطَعْنَا غُفْرَانَكَ رَبَّنَا وَإِلَيْكَ ٱلْمَصِيرُ

لأنها سهلة لعقولنا لأننا نراها ولأننا لا نستطيع إدراك معنى الخالق. فترى البعض عبد الشمس، والبعض الآخر عبد القمر أو الحجر أو عبد ما يمكن رؤيته. لهذا أرسل الله الأنبياء لينشروا حب الله والفضيلة بين البشر. والمنطق لو أنه هناك آلهة كثيرة لتقاتلوا فيما بينهم.

مَا ٱتَّخَذَ ٱللَّهُ مِن وَلَدٍ وَمَا كَانَ مَعَهُ مِنْ إِلَـٰهٍ ۚ إِذًا لَّذَهَبَ كُلُّ إِلَـٰهٍ بِمَا خَلَقَ وَلَعَلَا بَعْضُهُمْ عَلَىٰ بَعْضٍ ۚ سُبْحَـٰنَ ٱللَّهِ عَمَّا يَصِفُونَ

٩١ المؤمنون

أود مشاركتكم قصة وقعت لي، فقد تعرفت الى مهندس متعاقد كان يعمل في شركة للسيارات في أميركا. خلال وجبة العشاء، جلسنا نتحادث عما يمكن فعله بعد التقاعد، قال إنه يقضي وقته بدراسة الأديان الثلاثة، الإسلام والمسيحية واليهودية، مع العلم أنه من أصول بوذية. فسألني: لماذا يوجد خلاف بين الشعوب وتسود الكراهية بينهم، مع أن هناك تقارب كبير في الدين؟ الإجابة سهلة وواضحة وصريحة. قلت له لنفترض أنك مغرم بفتاة وهي بعيدة، فأرسلت لها رسالة عبر البريد. فقام ساعي البريد بقراءة الرسالة لها، ولكنها بدلا من أن تقع في حبك، وقعت في حبه. لقد وقع اليهود في حب

عقولهم من مخلوقات الله، ليس لها علاقة بمفهوم القوة المطلقة أو الخالق. الكل يتجاهل كم هي صغيرة مجرتنا مقارنة مع الكون غير المتناهي! وكل إبداعات الإنسان ما هي إلا استنساخ لما خلق الله (من الحيوانات والنباتات والأرض والسماء لا علم لدينا إلا ما أراد الله لنا أن نتعلمه). ونحن كمخلوقات لسنا مؤهلين لهكذا تخيل أو استنتاج لأننا لا نستطيع. فمهما كان تخيلك لله، فالله بخلاف ذلك. لا يمكننا أن نرسم شيئا لم نره من قبل! إذا نحن مخلوقون بحدود معينة وأراد الله لنا أن نعرف عظمته من خلال خلقه وأن نؤمن بالله وأن نحبه ونعبده، هذا هو الإيمان، وهذا هو الله عز وجل.

فَاطِرُ ٱلسَّمَٰوَٰتِ وَٱلْأَرْضِ ۚ جَعَلَ لَكُم مِّنْ أَنفُسِكُمْ أَزْوَٰجًا وَمِنَ ٱلْأَنْعَٰمِ أَزْوَٰجًا ۚ يَذْرَؤُكُمْ فِيهِ ۚ لَيْسَ كَمِثْلِهِۦ شَيْءٌ ۖ وَهُوَ ٱلسَّمِيعُ ٱلْبَصِيرُ

١١ الشورى

دعونا نؤمن بالخالق الذي يحبنا وننشر هذا الحب بين البشرية جمعاء، بدلا من شن الحروب وإزهاق الأرواح لغاية في نفس الآمرين بالسوء والشياطين. نحن كبشر، ومنذ بدء البشرية ونحن نبحث عن خالق لأننا ندرك بالفطرة أننا مخلوقات ولا بد من وجود خالق. ولأننا بشر نحن دائما نحب التجسيد

إِنَّ ٱللَّهَ لَا يَغْفِرُ أَن يُشْرَكَ بِهِۦ وَيَغْفِرُ مَا دُونَ ذَٰلِكَ لِمَن يَشَآءُ ۚ وَمَن يُشْرِكْ بِٱللَّهِ فَقَدْ ضَلَّ ضَلَٰلًۢا بَعِيدًا

النساء ١١٦

الغفران

لقد ذكر الله غفرانه في نفس السورة مرتين، ما أعظم رحمة الخالق غافر الذنب، إلا أن يشرك به. رحمته تفوق الخيال. إذا كان الله رحيما بالعباد، فلماذا لا نكون رحماء بيننا؟ لماذا الشرذمة في هذا الدين الحنيف؟ لماذا تتحكم الأنا الشيطانية في كل الطوائف؟ لماذا لا أحد يريد الإذعان لكلام الله؟ لماذا لا يجتمع أصحاب العمائم معا ليتناقشوا ويصلحوا، بدلا من أن يهدروا الدماء؟

الله جل جلاله

يجب علينا أن نفهم أن الله هو الخالق، هو القوة المطلقة وليس كمثله شيء. بتعبير آخر، إذا طلبت من كل من في العالم أن يرسموا الخالق، فكيف تظن قد تكون النتيجة؟ قد تكون بعض الصور عبارة عن رجل كبير أو سحاب كبير أو حتى أشكالا ترسخت في

الحفيد ذلك يصل بالسلة وهي فارغة لتسرب المياه منها ثم يعيد الكرة. وبعد عدة محاولات، استسلم وقال لجده: هذه المحاولات لا تجدي نفعا. فطلب منه الجد أن ينظر إلى السلة، وإذا بالسلة بها قد أصبحت نظيفة، وكذلك يفعل بك القرآن. بل سيجعلك قويا ضد الجهل والفتنة وينقي روحك وهو شفاء لك.

وَنُنَزِّلُ مِنَ ٱلْقُرْءَانِ مَا هُوَ شِفَآءٌ وَرَحْمَةٌ لِّلْمُؤْمِنِينَ وَلَا يَزِيدُ ٱلظَّـٰلِمِينَ إِلَّا خَسَارًا
١٨٢ الاسراء

الإسلام دين سلام، وهو تسليم نفسك لله في كل أمر ولله وحده. الأمر سهل وبسيط، فقط آمنوا بالله باعتباره القوة العليا، الخالق وليس له شركاء وأنت ضمنت الجنة لكي تكون مسلماً، كل ما عليك فعله هو الاستسلام لله.

الغفران

إِنَّ ٱللَّهَ لَا يَغْفِرُ أَن يُشْرَكَ بِهِ وَيَغْفِرُ مَا دُونَ ذَٰلِكَ لِمَن يَشَآءُ وَمَن يُشْرِكْ بِٱللَّهِ فَقَدِ ٱفْتَرَىٰ إِثْمًا عَظِيمًا

فَإِن لَّمْ تَفْعَلُواْ وَلَن تَفْعَلُواْ فَاتَّقُواْ ٱلنَّارَ ٱلَّتِى وَقُودُهَا ٱلنَّاسُ وَٱلْحِجَارَةُ ۖ أُعِدَّتْ لِلْكَافِرِينَ

٢٤ البقرة

أرجو أن يتمكن القارئ من إدراك عظمة القرآن في هذا التحدي. لذلك فإن تتبع أحاديث وأوامر مخالفة للنصوص القرآنية، هي نسف لمبدأ الرسالة الإسلامية والقرآن.

الثانية: أن القرآن الكريم قال إن محمد عليه السلام خاتم الرسل والنبيين، وها نحن اليوم بعد ألف وخمسمائة عام لا نبي أو رسول بعد محمد عليه الصلاة والسلام.

مَّا كَانَ مُحَمَّدٌ أَبَآ أَحَدٍ مِّن رِّجَالِكُمْ وَلَٰكِن رَّسُولَ ٱللَّهِ وَخَاتَمَ ٱلنَّبِيِّنَ ۗ وَكَانَ ٱللَّهُ بِكُلِّ شَىْءٍ عَلِيمًا

٤٠ الأحزاب

من أفضل القصص التي سمعتها وأود أ ن أشارككم إياها، هناك رجل مع حفيده، حيث سأله الحفيد: لماذا تقرأ القرآن ولا تحفظه؟ فطلب الجد من الحفيد أن يأخذ سلة متسخة بالسواد كانت تستعمل لنقل الفحم، وأن يعبئ فيها ماء من البحر ويحضره. كلما فعل

311

ترجمة القرآن واسعة وغير محدودة بزمان. لأن بعض الحقائق معروفة والبعض الآخر لم يتم اكتشافه بعد. فإن تفسير القرآن منذ ألف سنة مختلف كليا عن تفسيره الآن، لذلك فإنه لا حدود للمعجزات في القرآن، ولا يمكن أن نضعها في كتاب واحد، كما أن بعضها لم نعرفه بعد.

أريد أن أسلط الضوء على نقطتين لفتتا انتباهي في آيتين من القرآن الكريم:
الأولى: هي المعجزة بأن القرآن تحدى جميع الخلق على أن يأتوا بسورة مثل سورة من القرآن لما تحتوي من إعجاز، ولم ولن يستطيع أي مخلوق فعل ذلك.

أَمْ يَقُولُونَ ٱفْتَرَىٰهُ قُلْ فَأْتُوا بِسُورَةٍ مِّثْلِهِ وَٱدْعُوا مَنِ ٱسْتَطَعْتُم مِّن دُونِ ٱللَّهِ إِن كُنتُمْ صَـٰدِقِينَ
٣٨ يونس

وَإِن كُنتُمْ فِي رَيْبٍ مِّمَّا نَزَّلْنَا عَلَىٰ عَبْدِنَا فَأْتُوا بِسُورَةٍ مِّن مِّثْلِهِ وَٱدْعُوا شُهَدَاءَكُم مِّن دُونِ ٱللَّهِ إِن كُنتُمْ صَـٰدِقِينَ
٢٣ البقرة

توجد آيات في القرآن سهلة جدا، وإذا قرأتها ستفهمها فورا. وهناك آيات متشابهات، فما عليك إلا أن تأخذها كما هي، ولا تستطيع تأويلها. كما لا يستطيع تأويلها من يدعون العلم، فقط نؤمن بها كما هي. وهناك آيات تحاكي العلم والتقدم وما لم نعرفه بعد. فلذا، يجب أن نشجع العلم والمزيد من قراءة القرآن، لأن الرسول علم القرآن لمن سبقونا ولم يفسره وآمنوا به كما هو، من عند الله وآمنوا أن الله حق وسيرينا آياته في الآفاق. لذلك لا تدع أصحاب العمائم يمنعونك من قراءة القرآن بحجة أنك لن تفهمه، وأنك بحاجة إليهم كي تتعلم دينك. لقد تم تبليغ الرسالة، وهي القرآن، وكل ما تحتاجه موجود أو بالأصح كل ما يريده الله منك موجود فيه، فعد إليه لتقطع الطريق على الجهلاء. هل يعقل أن هذا الدين الحنيف العظيم لا يفهم إلا من خلال رجال الدين؟؟ نحن بأمس الحاجة إلى تعلم اللغة العربية أكثر من أي وقت مضى.

هُوَ ٱلَّذِى أَنزَلَ عَلَيْكَ ٱلْكِتَٰبَ مِنْهُ ءَايَٰتٌ مُّحْكَمَٰتٌ هُنَّ أُمُّ ٱلْكِتَٰبِ وَأُخَرُ مُتَشَٰبِهَٰتٌ ۖ فَأَمَّا ٱلَّذِينَ فِى قُلُوبِهِمْ زَيْغٌ فَيَتَّبِعُونَ مَا تَشَٰبَهَ مِنْهُ ٱبْتِغَآءَ ٱلْفِتْنَةِ وَٱبْتِغَآءَ تَأْوِيلِهِ ۗ وَمَا يَعْلَمُ تَأْوِيلَهُ إِلَّا ٱللَّهُ ۗ وَٱلرَّٰسِخُونَ فِى ٱلْعِلْمِ يَقُولُونَ ءَامَنَّا بِهِ كُلٌّ مِّنْ عِندِ رَبِّنَا ۗ وَمَا يَذَّكَّرُ إِلَّا أُولُوا ٱلْأَلْبَٰبِ

رجاء مشاهدة الفيديو.

معجزات القرآن الكثيرة

توجد في القرآن معجزات لا تحصى ومنها التي لم نعرفها بعد؛ هناك الإعجاز اللغوي حيث أن القرآن كنص قد صحح مسار اللغة العربية، ومن المستحيل أن يفعل رجل واحد شيئا مثل هذا. فالإعجاز العلمي والإعجاز الرقمي، والإعجاز الحسابي، والإعجاز الفلكي، ومعجزات كثيرة أخرى تجعل من القرآن كتابا إعجازيا من المستحيل أن يكون قد وُضع من طرف بشر. فلماذا لا نأخذ الوقت لقراءته والتمعن فيه.

بساطة القرآن

هل تعلم أن الله قد ذكر أربع مرات في القرآن أنه سبحانه وتعالى جعل القرآن سهل الفهم، فهل هناك من يقرأه؟؟

وَلَقَدْ يَسَّرْنَا ٱلْقُرْءَانَ لِلذِّكْرِ فَهَلْ مِن مُّدَّكِرٍ
القمر 17 22 32 40

لقد ذكرت هذه الآية أربع مرات! فكم مرة تريدها أن تذكر قبل أن تبدأ بقراءة القرآن؟

وترسم مسارًا دائريًا تقريبًا (مرة أخرى، بالنظر إلى الأسفل من الأعلى) يستغرق حوالي 230مليون سنة لإكماله بسرعة حوالي 137ميلاً (220كيلومترًا) في الثانية.

فيما يتعلق بمحور الدوران الخاص بها، فإن الشمس تتحرك عبر المجرة وهي مائلة بزاوية 60 درجة تقريبًا من مستوى المجرة نفسها. وينطبق هذا أيضًا على الكواكب التي تدور حول الشمس ـتمامًا مثل قرص مجرتنا، إذا نظرت إلى نظامنا الشمسي من الجانب، ستجد أن الكواكب تدور حول الشمس في مستوى مسطح نسبيًا .بشكل أساسي، تميل كل من الشمس والمستوى الذي تدور فيه أجسام النظام الشمسي حولها إلى الأمام بمقدار 60 درجة أثناء تحركهما عبر المجرة.

من الجدير بالذكر أيضًا أن الشمس لا يبدو أنها ترسم دائرة مسطحة ـفي مستوى واحد فقط ـأثناء تحركها حول المجرة. في الواقع، يبدو أنها تتحرك صعودًا وهبوطًا عبر القرص (نحن الآن في الأعلى، فوق مستوى القرص) أثناء تحركها، خلال فترة تقارب 60 مليون سنة.

<u>https://www.youtube.com/watch?v=KU dIQ7kvD7w</u>

يحتوي الخرطوم على أنبوبين، أحدهما يحقن اللعاب الذي يحتوي على مضادات التخثر ومسكن للألم، والثاني يسحب الدم بالفعل.

وهل قام أيضا بتشريح البعوضة؟؟

الكون

لَا ٱلشَّمْسُ يَنۢبَغِى لَهَآ أَن تُدْرِكَ ٱلْقَمَرَ وَلَا ٱلَّيْلُ سَابِقُ ٱلنَّهَارِ ۚ وَكُلٌّ فِى فَلَكٍ يَسْبَحُونَ

٤٠ يس

لسنوات عدة كان الاعتقاد بأن الشمس ثابتة. فحتى عام 1979، كانت لا تزال تدرس بالمدارس. بينما جاء القرآن ليقول بأن جميع الكواكب تسبح بما فيها الشمس. لم يحدد الحركة فقط، بل أيضا بالكيفية أي السباحة.

إذا تخيلت النظر الى أسفل على درب التبانة فان الشمس تقع على بعد حوالي 27000 سنة ضوئية من المركز. في منتصف الطريق تقريبا بين المركز وحافة مجرتنا على شكل قرص. وبالنظر من الجانب يكون القرص مسطحا نسبيا وتقع الشمس حاليا على ارتفاع 55 سنة ضوئية فوق مستوى قرص المجرة

مليغرام. وهي مقسمة إلى ثلاثة أجزاء أساسية :الرأس والصدر والبطن.

الرأس :الرأس مليء بالأجهزة الحسية التي تساعد البعوض في العثور على البشر والحيوانات والتغذي عليهم.

العيون المركبة لها عينان مركبتان كبيرتان مغطيتان بعدسات صغيرة تسمى ommatidia قادرة على اكتشاف أي حركة ولو كانت طفيفة.

في الجزء العلوي من رؤوسهم، لديهم أيضًا عيون حساسة بسيطة تكتشف الاختلافات في الضوء.

الهوائيات، تبرز قرون الاستشعار الخاصة بها، وهي أعضاء ريشية طويلة، إلى الأمام من رؤوسها وتحتوي على مستقبلات حساسة تكتشف ثاني أكسيد الكربون في أنفاس الإنسان من مسافات تزيد عن 100قدم .يلتقط ملامسة الفك العلوي بين الهوائيات رائحة الأوكتينول والمواد الكيميائية الأخرى المنبعثة في عرق الإنسان.

قي المنتصف يوجد أيضا خرطوم، وهو جزء فم طويل مسنن يستخدم لثقب الجلد وامتصاص الدم.

للنحلة معدة المحصول أو العسل هي بنية خاصة قابلة للتوسع. تقع بين المريء والجهاز الهضمي الحقيقي للنحلة العاملة.

النحلة تجمع مخزون المحاصيل من الرحيق حتى تصبح جاهزة للعودة إلى الخلية. لا يحدث هضم حقيقي في المحصول. العسل ليس من قيء النحل كما قد تقرأ في مكان آخر، فهذه القدرة على حمل الرحيق الخام في المحصول إلى الخلية مهمة. وبدون البطون لن يتمكن النحل من إنتاج العسل. فهل قام محمد عليه الصلاة والسلام بتشريح النحل؟

البعوض

إِنَّ ٱللَّهَ لَا يَسْتَحْىِ أَن يَضْرِبَ مَثَلًا مَّا بَعُوضَةً فَمَا فَوْقَهَا ۚ فَأَمَّا ٱلَّذِينَ ءَامَنُوا۟ فَيَعْلَمُونَ أَنَّهُ ٱلْحَقُّ مِن رَّبِّهِمْ ۖ وَأَمَّا ٱلَّذِينَ كَفَرُوا۟ فَيَقُولُونَ مَاذَآ أَرَادَ ٱللَّهُ بِهَٰذَا مَثَلًا ۘ يُضِلُّ بِهِ كَثِيرًا وَيَهْدِى بِهِ كَثِيرًا ۚ وَمَا يُضِلُّ بِهِ إِلَّا ٱلْفَٰسِقِينَ

البقرة ۞ 26

البعوض عبارة عن حشرات صغيرة نسبيا يبلغ متوسط طولها أكثر من 6 مم ويزن حوالي 2.7

أعماق المحيط

أَوْ كَظُلُمَٰتٍ فِى بَحْرٍ لُّجِّىٍّ يَغْشَىٰهُ مَوْجٌ مِّن فَوْقِهِۦ مَوْجٌ مِّن فَوْقِهِۦ سَحَابٌ ظُلُمَٰتٌۢ بَعْضُهَا فَوْقَ بَعْضٍ إِذَآ أَخْرَجَ يَدَهُۥ لَمْ يَكَدْ يَرَىٰهَاۗ وَمَن لَّمْ يَجْعَلِ ٱللَّهُ لَهُۥ نُورًا فَمَالَهُۥ مِن نُّورٍ *النور 40

تم مؤخرا اكتشاف وجود أمواج تحت الأمواج في قاع المحيط. لا أظنها صدفة أيضا!

النحل

وَأَوْحَىٰ رَبُّكَ إِلَى ٱلنَّحْلِ أَنِ ٱتَّخِذِى مِنَ ٱلْجِبَالِ بُيُوتًا وَمِنَ ٱلشَّجَرِ وَمِمَّا يَعْرِشُونَ النحل* ٦٨

ثُمَّ كُلِى مِن كُلِّ ٱلثَّمَرَٰتِ فَٱسْلُكِى سُبُلَ رَبِّكِ ذُلُلًاۚ يَخْرُجُ مِنۢ بُطُونِهَا شَرَابٌ مُّخْتَلِفٌ أَلْوَٰنُهُۥ فِيهِ شِفَآءٌ لِّلنَّاسِۚ إِنَّ فِى ذَٰلِكَ لَءَايَةً لِّقَوْمٍ يَتَفَكَّرُونَ *النحل 69

من بطونها وليس من بطن واحد، بل أكثر من بطن! كيف هذا!

لو جاء القرآن مع آدم عليه السلام، فلم يكن ليغير شيئا في البشرية. لذلك وجب إرسال كتب قبل القرآن، مثل الإنجيل والتوراة، حتى تكتمل الرسالة.
ما الذي يجعل القرآن معجزة؟
هناك العديد من الاكتشافات التي تبرهن معجزة القرآن، بعضه تعرفنا عليه وبعضه لم يحن وقته ولم يتم التعرف عليه بعد، لأنه لا حدود لحكمة الله وعلمه.

خلق الانسان

ثُمَّ خَلَقْنَا ٱلنُّطْفَةَ عَلَقَةً فَخَلَقْنَا ٱلْعَلَقَةَ مُضْغَةً فَخَلَقْنَا ٱلْمُضْغَةَ عِظَٰمًا فَكَسَوْنَا ٱلْعِظَٰمَ لَحْمًا ثُمَّ أَنشَأْنَٰهُ خَلْقًا ءَاخَرَ ۚ فَتَبَارَكَ ٱللَّهُ أَحْسَنُ ٱلْخَٰلِقِينَ المؤمنون ١٤

كيف عرف رجل من الصحراء هذا التفصيل الدقيق منذ ألف وخمسمائة عام، من دون اجراء العديد من الأبحاث والعمليات الجراحية والاختبارات لمواكبة تكون الجنين ومراحل نموه بهذا التفصيل الدقيق. نعم يمكنك القول بأنه صدفة ولكن كم من صدفة تحتاج لتيقن بأنه كتاب الله.

القرآن

القرآن هو المعجزة الحية منذ ألف وخمس مائة سنة وسيبقى إلى يوم القيامة بإذن الله جل جلاله، ففي كل عصر نكتشف المزيد عن هذه المعجزة.

لقد أرسل الله العديد من الأنبياء والرسل، نعرف بعضهم والبعض الآخر لم يقصصهم الله علينا. إن الرسالة واضحة وصريحة للحفاظ على البشرية والاستسلام والتسليم للإله وحده صاحب القوة العظمى.

دعونا نتخيل السيناريو التالي: أن الله عز وجل خلق آدم ولم يرسل أنبياء أو رسل! ماذا كان سيحصل! أكل لحوم البشر كان سيكون أمرا طبيعيا، والقتل كذلك وكل ما يقود إلى النهاية كان سيكون محللا، من كان سيعرف الخطأ من الصواب؟ كان العرب يدفنون البنات حتى ظهور رسالة سيدنا محمد صلى الله عليه وسلم!

لقد أرسل الله العديد من الرسل، وهذا سبب تطابق الرسالات السماوية عبر الكتب المقدسة. رغم اتباعهم الكتب المقدسة، فإن الناس يسارعون إلى القتال بينهم ونشر الكراهية بدلا من قراءة الكتب بتمعن. فلو فعلوا، لوجدوا أن الرسالة واحدة عند الرسل.

بِسْمِ ٱللَّهِ ٱلرَّحْمَٰنِ ٱلرَّحِيمِ

القرآن والإسلام

وَقَالَ ٱلرَّسُولُ يَارَبِّ إِنَّ قَوْمِى ٱتَّخَذُواْ هَٰذَا ٱلْقُرْءَانَ مَهْجُورًا الفرقان. ٣٠

شكر وتقدير

الحمد لله على إعطائي أكثر مما أستحق دائما وأبدا. يعطي الله جل جلاله الكثير للبشرية، وقليل هم الشاكرون. كم منا يأخذ من الوقت وقته ليتأمل ما أعطي ويشكر الله على ذلك.

شكر خاص لأصدقائي زاهر سعيد، عمار الجنيني، وأخي مصطفى الذين قضوا معي وقتا طويلا يتجاوز العشر سنوات من المناقشة والبحث والحوار. وهم أول من راجع مسودة هذا الكتاب.

شكرا لكل من كلير فوستر والدكتور محمد شحرور الذين ألهماني أن أتحدث بجرأة عن موضوع حساس كهذا.

وأخيرا، شكرا لكل من يقرأ هذا الكتاب بعقل منفتح وايمان بالله ورسوله، سواء أحب محتواه أم لا. وشكرا سلفا على الجهود التي سوف تبذل للتحقق من هذه النقاط، لأنه في النهاية، كلنا ننشد الإصلاح.

أسأل الله من كل قلبي الهداية لنا وللبشرية جمعاء.

وأن يصحح ما قيل خطأ بالبرهان والأدلة القاطعة. فبداية وأخيرا، أنا بشر، قد أخطئ وقد أصيب ولست مثاليا.

آدم، ونوح، وإبراهيم، وإسحاق، ويعقوب، ويوسف، وموسى، وهارون، ويحي، ومحمد عليهم السلام، ما هو القاسم المشترك بينهم؟
الله هو الذي أرسلهم بالنبوة والرسالة. إنما إلههم إله واحد ورسالتهم رسالة واحدة جمعتهم لهداية البشر إلى الله رغم كون السنين قد باعدت بين توقيت نزول الرسالة عليهم.

إذا كان هناك شيء خاطئ، فإن أولئك الذين لديهم القدرة على اتخاذ إجراءات للتصليح، واجب عليهم مسؤولية اتخاذ الإجراءات للتصليح.

بِسْمِ ٱللَّهِ ٱلرَّحْمَـٰنِ ٱلرَّحِيمِ

مقدمة

في عالم قد عدنا فيه إلى الظلام، حان الوقت للتوقف والعودة إلى الجذور والأسس الرئيسية الأصلية. الإسلام دين سماوي ممتلئ بالحب والعلم والعاطفة والإنسانية. القرآن الكريم هو أساس هذا الدين، وكتابي ليس إلا مجرد دعوة لكل مسلم، وكل رجل دين، وكل شخص يحب المعرفة ليأخذ دقيقة من وقته ويعيد التفكير في أين وصلنا وما أوصلنا إلى هنا، وما يمكننا القيام به لتصحيح المسار. ليس الهدف نهائيا عدم الاحترام أو الانتقاص من أي شخص أو أي دين، لأنني أومن بجميع الرسالات السماوية شخصيا، ولكن مشكلتي مع من نصّبوا أنفسهم آلهة. هذه الرسالة، وبنية صافية، مبنية على الحب والمعرفة، وإذا كان لدى أي شخص مشكلة مع ما كتب، فأمنيتي أن يناقش الموضوع بعلم وحب،

طُبع في الولايات المتحدة الأمريكية
الطبعة الأولى 2022
رقم ال ISBN:

ISLAM
HIJACKED
BY
MARWAN HACHEM